D1765774

WITHDRAWN

LIVERPOOL JMU LIBRARY

3 1111 01500 2528

A MORAL THEORY OF SOLIDARITY

A Moral Theory
of Solidarity

AVERY KOLERS

OXFORD
UNIVERSITY PRESS

OXFORD
UNIVERSITY PRESS

Great Clarendon Street, Oxford, OX2 6DP,
United Kingdom

Oxford University Press is a department of the University of Oxford.
It furthers the University's objective of excellence in research, scholarship,
and education by publishing worldwide. Oxford is a registered trade mark of
Oxford University Press in the UK and in certain other countries

© Avery Kolers 2016

The moral rights of the author have been asserted

First Edition published in 2016
Impression: 1

All rights reserved. No part of this publication may be reproduced, stored in
a retrieval system, or transmitted, in any form or by any means, without the
prior permission in writing of Oxford University Press, or as expressly permitted
by law, by licence or under terms agreed with the appropriate reprographics
rights organization. Enquiries concerning reproduction outside the scope of the
above should be sent to the Rights Department, Oxford University Press, at the
address above

You must not circulate this work in any other form
and you must impose this same condition on any acquirer

Published in the United States of America by Oxford University Press
198 Madison Avenue, New York, NY 10016, United States of America

British Library Cataloguing in Publication Data
Data available

Library of Congress Control Number: 2015958729

ISBN 978–0–19–876978–1

Printed in Great Britain by
Clays Ltd, St Ives plc

Links to third party websites are provided by Oxford in good faith and
for information only. Oxford disclaims any responsibility for the materials
contained in any third party website referenced in this work.

For John Cumbler,
who lives for justice.
"The people, united, might not
always inevitably be defeated!"

Foreword and Acknowledgments

I began thinking and writing about solidarity in 2001. In late 2012, the core normative thesis began to emerge. That keystone made it possible to organize and develop, over the intervening three years, a collection of ideas into a moral theory.

Some people have been through the whole fifteen years with me. Cheshire Calhoun, Karen Christopher, John Cumbler, Bob Goodin, Cindy Holder, and David Imbroscio have been invaluable sounding boards and sources of insight from the beginning. Bob Goodin, in particular, not only supported this project right from the first, but initiated the 2012 email conversation in which, together with Bob as well as Avia Pasternak, I hit on the normative thesis that became this book's keystone. Bob also encouraged me to visit Canberra for a six-week research fellowship, which I did—thanks to Christian Barry and the ANU Philosophy department—in 2015, and where I was able to immerse myself in the writing, revisions, and discussions that were essential to getting this book finished. So Bob is pretty much the *sine qua non* of this book. Cheshire Calhoun has also supported me and this project from the beginning, first as my department chair in Louisville, then over the years with probing questions, insightful suggestions, and unstinting encouragement. John Cumbler not only was an invaluable interlocutor and source of inspiration and insight over the years, but he also read the entire manuscript—parts of it repeatedly—as it neared completion, and helped me get key elements right, or at least, better.

In Australia I had the amazing good fortune to get to know people who—in addition to being lovely as friends and colleagues—were generous with their time and energy, reading chapters, massively improving particular arguments and the conceptualization as a whole. Among these were Christian Barry, Geoff Brennan, Cheshire, Bob, Sarah Hannan, Duncan Ivison, Seth Lazar, Chad Lee-Stronach, RJ Leland, Nic Southwood, Kai Spiekermann, and Lachlan Umbers. I hope it's clear from footnotes—despite the inevitable limitations of the form—how invaluable I found my time at ANU.

Over the years I have benefited from discussions of this material with—in addition to those already mentioned—Guy Dove, Suzi Dovi, Dan Farnham, Peter Fosl, Bryan Hall, Burke Hendrix, Kristen Hessler, Eileen John, Irfan Khawaja, Loren King, Holly Lawford-Smith, Amanda LeDuke, Justin Mog, Jim Molos, Cara Nine, David Owen, Richard Oxenberg, Nancy Potter, Linda Radzik, Andrea Sangiovanni, Sally Scholz, Stefan Sciaraffa, Hanoch Sheinman, George Sher, Yujia Song, Jennifer Szende, Leigh Viner, Tim Waligore, and students in various political philosophy classes. Many of these people read or heard article drafts and their comments and questions made the work better. In addition, I am grateful to Dominic Byatt and Will Kymlicka for supporting this work's adoption with OUP, to the two anonymous referees—one of whom I later learned was Greta Snyder—for careful reading of the draft manuscript and very helpful comments and suggestions for revision, and to Olivia Wells, Nishantini Amir, Kim Allen, and others for guiding this manuscript, and me, through the production process.

I presented earlier versions of parts of the book at the 2003 APA Central Division meetings; a 2009 brown bag at the Humanities Research Center, Rice University; the 2009 NASSP Conference in Philadelphia; a 2014 symposium on Solidarity at the APA Pacific Division meetings, with invaluable comments by Ami Harbin and ensuing phenomenal conversations with Cheshire Calhoun, Dan Farnham, Stephen Galoob, Cindy Holder, Naomi Scheman, and Sally Scholz; a Moral-Social-Political Theory workshop at Australian National University, and discussions with those already mentioned; and in the Philosophy Department of the University of Sydney, and conversations with Duncan Ivison, Miriam Cosic, Matthew Hammerton, Yarran Hominh, Dalia Nassar, and Luke Russell.

My initial research on solidarity was conducted during two summers as a visiting scholar at the University of Pittsburgh, where Michael Thompson and the Philosophy Department provided hospitality and research support. I also received research assistance from Sara Zizzo, funded by the University of Louisville's Vice President for Research. Research on Chapter One was supported by the Richard & Constance Lewis Foundation Fellowship in Latin American & Iberian Studies from the University of Louisville Latin American & Latino Studies Program, and by a matching grant from the University of Louisville Philosophy Department. This funding enabled me to visit Salamanca and Valladolid to research Vitoria and his contemporaries, and discuss the material in Chapter One with Javier Peña and Francisco Andrés. Some of the research was conducted during an External Faculty Fellowship at the Humanities Research Center, Rice University. I am grateful to Rice for the fellowship and the University of Louisville for the leave time. Finally, as noted above, writing and revisions were supported by a Visiting Fellowship in the Philosophy Department, Research School of Social Sciences, Australian National University.

Some material in the book appeared previously in print. I am grateful to Wiley-Blackwell for permission to reprint, free of charge, material from:

"Justice and the Politics of Deference," *Journal of Political Philosophy* 12 (2005), pp. 153–73.
"Dynamics of Solidarity," *Journal of Political Philosophy* 16 (2009), pp. 365–83.
"The Priority of Solidarity to Justice," *Journal of Applied Philosophy* 31 (2014), pp. 420–33.

In addition to philosophical colleagues, I have learned a great deal from activists whose example never fails to inspire and whose patience with my learning curve has been generous. Among these are—to name only a few— John and Judith Cumbler, Dawn Jenkins, Carol Kraemer, David Lott, David Owen, Attica Scott, Carla Wallace, Carter Wright, and the late Alice Wade and Blaine Hudson.

Anything I say about Karen Christopher can only be a pale reflection of what I wish I could say here. She could have been mentioned under most of the above headings: she is a lovely friend and colleague, she has read paper and chapter drafts, discussed material in various stages of incompletion, provided an example of solidarity, been unfathomably patient with more than just my learning curve, and so much more. She carried me on her shoulders while I was in Australia finishing this book. And, together with our children, Adam and Stella, she makes my life good, every single day.

Contents

List of Figures		xiii
List of Tables		xv
	Introduction	1
1.	Politics and the Limits of Conscience	9
2.	Loyalty and Justice	27
3.	Solidarity in Action	49
4.	Autonomy and Deference	72
5.	The Dilemma of Deference	92
6.	Solidarity as Equity	118
7.	The Ethics of Solidarity	141
8.	Equity and the Limits of Solidarity	166
Select Bibliography		181
Index		191

CONTENTS

List of Figures

4.1 Forms and levels of deference   83
5.1 A process of relationship deference   98

List of Tables

4.1 Deference to bad decisions   87

7.1 *Group Responsibility*   163

7.2 *Conspiracy*   163

7.3 *Shared Responsibility*   164

Introduction

1. "SHALLOW UNDERSTANDING FROM PEOPLE OF GOOD WILL"

In his classic "Letter from Birmingham City Jail," Martin Luther King, Jr. confesses to having become "gravely disappointed with the white moderate."[1] Even more than the members of White Citizen's Councils and the Ku Klux Klan, it is "white moderates" who, in Dr. King's view, have become "the Negro's greatest stumbling block in his stride toward freedom." For the white moderate

> constantly says: 'I agree with you in the goal you seek, but I cannot agree with your methods of direct action'.... Shallow understanding from people of good will is more frustrating than absolute misunderstanding from people of ill will. Lukewarm acceptance is much more bewildering than outright rejection.[2]

From a liberal perspective, it is obvious that we should not be Ku Klux Klanners. From the perspective of today, it is also obvious that we should not have been the "white moderates" whom Martin Luther King challenges here. Yet the fact is, on most issues, most of the time, most of us—white, black, male, female, whatever—are just such "white moderates." Occasionally we might worry about this, perhaps stressing about what "future generations [will] condemn us for,"[3] but on the whole not changing our behavior or being galvanized even on these issues.

Meanwhile, the liberal tradition venerates the lone individual who bucks convention or common opinion, who is not just a statistic or a face in the crowd, but who stands up for what he or she believes in. "Above all, to thine

---

[1] Martin Luther King, "Letter from Birmingham City Jail," in *A Testament of Hope: The Essential Writings and Speeches of Martin Luther King, Jr.*, ed. James M. Washington (San Francisco: HarperSanFrancisco, 1986), 295.

[2] Ibid.

[3] Kwame Anthony Appiah, "What Will Future Generations Condemn Us For?," *Washington Post*, 26 September 2010. Appiah's answers: our prison system, industrial meat production, institutionalizing and isolating the elderly, and the environment.

own self be true," and so on—never mind that it is the fatuous Polonius who says this, rather than some tragic hero at his moment of reckoning.

Why is it, then, that we want to stand up against convention, be true to our individual selves, and avoid behaving in ways that our grandchildren will condemn; and yet by and large we live conventionally? Have we been bought off? Have we internalized the logic of the prisoner's dilemma to the extent that we would rather live condemnably than get the sucker's payoff? Philosophers seem to worry about these issues a lot more than most. And yet, by and large, philosophers live conventional upper-middle-class lives, albeit with a tweak here and there—vegetarianism, Oxfam, what have you. We treat it as a criterion of adequacy for an ethical theory that it can avoid the problem of demandingness. Those of us who have tenure don't even rock the boat of contingent academic labor very much. Liberals love the lone Jeremiah, but on the whole, liberals *live* the Company Man.

I think one key problem here is a tendency to forget the essential third option. We do not need to choose between conformity to convention and total self-abnegation. We have a better choice: solidarity.

Though some excellent work has appeared in the past twenty years, solidarity has been a great neglected subject of recent political philosophy. This is strange, since, in the first place, solidarity is the essential and sometimes the only weapon of all popular politics and justice movements, and second, recent political philosophy emerged out of the 1960s. One of our principal journals was founded precisely to give voice to the new ferment of those times. How then to explain the dearth of careful thinking about solidarity?

It is possible to blame John Rawls. In Rawls's hands, solidarity was "fraternity," fraternity was the difference principle, and the difference principle's purpose was to authorize differential rewards for differential merit.[4] Further, in Rawls's hands civil disobedience was principally a means of democratic communication, pitting the lone voice of Constitutionalism against the majority; and conscientious refusal was about the draft.[5] All of these tend to individualize political life, even political opposition. One current in contemporary political philosophy, continuous with Rawls, uses the term "solidarity" to denote exclusively the basic attitude of support for the welfare state or social-democratic redistribution, notwithstanding the challenges posed by diversity and inequality.[6] Even more explicitly than

---

[4] John Rawls, *A Theory of Justice, Revised Ed.* (Cambridge, MA: Belknap/Harvard University Press, 1999), 90.

[5] Ibid., 319–44.

[6] On solidarity in the face of diversity, see David Kahane, Daniel Weinstock, and Alison M. Jaggar, "Symposium: Diversity and Civic Solidarity," *Journal of Political Philosophy* 7 (1999). On solidarity as a strategy for transcending inequalities, see Carol Gould, *Globalizing Democracy and Human Rights* (New York: Cambridge University Press, 2004). For discussion of "civic solidarity" as such, see Sally Scholz, *Political Solidarity* (University Park, PA: Penn State University Press, 2008), 27–33.

Rawls, this approach gives up on the solidarity that mans the barricades in favor of the "solidarity" that files the tax return. Whereas Locke's contractors delegate their right to punish, Rawls's parties delegate their role in political struggle.[7] Just as a criminal justice system absolves us of the duty of exacting retribution from those who wrong us, so bureaucratic transfer payments absolve us of the duty of street-level solidarity with those who are oppressed.

It is possible to blame some of Rawls's followers and critics, who treated certain of his simplifying assumptions as ground rules for the very possibility of political philosophy, and whose particular interest in specific aspects of the theory—however important in their own right—inevitably distorted the whole. A principal problem in this zone was the focus on "ideal theory" and the indefinite postponement of nonideal justice, given that solidarity has typically been understood as required for *building* justice.[8] That the Rawlsians inhabited the "left wing"—as against libertarians and communitarians—in most philosophical debates of the 1970s, 1980s, and 1990s, did not, of course, help.

It is also possible to blame the Vietnam War. As occurred once again during the more recent Iraq catastrophe, wars, even overseas wars, have a way of sucking up all political energy. It becomes difficult to get traction in critique of anything else. Political opposition to the regime is either muted by nationalist sentiment or redirected towards opposition to the war. And opposition to aggressive wars like those in Vietnam or Iraq is not especially conducive to solidarity, since it is hard to communicate with the victims, and what they want seems too obvious to require finding out about—they want us to stop killing them.

It is possible, finally, to blame the demographics and power structure of analytic political philosophy. The great recent work on solidarity has principally been due to philosophers from groups that are euphemistically called "traditionally underrepresented" within philosophy. Many of these works also emerge out of debates and fields that were marginal to, or outside of, analytic political philosophy per se, and continue to be largely ignored within it—particularly philosophy of race, ecofeminism, and feminism more broadly.[9] Moreover, the tenured white men who have dominated political philosophy

[7] G. A. Cohen, *Rescuing Justice and Equality* (Cambridge, MA: Harvard University Press, 2009), 44.

[8] Rawls, *A Theory of Justice, Revised Ed.*, 212.

[9] Greta Gaard, ed. *Ecofeminism* (Philadelphia: Temple University Press, 1993); Jodi Dean, *Solidarity of Strangers* (Berkeley and Los Angeles: University of California Press, 1996); Chandra Talpade Mohanty, *Feminism without Borders: Decolonizing Theory, Practicing Solidarity* (Durham, NC: Duke University Press, 2003); Tommie Shelby, *We Who Are Dark: Philosophical Foundations of Black Solidarity* (Cambridge, MA: Harvard University Press, 2005); Scholz, *Political Solidarity*.

tend to think themselves—and I don't mean to exclude myself here— particularly good in the deployment of reasoning and, especially, moral reasoning. Yet as I shall argue at length in this book, a key element of solidarity is *deference* on questions of prudential judgment and conscience. A proper mistrust of our own conscience—particularly if we are among the privileged— is a particularly valuable habit of a just person. But deference does not, to say the least, come naturally to tenured white male political philosophers; nor, obviously, is mistrust of our own moral reasoning inculcated into us in graduate school or rewarded in publication. And anyway, if voiced uncare- fully, the idea of deference on moral or political questions sounds like that most illiberal of political orientations, conformity to the mob or to illegitimate authority.

2. SOLIDARITY ITSELF

Before going overboard pointing the finger of blame it may be better to consider whether solidarity's earlier unpopularity had to do with the concept itself. "Solidarity" is first of all very fuzzy. It is used in many different ways. *Human* solidarity supposedly grounds a love of all humanity such that we should support peace and the elimination of poverty beyond national borders.[10] *National* or *civic* solidarity supposedly inclines us to support our compatriots with social welfare schemes, despite the fact that we are also concomitantly locked in economic competition with them.[11] *Class* solidarity supposedly does or should unite social classes, particularly the working class, to overcome the prisoner's dilemma-type situation in which capitalism places them. *Racial* and *ethnic* solidarity supposedly lead us to treat our co-ethnics with special regard and support.

Each of these notions seems to presuppose an antecedent group whose boundaries also delimit the solidarity in question.[12] Each also, perhaps for that reason, seems to assume that solidarity is something like a feeling or an inclination rather than a reason. It should be unsurprising, then, that liberals are skeptical of solidarity. We don't need to lay any blame on liberals or liberalism; instead we should blame the communitarianism of solidarity, its fundamentally illiberal commitment to the existence of antecedent groupings and an irrationalist politics based on fellow-feeling. Groups and fellow-feeling

---

[10] Kevin Watkins, "Human Development Report 2007–2008: Fighting Climate Change: Human Solidarity in a Divided World" (New York: United Nations Development Program, 2007).

[11] David Miller, *Citizenship and National Identity* (Cambridge, UK: Polity Press, 2000).

[12] Ulrich K. Preuss, "National, Supranational, and International Solidarity," in *Solidarity*, ed. Kurt Bayertz (Dordrecht: Springer, 1999), 281.

might have a place in liberal political philosophy, but they can only be derivative on justice.

Much of the recent work mentioned in the preceding paragraphs, however, particularly the feminist and ecofeminist work of Scholz, Gaard, Lugones, and others, denies that solidarity must be built out of antecedent groups. Rather, solidarity has an essential role in constructing the group. Scholz valuably distinguishes between "social" solidarities, which are predicated on antecedent group membership, and "political" solidarity, which is not.[13] She thus renders "political solidarity" safe for liberalism—safer, indeed, than the "civic" solidarity that supports welfare schemes for all and only those who find themselves within our borders—and in this respect my approach is an account of political solidarity.

Yet my approach departs from some of this recent work in being more skeptical of relationships, trust, and sympathies. My approach is Kantian. In one respect this Kantianism makes my view even safer for liberalism, given its individualistic orientation. But in a deeper sense my approach challenges liberalism more sharply, since the whole idea is that we should be in solidarity despite disagreement, despite the lack of relationships of trust or mutuality, despite lack of sympathy. The argument for solidarity can thus override our conscience even without grounding in emotions or communities. Consequently, I dwell at length on distrust of individual conscience and on deference to the group.

There is another reason for my departure from some earlier work, namely, that my theory of solidarity principally addresses not the oppressed themselves, but the person who joins when the oppressed call. I understand solidarity, in the first instance, as political action *on others' terms*. If solidarity is justified by siding with the oppressed, then, by taking the perspective of the "joiner" rather than the "caller," I have perforce taken the perspective of the more privileged. By contrast, feminist and critical race theorists might be inclined to understand solidarity as political action *on collective terms*—without the self/other distinction—taking the perspective of those who struggle to overcome their own oppressions. I admit this difference in orientation; and some of my principal cases, from Spanish critics of the *Conquista* to white southerners under Jim Crow, do indeed take the perspective of the more privileged person called to lay aside that privilege. I think this is one of the most theoretically interesting and politically important sites of solidarity, and, often, one of the most glaringly absent, especially from liberal thought and practice. This belief is grounded in my own experience of both philosophy and politics, to be sure, but it is also grounded in reflection on Dr. King's powerful words about "white moderates."

I also insist that there is no one who counts as worst off in all contexts. Those who are oppressed in circumstances *Z* might be called upon to support

---

[13] Scholz, *Political Solidarity*, 21.

victims of oppression in *Y*; nothing requires that the former are "privileged" *simpliciter*, or even that they are *more privileged* than the latter on any reasonable measure. My orientation, distinguishing between caller and joiner, makes better sense of this fact, and more easily avoids certain problems of essentialism and antecedent group identity, than does thinking about solidarity in terms of the collective struggle of those who are oppressed or who antecedently agree. And moreover, even the oppressed, once in solidarity, must defer to collective judgment in the ways I describe. The fact that the goal of solidarity is their own collective interests rather than the interests of some other group does not entail that every participant will personally agree with every means adopted by the group, or even every goal it pursues. To the contrary; each is an individual. Thus my orientation is less from the perspective of *the privileged* than from that of *the joiner*, who need have no antecedent link, be it cognitive, identitarian, or structural, to the caller. This kind of case isolates the normative force of solidarity, and for that reason it is my core case.

By contrast, much recent work on solidarity, including on "political solidarity" as Scholz understands it, assumes that we—the "we" of the group—broadly agree on where justice lies, that we gain strength and affirmation through our participation in the group, and consequently, that our unification in solidary action brings a meeting of minds and hearts. That may indeed happen. Nonetheless, my worries regarding this "collective" approach are twofold. First, methodologically, it generates a theory of solidarity for the easy cases, where the function of the call to solidarity is merely to solve collective action problems and motivate us to do what we already know is right. Solidarity is then understood teleologically as a collective effort to bring about ends for which we have a compelling independent justification. The real test of solidarity, however, comes when we are called to do something we think prudentially or even morally unwise, or to support someone whose judgment we question. This is when we demand a justification of why we should do what solidarity requires (*de dicto*)—why solidarity in itself is morally worthy. The answer cannot appeal to the evident justice of the cause, since that is what we doubt. Nor can it rely on convincing us of the rightness of the act in question (*de re*), since then solidarity per se does no moral work.

Second, the collective approach tricks us into moralizing the concept of solidarity, as though solidarity were necessarily about pursuing justice. This orientation seems to me both too narrow and too broad. It is too narrow because many cases of solidarity aim at injustice or perpetrate injustice along the way. Nazis, for instance, seem to be capable of solidarity, as do violent revolutionaries of all stripes. A moralized conception makes Nazi solidarity *conceptually impossible*. But it is not; it is morally wrong, but it is still solidarity. The moralizing conception is also too broad, because some cases of acting together for justice are not solidarity. Solidarity seems to require acting with others *because that's what they ask of us*, not because we happen to agree on ends. I might join a political party because I agree with its platform, but I join a solidarity movement because I am asked. Solidarity thus requires at least a counterfactual disposition to do what the agent disagrees with.

Solidarity is, then, about working together, but insofar as it is a morally distinctive notion it is working together *irrespective of whether we agree.* Just as political solidarity must depart from the antecedent *social* unity that delimits our fellow-feeling, so it must depart from the antecedent *moral* unity that delimits our collective action.

3. OUTLINE OF THE BOOK

A Moral Theory of Solidarity is divided into eight chapters that together try to solve three fundamental problems. The first is the *conceptual* problem of defining solidarity, which consumes Chapters Two and Three. I start with a preliminary definition of solidarity as *political action on others' terms.* This means that in solidarity we act as others direct or would direct—in effect, we act as their understudy or their surrogate. If I am in solidarity with you then I am disposed to act, on the front end, as you would, and I am disposed to accept, on the back end, the same treatment as you receive. Thus the definition captures both deference in the choice of action and shared fate in the acceptance of consequences. The definition is, importantly, nonevaluative. Nazis are perfectly capable of solidarity. Yet the preliminary definition is inadequate by itself, and must be both fleshed out more fully and operationalized in a plausible social ontology and a theory of collective action. That is the task of Chapter Three.

The second problem, which principally comprises Chapters Four and Five, is the *agency* problem of how to understand individuality and autonomy in agents who are in solidarity. The key here is that deference departs from autonomy. In solidarity I choose as directed, on both moral and prudential matters. This rejection of the sovereignty of conscience seems like a radical departure from a liberal orientation. I argue, however, that a certain strand of liberalism is perfectly comfortable with deference, in some forms. But this raises an obvious question, or indeed, what I call a "dilemma of deference." If we must defer on conscientious questions, what is to stop us deferring to Nazis? But if we can avoid deferring to Nazis, isn't that going to require that we deploy our autonomous moral reasoning? And if so, then the sovereignty of conscience comes in through the back door. I dissolve this dilemma with a structural criterion of deference: we can defer to the least well-off, which is cashed out as those who suffer inequity.

Which leads us, finally, to the *justificatory* problem: when ought we to be in solidarity, with whom, and why? Is solidarity ever obligatory, or is it merely (sometimes) permissible? Subsidiary to the justificatory problem are other questions about the ethics of solidarity. For instance, if solidarity is about submerging one's conscience, who is responsible for morally problematic actions taken in solidarity? Is violence ever permissible? These issues consume Chapters Six through Eight. My account is Kantian and deontological. Solidarity with those who suffer inequity constitutes equitable treatment of them. As equitable treatment, solidarity is a perfect duty; solidarity is partly constitutive of equity, and since equity is what Joseph Raz calls an "ultimate value,"[14] it follows that *solidarity with the least well-off is intrinsically valuable even when it does not bring about justice*. This seems to me to be the right result. Dr. King sits in Birmingham City Jail in 1963 before passage of the Civil Rights Act, before the Voting Rights Act. He has no idea how the movement will turn out. For all he knows it will lead to a hardening of white reaction. Indeed, that is a plausible partial analysis of how it actually did turn out over the next twenty years and beyond.[15] Still, there is simply no doubt which side we should be on. Similar things can be said about the Denmark Vesey uprising, the Warsaw Ghetto Uprising, and indigenous peoples' struggles against colonial rule. Solidarity is not about picking winners, it is about taking sides.

As a perfect duty of equity, as an instance of equitable treatment, solidarity is not optional. Responding to the call for solidarity from those who suffer inequity is analogous to returning someone's wallet when you find it: if you don't do it, you have wronged them. But this returns us to the problem of demandingness. I argue in Chapter Seven that all that we can demand of ourselves and others is that we live for justice, in a meaningful sense of this idea.

It all begins, though, in 1511. Chapter One reflects on the contrasting politics of Francisco de Vitoria and Bartolomé de las Casas in the first century of the Spanish *Conquista*. Both were opponents of the conquest; Vitoria, the leading jurist of his day, even argued that the Spanish transatlantic enterprise was illegal. Yet Vitoria remained, as it were, a prisoner of his own conscience—he could not break out of a conscientious orientation, where the limits of his own capacity to tolerate others defined the limits of his moral imagination. In contrast, for all his own limitations, Las Casas was able to transcend his conscience and defend the Indians even in behavior that he believed to be unconscionable. We see Las Casas here taking sides with those who were least well-off and submerging his own conscience under theirs. Though Las Casas is sometimes called the conscience of the empire, he is better understood as having overcome conscience in the name of solidarity. His case sets the stage for the book as a whole.

[14] Joseph Raz, *The Morality of Freedom* (Oxford: Clarendon Press, 1986), 177.
[15] Rick Perlstein, *Nixonland: The Rise of a President and the Fracturing of America* (New York: Scribner, 2008).

1

Politics and the Limits of Conscience

In 1538 the great Spanish Thomist Francisco de Vitoria, founder of the "School of Salamanca," delivered his courses on the "recently discovered Indians" of the Americas.[1] Perhaps due to political pressure he never published these lectures, but they had an immediate impact and his students' presumably faithful lecture notes were compiled and published after his death. Although it was reports from the conquest of Peru in particular that made Vitoria's blood freeze in his veins,[2] we can assume that Vitoria was influenced in part by the writing and activism of Bartolomé de las Casas, who had, since the 1510s, been struggling to lighten the burden of Spanish rule on the Americans.[3] Las Casas himself was initially spurred by the priest Antonio de Montesinos, whose sermons in Española (now the Dominican Republic) in 1511 lashed out at the Spanish conquistadors:

> Are these not men? Do they not have rational souls? Are you not obligated to love them as yourselves? Do you not understand this? Do you not feel this? How could you be in so deep and lazy a slumber?[4]

---

[1] Francisco de Vitoria, *Political Writings* (Cambridge: Cambridge University Press, 1991). Throughout this chapter I will mostly use "Indians" to describe the indigenous peoples of the Americas. I do this because I want to follow the usage of the authors I am discussing, but also because, as I understand it, this term is not, or no longer, considered inappropriate. See Taiaiake Alfred, *Peace, Power, Righteousness: An Indigenous Manifesto* (Toronto: Oxford University Press, 1999), xxvi.

[2] See Vitoria's "Letter to Miguel Arcos" in Vitoria, *Political Writings*. See also the discussion in Juan Goti Ordeñana, *Del Tratado De Tordesillas a La Doctrina De Los Derechos Fundamentales En Francisco De Vitoria* (Valladolid: Secretariado de Publicaciones e Intercambio Científico, Universidad de Valladolid, 1999), 212–13.

[3] Daniel Castro, *Another Face of Empire: Bartolomé De Las Casas, Indigenous Rights, and Ecclesiastical Imperialism* (Durham, NC: Duke University Press, 2007); Lawrence A. Clayton, *Bartolomé De Las Casas: A Biography* (New York: Cambridge University Press, 2012).

[4] "¿Estos, no son hombres? ¿No tienen ánimas racionales? ¿No sois obligados a amallos como a vosotros mismos? ¿Esto no entendéis? ¿Esto no sentís? ¿Cómo estáis en tanta profundidad de sueño tan letárgico dormidos?" Mercedes Serna, ed. *La Conquista Del Nuevo Mundo: Textos Y Documentos De La Aventura Americana* (Madrid: Castalia, 2012), 241–2.

Vitoria, in turn, incited a national crisis of conscience regarding the American adventure. "La duda vitoriana"—the Vitorian Doubt—spread through the Spanish elite, all the way up to Emperor Charles V.[5] Vitoria's critique was strengthened and refined by later Salamancans, including his student and successor in the Prime Chair of Theology, Melchor Cano, and Juan de la Peña.[6]

It is a staggering irony that one of the greatest wrongs in the history of the world—the Iberian conquest of what is now Latin America, which caused or constituted what is likely the largest demographic collapse ever[7] and inaugurated the Trans-Atlantic slave trade—was explicitly and self-consciously undertaken as a moral enterprise, under conscientious moral scrutiny. Conscience, be it in royal decrees, hearings and inquests, the establishment of a "Defender of the Indians," a monastic order dedicated to their protection, and influential pronouncements from the most prominent theologians of the day, was for the first century of the conquest always in play. And although the voice of conscience was explicitly Catholic, it was in many respects recognizable as a nonsectarian moral call to treat people as full equals and to respect human rights. The *Conquista* was carried out under the flag of a kind of moral universalism.[8]

In this chapter I want to perform an "ethical autopsy"[9] of the Spanish conscience in the sixteenth century. I want to show that conscience is not

---

[5] See Luciano Pereña's introduction to Juan de la Peña, *De Bello Contra Insulanos: Intervención De España En América: Escuela Española De La Paz, Segunda Generación, 1560–1585: Testigos Y Fuentes*, ed. L. Pereña, Corpus Hispanorum De Pace (Madrid: Consejo Superior de Investigaciones Científicas, 1982).

[6] Ibid.; Anthony Pagden, "Conquest and the Just War: The 'School of Salamanca' and the 'Affair of the Indies'," in *Empire and Modern Political Thought*, ed. Sankar Muthu (New York: Cambridge University Press, 2012), 48; María Lourdes Redondo Redondo, *Utopía Vitoriana Y Realidad Indiana* (Madrid: Fundación Universitaria Española, 1992).

[7] Tzvetan Todorov calls it a genocide: "If the word genocide has ever been applied to a situation with some accuracy, this is here the case. It constitutes a record not only in relative terms (a destruction on the order of 90 percent or more), but also in absolute terms, since we are speaking of a population diminution estimated at 70 million human lives." However, as Larry May notes, the *crime* of genocide requires *mens rea*. And it seems clear that the Spaniards lacked the intent to commit genocide. (Though other crimes they certainly intended, and a demographic collapse they certainly caused.) Tzvetan Todorov, *The Conquest of America: The Question of the Other*, trans. Richard Howard (New York: Harper & Row, 1984), 133; Larry May, *Crimes against Humanity: A Normative Account* (New York: Cambridge University Press, 2005), 168–70.

[8] Anthony Pagden, "Human Rights, Natural Rights, and Europe's Imperial Legacy," *Political Theory* 31, no. 2 (2003); Carole Pateman and Charles Mills, *Contract & Domination* (Cambridge: Polity Press, 2007). See also Burke A. Hendrix, "Political Theorists as Dangerous Social Actors," *Critical Review of International Social and Political Philosophy* 15, no. 1 (2012).

[9] Allen E. Buchanan et al., *From Chance to Choice* (New York: Cambridge University Press, 2000), 42. Buchanan has reconsidered this ethical autopsy in ways that I find deeply instructive; see Allen Buchanan, "Institutions, Beliefs and Ethics: Eugenics as a Case Study," *Journal of Political Philosophy* 15, no. 1 (2007).

enough to guide theory or practice in politically charged situations. Conscience defaults to hegemonic frames and fails to bridge gaps of culture or familiarity. Something else is needed if we are to break free of these intellectual bonds. That is the thesis of this chapter. Bearing this thesis out are the limitations of Vitoria's doctrine as well as Las Casas's decisive shift from slave-owning voice of conscience to abolitionist and apologist for unconscionable Indian practices such as human sacrifice and anthropophagy.

I borrow the idea of an ethical autopsy from Allen Buchanan and his coauthors, who use this method to dissect the eugenic ideal of the late nineteenth and early twentieth centuries.[10] Although everyone knows eugenics is a moral "dead letter," we pay little attention to what killed it. Indeed, precisely the unanimity on this matter prevents our paying attention, because everyone assumes that the answer would be obvious. In reality, the ethics of eugenics is messy. Buchanan et al. remark upon "the complexity of the eugenics movement," arguing for the

> Importance…of informing our moral evaluation of past events and actors with an understanding of how the world seemed through their eyes.…The 'real' story is less tractable, less teachable, and harder to mine for bioethical insights. Attempts to draw lessons from this history require great caution.[11]

An ethical autopsy can be a powerful antidote to anachronism and Whiggish history. It can also offset the dangerous temptation to see great evils as the work of unique monsters who are utterly unlike ourselves. As Tzvetan Todorov and others have argued, having reflected on extreme cases of historical evil, the world is generally populated by "neither monsters nor beasts," but by ordinary people who are—probably like all of us—capable of horrific evil if they find themselves caught up in situations or social structures that magnify ordinary vices.[12] Such perverse circumstances as extreme honor cultures; ascriptions of subpersonhood to an identifiable other; the enjoyment of power over these putative subpersons; and the ability to bifurcate one's mind to prevent full awareness enable ordinary people to do great evil. Such circumstances seem to have existed in Spain and particularly among the conquistadors in the fifteenthth–sixteenth centuries. Ascriptions of extreme evil to some people—such as Columbus or Sepúlveda—as individuals tend to just re-ask a question rather than offer useful answers.

For similar reasons, ethical autopsy can also teach us something about our own times. "Evildoers" in our times are in the above respects most often like "evildoers" in other times. This neither excuses nor minimizes the evil that they do. But it does enable us to see anew the social conditions that enable evil,

---

[10] Buchanan et al., *From Chance to Choice*, 42ff.   [11] Ibid., 29.
[12] See Tzvetan Todorov, *Facing the Extreme: Moral Life in the Concentration Camps*, trans. Arthur Denner and Abigail Pollak (New York: Metropolitan Books, 1996), 121ff.

including the conditions surrounding ourselves that make us capable of grave wrongs, and to diagnose the problem more accurately.

There are important moral parallels between Spain in the sixteenth century and the wealthy "West" today. In particular, in an age of globalization, we find ourselves participating in morally problematic institutions and processes that have thrown societies worldwide into upheaval. The most powerful negative effects fall on distant strangers and others whose voices we rarely hear, and when we do hear them it is, often as not, because some of them wash up on our shores while others commit acts of terrorism. It is exceedingly hard to know whether our global institutions are for the best in either the short- or the long-term; and even if it might have been better had some policy never been adopted or institution never created, it is not clear whether it should or could be scrapped or dialed back. We may suspect that our comfort or our preoccupations are preventing us from taking moral outrages with adequate seriousness, or that our prejudices are allowing us to shrug at real harm. We might even, like those before us who profited from slavery, be living irreme- diably blighted lives.[13] Recognizing these similarities between ourselves and others whose moral situation is perhaps clearer—to us, now—may help us get some critical perspective on our own situation, and thus learn about it. As there are today, among the Spaniards of the sixteenth century there were people of conscience, creativity, and courage. Taking at face value the language of conscience that these thinkers and political actors employed, we can discern the limits of conscience.

"Conscience" is itself a fraught notion. I understand it to mean a distinct- ively and recognizably *moral* impulse that nonetheless falls short of a full moral theory. Conscience is bound by criteria of rationality or reasons-respon- siveness—though sometimes conscience might lead us to stamp our foot because of a moral intuition for which we lack good arguments but which we are currently unwilling to reject. It is also bound by rational consistency; though perfect consistency cannot be expected, the agent moved by conscience is normally one who is concerned to be consistent and especially not to be hypocritical. Conscience is typically informed by religious or other external commitments, and when push comes to shove the person of conscience might fall back on religious authority to ground conscience. Conscience principally challenges the self, be it the individual self or the collective self, such as the nation or family to which one belongs. Consequently, conscience can put some limits on loyalty and prejudice, but it can also serve as the voice of the

---

[13] This is Stephen Gardiner's powerful and disturbing suggestion regarding our contributions to global warming. See Stephen M. Gardiner, *A Perfect Moral Storm: The Ethical Tragedy of Climate Change* (New York: Oxford University Press, 2011). See also Christopher Kutz, *Com- plicity: Ethics and Law for a Collective Age* (New York: Cambridge University Press, 2000), 184–91.

group or of conventional prejudice when we depart from what is expected.[14] Sincere appeals to conscience are not willy-nilly or fleeting. Right or wrong, the appeal to conscience is an assertion of a commitment to be bound by the dictate so discovered. We might fail in, or override, this commitment; and it might well be wrong; but it is a commitment nonetheless.

Conscience can be—and in sixteenth-century Spain, was—a trenchant voice in critique of power. I shall show, however, that conscience *just isn't enough* to enable us to comprehend the nature of grave evils or our role in them. It is inadequately perceptive and, although it can lead people to take real risks and even reshape their lives in morally admirable ways, conscience is in its own way inadequately demanding. Or perhaps better, it can demand both too much and too little, damaging us and our causes in both respects. Ultimately we must *overcome* conscience in favor of solidarity.

A note on method before moving on. I will be taking the writings and motives of the Spaniards, including the Crown, at face value. There can be no doubt that their motives were—to say the least—compromised. But even if their putatively conscientious motives were not their true motives, one can argue that "hypocrisy is the homage that vice pays to virtue," and we can learn about what the Crown believed to be morally important by what justifications it gave for its policies.[15] Moreover, as Todorov emphasizes,[16] to deal honestly with Columbus and others of his time we need to get into their worldview rather than impose our own. They really did think they were doing God's work, and the breathtaking events occurring around them—subduing mighty empires with vastly outnumbered forces, for instance—seemed to them to be confirming this belief. We may know that they were wrong about that, but they did not.

1.1 CONSCIENCE IN CONQUEST

Todorov begins his study of "the question of the Other" not with the singular encounter between Columbus and the Indians but with that between ourselves as readers and the man Columbus. It takes a feat of the imagination to get inside his head. He was a medieval religious zealot, not so much interested in wealth and power as the word and deed of God. When he sailed, Columbus could not initially have intended *conquest*; he thought he was going to India

---

[14] On the place of prejudice and bias in conscience see Hannah Arendt, *Eichmann in Jerusalem: A Report on the Banality of Evil* (New York: Viking Press, 1963), 148–50; Chloë Fitzgerald, "A Neglected Aspect of Conscience: Awareness of Implicit Attitudes," *Bioethics* 28, no. 1 (2014).

[15] Michael Walzer, *Just and Unjust Wars*, Second ed. (New York: Basic Books, 1992), 19.

[16] Todorov, *Conquest*, 10.

LIVERPOOL JOHN MOORES UNIVERSITY
LEARNING SERVICES

and China, countries that were well known to have advanced political systems and military might that Spain, a mid-level power even by European standards, could not hope to match. A man of profoundly medieval sensibilities, Columbus wanted to visit the Grand Khan because Marco Polo had reported that the Khan desired to hear the Gospel.[17]

From the beginning, the Spanish Crown sought to conduct its affairs in a morally upstanding way. Roman law permitted enslavement of captives from a just war. The medieval Christian worldview implied that infidels lacked legal personhood and could consequently be enslaved. The Spanish Crown accepted neither doctrine in the case of the Indians, instead repudiating their enslavement altogether. In 1493, Pope Alexander III had supposedly "donated" the world to the Crowns of Spain and Portugal, to be governed in the interests of the inhabitants, principally in the sense of bringing Christianity to them. As Queen Isabella understood these Bulls of Donation, it followed that those Indigenous Americans who were resident in the Spanish zones were *already subjects of the Crown of Castilla*. Spaniards could not enslave or make war on subjects of the Queen. Indians who resisted were traitorous or uninformed subjects, not enemy armies, and once the perpetrators were subdued and converted there was no cause for war.

Consequently, first Queen Isabella, then her widower Ferdinand, and then their grandson Charles, repeatedly sought to rein in abuses of Indians. In 1500, Isabella commanded the repatriation of any American slaves brought to Europe and proclaimed those who had been enslaved to be free.[18] In 1502 her emissary Nicolás de Ovando arrived to carry out this proclamation. Unfortunately, the means for doing this in turn caused the most catastrophic period of the Conquista. In 1503 Ovando created the *encomienda*, a kind of feudal plantation where Indians were the property of Spaniards. Juan Goti Ordeñana argues that the *encomienda* was intended as a *response* to the catastrophic collapse of the Indian population up to 1503. The idea was to require that Spanish colonists take responsibility for the welfare of "their" Indians. This was the responsibility that Montesinos reminded them of eight years later, in 1511: to

> give them food and cure their illnesses,...to teach them to know God their Creator, to be baptized, to hear mass, and to keep the Sabbath and holy days.[19]

Yet even if the intentions reflected a kind of constrained humanitarianism, the *encomienda* became one of the most horrific institutions ever devised. The

---

[17] Ibid.

[18] This discussion relies on Goti Ordeñana, *Tratado*.

[19] Serna, *Conquista*, 242. "...sin dalles de comer ni curallos en sus enfermedades...? ¿Y qué cuidado tenéis de quien los doctrine, y conozcan a su Dios y criador, sean batizados, oigan misa, guarden las fiestas y domingos?"

encomienda "became a means of exploitation of the Indians. They were disappearing because of epidemics, forced labor, suicide, enslavement, and war. The years from 1504–1511…were the worst years of the entire Spanish colonial period."[20] Las Casas blames this horror on the disorder at the top caused by Isabella's death and the extended interregnum while her husband Ferdinand—who was only King of Aragón, not of Castilla—exercised sovereignty on behalf of their daughter. Las Casas writes,

> It is of note that all these island territories began to go to the dogs once news arrived of the death [in 1504] of our most gracious Queen Isabella…. Up to then, only a small number of provinces had been destroyed through unjust military action, not the whole area, and news of even this partial destruction had been kept from the Queen, because, she…took a close personal interest in the physical and spiritual welfare of the native peoples.[21]

Ferdinand eventually tried to stop the carnage. In 1511, upon hearing of Montesinos's sermons and his refusal to hear confession from *encomenderos*, Ferdinand convened the Junta of Burgos to do a moral review of the transatlantic enterprise. Montesinos himself represented the Dominican order at the Junta. The result was the Burgos Laws and the Valladolid Laws of 1512–13, which amount to the first modern human-rights statute. They decreed that Indians were free and were to be instructed in the faith, and that their work was to be voluntary, justly remunerated, punctuated by breaks, and never so onerous as to interfere with their religious instruction.[22] But as with Isabella's proclamation a decade earlier, the good intentions of the Burgos laws became the engine of their spectacular failure. For the Burgos laws introduced the *Requerimiento*, a document that conquistadors were required to read to Indians before assuming political power or assigning Indians to *encomiendas*.

It is possible that the Crown genuinely thought the *Requerimiento* would help protect Indians from coercion, since it acknowledged their moral and political freedom, hence their full personhood. Read in Spanish, without interpreters, to newly encountered Indians, the *Requerimiento* informed them of the Sovereignty of the Crown and the divinity of Jesus and demanded that they submit—freely, of course—to the Crown (and the *encomienda*). If they refused, the ensuing war, depredations, and enslavement would be just, because voluntarily chosen by the Indians themselves. It is hard to know

---

[20] Ibid., 232. "Pero la encomienda se convirtió en un medio de explotación de los indios. Estos fueron desapareciendo a causa de las epidemias, los trabajos forzados, los suicidios, la esclavitud o las guerras. Los años que van de 1504 a 1511, indica Lesley B. Simpson, fueron los peores de toda la colonización española [citing Simpson, *The Encomienda in New Spain*, Berkeley, 1929, p. 41]."

[21] Bartolomé de las Casas, *A Short Account of the Destruction of the Indies* (New York: Penguin, 1992), 25.

[22] Serna, *Conquista*, 253–88; Goti Ordeñana, *Tratado*, 191.

now whether anyone was ever sincerely convinced by the sheen of legitimacy that the *Requerimiento* provided, but I think that some were. By the time Vitoria decisively repudiated it in 1538 (on which, more later), it was obvious to many people that the *Requerimiento* was an absurd and transparent fig-leaf for imperialism.[23] But that does not mean it was completely insincere at the time. Indeed it fits into a long history of merely formal but in reality coercive "agreements" and duties to inform, which, to this day, characterize relations between actors with stark power differentials—think of powerful employers and putatively free labor,[24] or bomb-droppers and the civilians who receive warning leaflets or "knocks on the roof" in advance—yet which serve to hide, *from the powerful*, the real moral weight of what they are doing. The philosophical history of moral universalism and individual autonomy is polluted not only by empire but by the frequency of such "coercive offers."[25]

Another major milestone in Spanish efforts to act in a justifiable way was the famous Valladolid debate of 1550–51, pitting Las Casas against Sepúlveda and judged by a panel of theologians and jurists. The debate was officially sponsored by the Crown because Sepúlveda—the leading Aristotelian of the time—had written a book purporting to justify the *Conquista* on grounds that the Indians were Aristotelian "natural slaves," and arguing that it was consequently right to compel them to give up their putatively evil practices and adopt Christianity. But he could not get permission to publish. Nor was he able to win that right at Valladolid, from which result Las Casas, at least, inferred that Sepúlveda's views were discredited. It should be emphasized that his conclusions would have been convenient for the Crown. But for reasons of conscience the Crown rejected them.

If the Crown was so conscientious, it may be wondered why Charles V did not simply call off the *Conquista* altogether and abandon the Americas. One answer is that this is less far-fetched than it seems. In 1549 the Council of the Indies "advised the king that the dangers both to the Indians and to the king's conscience which the conquests incurred were so great that no new expedition ought to be licensed without his express permission and that of the Council."[26] And as noted above, on April 16, 1550, Charles ordered "that all conquests be suspended in the New World" until the conclusion of the Las Casas–Sepúlveda

---

[23] Serna, *Conquista*, 296; Lewis Hanke, *Aristotle and the American Indians: A Study in Race Prejudice in the Modern World* (Chicago: H. Regnery Co., 1959), 16; see also Charles W. Mills, *The Racial Contract* (Ithaca: Cornell University Press, 1997), 22–3.

[24] Kevin Bales, *Disposable People: New Slavery in the Global Economy* (Berkeley and Los Angeles: University of California Press, 1999), chap. 1.

[25] On "coercive offers" see Lisa Fuller, "International NGO Health Programs in a Non-Ideal World: Imperialism, Respect and Procedural Justice," in *Global Justice and Bioethics*, ed. J. Millum and E. Emanuel (New York: Oxford University Press, 2012), 220–2.

[26] Hanke, *Aristotle and the American Indians*, 35–6.

debate.[27] Evacuating Spanish colonists from the New World was a different story. By the mid-sixteenth century it would likely have been impossible anyway. The Emperor did in fact ban the *encomienda* but later reneged on this because the *encomenderos* were too powerful. They had become a fifth column of powerful settler extremists who were armed and dangerous and had frontier sensibilities, emboldened by the fact that Spain had come to depend on them for the infusions of gold and other precious metals that could only temporarily allay the consequences of the hyperinflation caused by this very same plunder.[28]

It may also be that Charles thought he had no right to abandon the enterprise. As far as he was concerned, the Bulls of Donation made the Americas as much a part of Spain as Seville. Spaniards also ironically feared that abandoning the Americas would cause a humanitarian catastrophe, since the Indians no longer had the skills or religion, the demography or geography that they had had in 1491. Again, the Emperor may well have been wrong about these things, but to explain his action what we need to know is not what the truth of the matter was, but what he believed it to be. And in the belief that abandoning the transatlantic enterprise would be a humanitarian catastrophe, he appears to have been joined by the entire spectrum of elite opinion in Spain. Even Las Casas, in his *Apologia*—his defense of the Indians against Sepúlveda at Valladolid—assumes that at least a nominal Spanish presence is necessary. Anthony Pagden notes that Las Casas also accepted the Donation, using its putatively humanitarian core to argue for the overthrow of the *encomienda*.

It was not Las Casas but Vitoria who repudiated the Alexandrine Donation. Indeed, although Vitoria reads today as considerably less critical of empire than Las Casas,[29] in one key respect at least Vitoria was the more radical. For not only did he object morally, as Las Casas did, to the conduct of the Conquista and the *encomiendas*,[30] but Vitoria systematically smashed the legal and theological foundations of the entire enterprise. Vitoria of course rejected the "natural slaves" thesis that, as we have seen, even the Crown

---

[27] Ibid., 36–7.

[28] Clayton, *Bartolomé De Las Casas: A Biography*. For some discussion of monetary issues see André A. Alves and J. Moreira, *The Salamanca School* (New York: Continuum, 2010).

[29] Or at least, the Vitoria of 1538 reads as less critical than the Las Casas of 1554. It is unfortunate that we have only a snapshot of Vitoria on this question, in contrast to the relatively clear picture of evolution that we see in Las Casas from 1511 to 1566. I shall discuss Las Casas's radicalization in section 1.2. For discussion see Enrique Dussel, "Orígen De La Filosofía Política Moderna: Las Casas, Vitoria, Y Suárez (1514–1617)," *Caribbean Studies* 33, no. 2 (2005). On Vitoria's (in)famous doctrine of hospitality, see Timothy Waligore, "Cosmopolitan Right, Indigenous Peoples, and the Risks of Cultural Interaction," *Public Reason* 1, no. 1 (2009).

[30] His most personal cry of conscience is found in his Letter to Miguel Arcos, in Vitoria, *Political Writings*, 331–3. His *relectio* "On the American Indians" contains a more understated critique at Question 2, article 4, in ibid., 271–2.

would not endorse. But more importantly he repudiated the Alexandrine Donation on grounds that the world was not the Pope's to give:

> [E]ven if the barbarians refuse to recognize any dominion (*dominium*) of the pope's, war cannot on that account be declared on them, nor their goods seized. This is obvious, because the pope has no such dominion.
>
> [...]
>
> It is clear from all that I have said that the Spaniards, when they first sailed to the land of the barbarians, carried with them no right at all to occupy their countries.[31]

Vitoria also rigorously repudiated the *Requerimiento*. He denied that the Indians knew what they were agreeing to, and noted that even if they agreed knowingly, they did so in a state of fear and thus their agreement was coerced. He also argued that one cannot change one's ruler without cause, so that even if there were knowledge and no fear, the Indians would not be in the right to willy-nilly secede from their country and deliver themselves over to Spain.[32] Other familiar justifications of empire, including the now bizarre idea that the Holy Roman Emperor was the legitimate ruler of the entire Earth, also met with Vitoria's scorn.[33] But his rejections of the Alexandrine Donation and the *Requerimiento* were fundamental because these were the essential bases on which the Crown itself justified its enterprise in the New World. Vitoria had ruled that the Spanish transatlantic enterprise was illegal. Worse, he had done so in a way that seemed to overthrow both Pope and Emperor.

Nonetheless, Vitoria sadly makes a poor poster child for anti-colonialism because he appears immediately to take back with the left hand what he had given with the right. After repudiating the seven "unjust titles" for war against the Indians he catalogues "*eight* just and legitimate ones."[34] A lively debate has arisen around why he would do this. I think that this apparent about-face is highly informative regarding the place of conscience in the *Conquista*, and our ethical autopsy will be advanced by trying to understand Vitoria's thinking.

1.2 UNDERSTANDING VITORIA

Among Vitoria's eight just titles, the ones most remarked upon today are the right of harmless traveling traders to hospitality and to a basic suite of liberal rights such as the right to trade, to a presumption of innocence, to free

---

[31] Ibid., 263–4.   [32] Ibid., 275–6.

[33] Charles V was not merely King of Spain but Holy Roman Emperor. He redivided the two empires upon his abdication, installing one son as Holy Roman Emperor and the other as King of Spain.

[34] Vitoria, *Political Writings*, 252; 77–91. Emphasis added.

movement, and so on,[35] and the right or duty of humanitarian intervention to protect innocent victims of human sacrifice or anthropophagy.[36] He also justifies war if the Indians refuse to hear the Gospel;[37] if a majority of them, having converted, choose to give their state over to a Christian prince; or if they ask for outside help in a just war against a common enemy.[38]

It is not clear just how far Vitoria intended to endorse war in these cases, or even why he laid them out at all. He had just undermined the *actual* ideological foundations of empire; why, then, lay wholly new and innovative foundations to replace the ones just repudiated? Enrique Dussel, Antony Anghie, and others find in these "just titles" a commitment to the superiority of Europe and a denial that the Indigenous peoples' cultural practices have any value and even of the very idea that Indians can be sovereign.[39] By contrast, G. Scott Davis argues that Vitoria is simply following the scholastic practice of trying to exhaust logical space, and that his justifications for war apply only *in principle*; they would be applicable only under conditions that Vitoria insisted did not, in fact, hold.[40]

More accurate than either reading, to my mind, is that Vitoria is a proto-liberal who intends to justify coercive interventions but only, and only to the extent that, they are proportional and exercised in defense of human freedom and dignity; and who, like many present-day Americans reflecting on Kosovo[41] or Libya,[42] believes that for lack of a better candidate, the leading power is eligible to intervene in these ways. The key is that the motive and justification of military interventions have to be found in free trade, freedom of conscience, and rescue from tyranny, and cannot be found in efforts to spread the faith coercively or seize other peoples' "dominion." It follows on this reading that he proposes the innovative "just titles" because he sincerely believes that these should be asserted publicly as the pillars not just of the Spanish transatlantic enterprise, but of *any* overseas endeavor as a matter of *jus gentium*, and that such engagements should continue only insofar as the eight titles allow. The argument for this interpretation is that Vitoria is

[35] Ibid., 278–84; for discussion see Dussel, "Orígen," 52; Martti Koskenniemi, "Empire and International Law: The Real Spanish Contribution," *University of Toronto Law Journal* 61, no. 1 (2011).

[36] Vitoria, *Political Writings*, 287–8; see also 25–6; Antony Anghie, *Imperialism, Sovereignty and the Making of International Law* (New York: Cambridge University Press, 2005).

[37] Though they are not, or not immediately, required to convert to Christianity.

[38] Vitoria, *Political Writings*, 287–90.

[39] Anghie, *Imperialism*, 26–8; Dussel, "Orígen."

[40] G. Scott Davis, "Conscience and Conquest: Francisco De Vitoria on Justice in the New World," *Modern Theology* 13, no. 4 (1997).

[41] Allen Buchanan, *Justice, Legitimacy, and Self-Determination: Moral Foundations for International Law* (New York: Oxford University Press, 2004), 444.

[42] Jonas Claes, "Libya and the 'Responsibility to Protect'," (2011), http://www.usip.org/publications/libya-and-the-responsibility-protect.

evidently committed to individual freedom, the inviolable status of the human person, and the unity of the world community such that all men are neighbors. Indeed it is this idea—that we are all neighbors—that justifies both humanitarian intervention and the coercive assertion of the rights of harmless traders.[43] Similarly, Juan de la Peña revisits many of Vitoria's arguments and even seems to double down on humanitarian intervention, specifically on grounds of human solidarity.[44] It is arguably, then, not a sense of European superiority but, quite the opposite, an ingenuous belief in universal equality and comity that leads him to understand *encomenderos* as mere travelers and traders who sometimes act badly; conquistadors as in some cases merely helping some overseas friends rebel against their Aztec oppressors; missionaries as harmless pious men seeking only to share the Gospel. Unable to see power imbalances written into a social order—seeing harms as the one-off and fundamentally correctable acts of cruel individuals—Vitoria is not the viciously racist Sepúlveda; he is a sixteenth-century "white moderate."

Both Peña and Melchor Cano chide Vitoria for failing to recognize that Alexander the Great was not just some traveler, or that political communities may decide under what conditions to admit foreign visitors who are not literally refugees.[45] Hence seeing the reality more clearly was not impossible, even for a theologian in an ivory tower. The outstanding question, then, is what blocks Vitoria's vision. I think Las Casas has it right, blaming what he calls Vitoria's "careless[ness]" on a wish "to moderate what seemed to the Emperor's party to have been rather harshly put."[46] Which is to say, Vitoria did not want to be impolite to the King. What Las Casas puts his finger on here is that individual conscience is something of an "antipolitics machine."[47]

In his powerful critique of quantitative metrics such as citation indices and standardized testing, James C. Scott calls each of these tools an "'antipolitics machine' designed to turn legitimate political questions into neutral, objective, administrative exercises governed by experts."[48] The success of such a machine "depends absolutely on appearing totally nonpolitical: objective,

---

[43] See Alves and Moreira, *The Salamanca School*. Not only Vitoria but Sepúlveda justified war on the putatively humanitarian grounds that "all men are neighbors." See the extract from Sepúlveda in Serna, *Conquista*, 363–81; esp. 80 for the argument from humanitarian intervention. See also the "Summary of Sepúlveda's position" in Bartolomé de las Casas, *In Defense of the Indians* (DeKalb: Northern Illinois University Press, 1974), 13–14.

[44] See Peña, *De Bello Contra Insulanos*, 233. The word translated as "solidarity" (*solidaridad*) is *societatis*.

[45] Quoted in Vitoria, *Political Writings*, xxvii. I am grateful to Javier Peña Echeverría for discussion of this retort.

[46] Casas, *Defense*, 341.

[47] James C. Scott, *Two Cheers for Anarchism* (Princeton, NJ: Princeton University Press, 2014), 111.

[48] Ibid.

nonpartisan, and palpably scientific."[49] While Scott's focus is on standardized quantitative measures, I want to emphasize that appeals to conscience—and particularly that of putative religious experts—can have the same effect. Such appeals privatize and shield from public scrutiny the grounds of evaluation. Conscience purports to be a precondition of rationality, prior to and regulative of our politics.[50] And it purports to be subject only to the individual's sovereignty: "everyone's entitled to an opinion." But appeals to conscience turn essentially political judgments, which are required to be grounded in facts and reasons, into matters of unaccountable personal prerogative. Thus the appeal to conscience is the mirror image of the standardized test: it depoliticizes intensely political questions, in this case not by seeming to make them objective and measurable, but by seeming to make them subjective and unaccountable. But when subjective and unaccountable mental states have objective political impacts, they must be challenged as political action.

Las Casas, importantly, diverged from Vitoria at just this point. Starting out as a conquistador himself—he participated in the conquest of Cuba and "owned" Indians as an *encomendero* in Española at the time he heard Montesinos's sermon—he proceeded over the course of his life toward an increasingly pro-Indian attitude. But a decisive break seems to have occurred as he prepared for his dispute with Sepúlveda. Until then he was still trying to secure royal funding for peaceful colonies such as Vera Paz, aiming to proselytize without violence. But at Valladolid he concluded that the entire enterprise should be given up, and indeed that if war should be waged it should be against the *encomenderos*. In the remaining fifteen years of his life he wrote increasingly strident pieces against the wars and against Spain's political elite.[51] Unlike Vitoria, Las Casas makes a genuine about-face; from "another face of empire" to an Isaiah.[52]

The Valladolid debate forced Las Casas to do two things that he had not done before: not just to plead in defense of the Indians but to speak *on their behalf*; and not just to make the standard arguments against the natural slaves thesis, or catalogue Spanish cruelties, but to defend the Indians against the most outrageous and decisive arrow in Sepúlveda's quiver, human sacrifice

---

[49] Ibid., 125.

[50] See John Finnis, *Natural Law and Natural Rights*, second ed. (New York: Oxford University Press, 2011), 125–6.

[51] Of course he regarded himself as writing in favor of Spain, since he thought he was a prophet saving it from eternal damnation. See Luis N. Rivera-Pagán, "A Prophetic Challenge to the Church: The Last Word of Bartolomé De Las Casas," *Inaugural lecture as Henry Winters Luce Professor in Ecumenics and Mission, delivered at Princeton Theological Seminary* (2003), http://www.lascasas.org/Rivera_Pagan.htm.

[52] For a critical picture see Castro, *Another Face*. For a meditation on Las Casas' last years, see Rivera-Pagán, "A Prophetic Challenge." Todorov describes Las Casas as undergoing a series of "crises," "conversions," or "transformations," between 1514 and 1550. See Todorov, *Conquest*, 186.

and anthropophagy. On the first issue, we might draw a sharp distinction between acting *in* behalf of another, and acting *on* their behalf. Whereas the former is the attempt to benefit them, the latter is the attempt to *do what they would do* in the situation. Often, of course, these two agendas converge. Though Las Casas had spent the latter half of his life working *in* behalf of the Indians, at Valladolid he had to argue *on* their behalf, not least because two indigenous communities explicitly delegated him to speak for them.[53] It's one thing to appeal for their well-being, and another to speak as their mouthpiece.

As to human sacrifice and anthropophagy, these were the scandalous practices that had played a huge role in Spanish propaganda and in the total annihilation of Caribbean Island Indians.[54] Rescue from these was one of Vitoria's "eight just titles."[55] Todorov argues that what changed Las Casas was his reflection on this practice of human sacrifice and anthropophagy; to defend the Indians on this score he is "led to" a kind of religious "perspectivism" on which each person's path to God is her or his own, not to be judged by a different religion. On this view, as Todorov represents it, "their god is true for them—[which is] a first step toward another acknowledgment, i.e., that our God is true for us—and only us."[56] But this seems to take Las Casas in the wrong direction. Las Casas never suggests that Christianity is anything but *the* true religion. What is essential is not the *truth* of the matter but the reasonableness of the belief-system of Indians who believe themselves permitted or even obligated to engage in human sacrifice and anthropophagy. Las Casas argues that reasoning about religious matters is probable reasoning, and because of their circumstances the Indians would be rationally compelled to believe that human sacrifice and anthropophagy were compulsory. Consequently, while he continues to hope that they will eventually adopt what he takes to be the true religion, he insists that the Spaniards may impose no such demands on them. This insistence that no such demands be imposed is crucial; it rests on an *actual consent* requirement for the imposition of a new political regime. The Spaniards may continue to proselytize and encourage the repudiation of objectively horrific practices. But if consensus is to be free then it cannot be coerced, and if it is not to be coerced then the process of reasoning and reflection has to be allowed to continue in perpetuity. The Indians do not *owe* the Spaniards a decision, any more than they owe them their political submission. If there were a right to demand a decision, there would have to have been a right of conquest in the first place.[57]

If this is correct, then Las Casas's great achievement is not to have been the voice of conscience in the sixteenth century, but to have *overcome* conscience. *Of course* human sacrifice is unconscionable. He makes no bones about this.

---

[53] Hanke, *Aristotle and the American Indians*, 29–30.   [54] Ibid., 18–19.
[55] Vitoria, *Political Writings*, 225; 87–8.   [56] Todorov, *Conquest*, 189.
[57] Dussel, "Orígen," 44.

But in the *Apologia*, this fact *just doesn't matter*. What matters is that the people he represents are not unreasonable to believe that it is not only conscionable but required. So this is the position he defends. The achievement here, then, is to have replaced his own voice with the collective voice of which his is the delegate; and to have replaced his own conscience with that of the collective he represents. Whereas Vitoria's conscience provides cover for depoliticizing an intensely political matter, insulating it from careful reasoning and leaving unaccountable its convenient alignment with popular prejudice and the *status quo*, Las Casas's decisive shift is to join with the Indians in solidarity.

1.3 SOLIDARITY OVER CONSCIENCE

Vitoria's writings reflect the power—but also the limits—of conscience. Vitoria discusses the question of the "barbarians" in pseudo-anthropological terms—it is *about* them, but not *with* or *from* them, that he reaches his conclusions. Vitoria positions himself rhetorically and politically as an adviser to the Emperor—the voice of conscience in his ear—rather than as part of a political movement against conquest and empire, or still less, a liberation struggle led by Indians themselves. When push comes to shove, he holds the Indians to parochial Spanish standards, and defaults in favor of the interests of Spain, that is, his own "side," even while wrapped in the austere objectivity of scholasticism. These are the perennial flaws of conscience.

Vitoria's methodology is attractive on its face. In the absence of a shared moral or cultural framework such as that which unifies Christian Europe, Vitoria appeals not to (unshared) divine or civil law, but to *jus gentium*, the law of nations. He explicitly and repeatedly denies that the Emperor or the Pope has jurisdiction over the Indians and, consequently, denies that Spaniards may judge or punish Indians. The available positive law all points away from the legality of the empire. Vitoria understands the law of nations as the intersection of all systems of positive law; thus for instance a law against murder is presumably shared in all countries, and so murder violates the law of nations.[58] The problem is that with this merely positive foundation, the law of nations cannot give him any critical purchase on any actual code of positive law. Consequently it cannot rule out any moral enormity that is practiced under color of law in any country. In order to use it as a tool of normative analysis, Vitoria treats the law of nations as a kind of law-of-nature "lite," which generates what we might call the Vitorian Circle: the law of

---

[58] Vitoria, *Political Writings*, 40; see Pagden's discussion in his Introduction at xv–xvi.

nations describes the limits of what Vitoria can tolerate; the content of the law of nations is supposed to be given by what is universally shared; but Vitoria knows that it is universally shared because it falls within the limits of what Vitoria can tolerate.

This effort at universality is commendable in its own right, and arguably pushes Vitoria farther than could otherwise have been expected. He tries to model the Indians' reasoning about religious matters, recognizing that their perspective is genuinely different from that of the Spaniards. This recognition drives his demolition of the standard justifications for war and empire. It is Vitoria, not Las Casas, who first attempts to model the epistemic situation of Indians confronted by the news of the Gospel, and who argues that for them this is a case of "probable" reasoning rather than divine revelation. He argues that Indians have not (yet) been given good reason to believe the truth of Christianity, and are therefore not (yet) obligated to convert. Being non-Christian is in their case a misfortune rather than a sin.[59] But Vitoria cannot take the next step of arguing that they should be left alone. And although he insists that no one is obligated to accept the truth of Christianity—at least, not until its truth has been proven with good works and miracles—any refusal to *listen* to the Gospel is a crime that merits war.

This judgment of what is surely the most bizarre candidate for an international provocation ever imagined—refusal to listen to a foreigner talk—is putatively founded in familiar liberal rights of freedom of conscience, freedom of movement, and the presumption of innocence. But what really does the work is the unexamined identifications and prejudices that generate the voice of conscience. Conscience is directed at ensuring one's own moral integrity rather than at fostering the political movement that could secure moral results that challenge one's standing. Vitoria was under no illusions about the immoral behavior of the conquistadors. Yet it simply did not occur to him that his politics on the issue should be driven, in the least, by *the views of the victims*. The law is as stern a master for them as it is for the oppressor. Nor did his views about the Gospel make any reference to whether the Indians *wanted* to hear it, or had any use for Christianity.

Before Valladolid Las Casas suffered from the same flaws. Though supposedly among the more humane of *encomenderos*, in 1514 Las Casas gave up "his" Indians despite knowing they would be captured and most likely killed by a less humane *encomendero*.[60] In 1518, by his own report, "in order to free the Indians" he arranged that "the Spaniards of these islands would be allowed to take some Negro slaves from Castile," thereby perhaps contributing to—and certainly providing ideological cover for—the African slave trade. He

---

[59] Ibid., 265–70.   [60] Castro, *Another Face.*

himself continued to own African slaves until 1544.[61] He repeatedly sought and won the right to set up peaceful settlements dedicated to "The Only Method of Attracting All People to the True Faith."[62] Las Casas never wavered from his dogmatic personal belief that everyone would be better off as a Catholic. Nor does he seem ever to have rejected the Alexandrine Donation. As long as he was driven by conscience, his moral critiques of empire were limited. What allowed him to supersede these limits was speaking as the mouthpiece of political resistance rather than as a voice of conscience.

Notwithstanding the obvious moral wrongness, even then, of much that occurred, the Spanish transatlantic enterprise raised moral, epistemic, psychological, and other questions that were difficult at the time to understand; their contemporary analogues remain so today. I have tried to treat seriously, and without anachronism, the moral reasoning of some of the leading critical voices of the time. This ethical autopsy sheds important light not just on the era but on conscience as a phenomenon. For instance, we can see that the Spanish Crown endeavored to act rightly, and by "rightly" they meant by and large what we mean. Both the Crown and Vitoria failed, however—and even Las Casas ultimately succeeded only four decades after hearing the sermon of Montesinos—to *overcome* their conscience, with its in-built parochialism. Only having treated their moral situation seriously can we see why conscience is a mediocre action-guide. We do not know enough, in the thick of things, to discern the moral truth. We have prejudices, such that the *sources* of our conscientious judgments are opaque to us; they may lie in nonrational loyalties to "our" side as we understand it. Whatever criticisms we might have of our side, we simply cannot imagine crossing over to the other. These flaws, observable in sixteenth-century Spain, are shared with democratic politics today, particularly in powerful countries such as the contemporary United States: Americans are capable of vigorous debates about the management of empire, but rarely able to question the basic legitimacy of a world order where any country is a "superpower." Conscience makes things worse: it turns political judgments into unaccountable intuitive "seemings," and it inverts the relationship between evidence and output, making the evidence conform to the seeming rather than the other way around. Conscience operates as an antipolitics machine; and like all such machines it is not just political but partisan.

In the thick of things, we must overcome the default to "our" side, and take extra steps to determine where the moral chips have fallen. We cannot do this

---

[61] The report is from his own *History of the Indies*, and he expresses horror at having played this role. See Bartolomé de las Casas, *Witness: Writings of Bartolomé De Las Casas* (Maryknoll, NY: Orbis Books, 1992), 85–6. For more on the role and views of Las Casas on African slavery see David Brion Davis, *Inhuman Bondage: The Rise and Fall of Slavery in the New World* (New York: Oxford University Press, 2006), 73; 354–5; Clayton, *Bartolomé De Las Casas: A Biography*, 135–8; 420–8. I shall briefly return to this issue in Chapter Two.

[62] Casas, *Witness*, 137–42; for critical discussion see Castro, *Another Face*.

alone; but nor is it much help to seek out others who are similarly situated. We must ask the victims how they see their situation, and join with them in trying to alleviate it. We might do this even if their perspective is wildly different from our own, and we genuinely think that they are wrong. It does not follow that conscience has no place, but that it must be governed by solidarity.

The remainder of this book is an attempt to bear out this judgment, to explain why it is that self-reliant conscience cannot be trusted, how to discern who the victims are, and why we should defer to them in governing our conscience. But if conscience is dangerous, deference is no less so. The book therefore defends a kind of solidarity with the least well-off that is driven by the basic practical commitment to equity. The first challenge is to understand what solidarity is and why it is dangerous. From there we can go on to explain why, when, to what extent, and with whom we should accept this danger and join up in solidarity.

2

Loyalty and Justice

In Chapter One our ethical autopsy indicated that conscience does not reliably determine what is right, or move us to do it. Francisco de Vitoria and, before 1550, Bartolomé de las Casas—theologians who were the conscience of the empire—were able to sympathize with the Indians who were victims of aggression, but unwilling or unable to take on the Indians' struggle as their own. Conscience served as an antipolitics machine, securing factual and moral judgments behind a wall of unaccountability, and inhibiting them from taking a mental or physical leap of faith away from the solid ground of moral conventions. This changed for Las Casas when he was required, at Valladolid, to speak on behalf of indigenous communities and, in particular, to stand up for the non-culpability of practices—human sacrifice and anthropophagy—that he himself found unconscionable. Las Casas overcame his own conscience. While living as a voice of conscience is in many ways admirable, we can learn from these limits, and from the power of Las Casas's *Apologia*. Solidarity with the Indians—and not conscience—was what was needed.

Even if we grant that we should be in solidarity, though, we might wonder what that demands of us, and by what right it demands these things. Further, if it's true that conscience is unreliable, we might ask how we can tell whether our own conscience is also inadequate, and what we are required to do if it is. Can we really be expected to *jettison* conscience? Without conscience, how can we distinguish Indians from conquistadors, or Martin Luther King from Bull Connor? These questions point to three interrelated core problems that any theory of solidarity must resolve:

Concept: what is solidarity, and when is someone "in solidarity"? How if at all does it differ from collective action, loyalty, sympathy, and so on?

Agency: what is the relationship between the individual agent in solidarity, and other agents, both individual and collective? When or in what respects is an action carried out by individual hands also, or instead, an action done by the group? Contrariwise, when does an individual share in responsibility for actions that others' hands or voices carried out? Is solidarity just a matter of doing together what can't be done alone, or feeling akin to others in a certain way? Or do other people have a deeper role? What is the rational structure of individual agency in solidarity?

Justification: When and why is solidarity valuable and permissible? Is it ever morally *required*? Does its value depend on its tendency to bring about justice or some other end, or is its value partly or wholly independent of ends? Is it merely instrumentally valuable or does it have intrinsic value?

The current chapter focuses on the concept because answers to that first question have significant implications for the other two. I proceed by critically discussing two approaches coming from opposite directions: one, "teleological solidarity," conceives solidarity as joining together to promote shared goals; the other, "loyalty solidarity," conceives solidarity as a species of loyalty, of deference to one's group. I suggest a middle path between these two, one yoked to both justice and deference, but in ways that diverge sharply from these two approaches. Chapter Three begins my affirmative response to these problems, which I believe best captures the key moral insights of the ethical autopsy and supersedes both teleological and loyalty approaches. There I will flesh out the concept of solidarity as I understand it, isolating the features that I think are essential, but which are too often missed in accounts of solidarity. The basic definition of solidarity as *political action on others' terms* is a descriptive definition, leaving entirely open the question of aims and means, as well as the justificatory question of whether one should ever act in solidarity, and if so, when. The definition will become clearer over the course of this chapter and the next.

Because I define solidarity descriptively, in this chapter I neither argue nor assume that solidarity is ever morally permissible, let alone required. That depends on the answer to the justificatory problem, and answers to that problem are part of what is at stake in this and later chapters. So I take no position here on the ethics of solidarity. The views we will canvass have implications for when if ever solidarity is morally permissible or required, but my discussion does not turn on that question of moral justification. Still, I do presume that solidarity at least sometimes *represents itself as* required, and that this normative heft is part of the concept. For instance, suppose Rosa Parks sits down on the bus and remains seated when a white passenger boards and finds no place up front to sit. The driver demands that Mrs. Parks yield her seat and, when she refuses, has the police remove her from his bus. It seems built into the concept that *solidarity* with Rosa Parks would require each of us, if we were on that bus, to get off the bus with her—to refuse a public service to which we were entitled and for which we had paid. That seems like a plausible moral demand to make of us. Yet irrespective of whether it is ultimately *morally* obligatory, it seems to be a valid *hypothetical* imperative grounded in the concept of solidarity: *if* you want to be in solidarity with Rosa

Parks, you must get off the bus when she is removed. You cannot both be in solidarity and fail to get off the bus. We are not in solidarity if we sympathize with her but do nothing, or wish the law were different, or vow to write our elected officials when we get home. These might all be morally praiseworthy, but they are not solidarity. At any rate, solidarity demands action. This demand seems to me to be a conceptually necessary condition of solidarity. In what follows I will assume that it is, and in Chapter Three I shall complete the definition of solidarity by grounding it in the theory of collective action. What remains open to question, and postponed till Chapter Six, is whether and why the demand for action is ever a *moral* demand.

2.1 TELEOLOGICAL SOLIDARITY

One initially plausible approach to solidarity is to understand it as *the pursuit, together with others, of shared political goals*. It is, in other words, *instrumental collective action*. Its moral worth then depends on that of its goals and the means chosen to pursue them, where the "means" include the organizing rules such as whether the group is based in an ascriptive identity, whether the group is run democratically, and so on. The basic difference between solidarity with indigenous peoples and with conquistadors is that the former aims to alleviate oppression while the latter aims at its imposition and continuation, and hence the former is presumptively justified and the latter presumptively unjustified.

Call this conception of solidarity *teleological*, not to imply that the justification must be consequentialist, but only that the solidarity is characterized and justified by appeal to the ends that the agents seek. If we assume that ordinary political participation runs to such activities as speaking one's mind and voting for one's preferred candidate, then solidarity is extraordinary political participation such as protests, boycotts, and direct action. We tend to think that such extraordinary modes of participation are called for when the injustice that they seek to overcome is great. There is then a straightforward parallel between teleological solidarity and the theory of the just war or revolution. Solidarity is an extraordinary means which is justifiable only if it is required for morally compelling and important ends.[1] However, even when pursued for just ends, solidarity might be executed unjustly, as for instance if picket lines become violent or dissent is silenced. These two clauses of the approach parallel *jus ad bellum* and *jus in bello*. And this parallel is appropriate since arguably war is an extreme instance of teleological solidarity.

---

[1] For some examples of solidarity so understood see Shelby, *We Who Are Dark*; Scholz, *Political Solidarity*; Carol Gould, "Transnational Solidarities," *Journal of Social Philosophy* 38 (2007).

2.1.1 Teleological Justification

The just war analogy provides a straightforward answer to the justificatory problem and suggests a solution to the agency problem. For teleological solidarity, agents themselves are responsible for their actions performed in solidarity, and thus agents ought to do in solidarity only what is just, or most just. Logically, then, endorsement of the moral rightness of the cause and of the action taken in its name is prior to the decision to act. One *first* determines what justice requires, and *then* joins up with others who think alike in order to magnify power; should those others take a wrong turn, one should not do so with them. Solidarity is valuable when and because it is the best means to bring about justice or alleviate oppression; it is neutral when it harmlessly serves some other permitted but not morally significant purpose, such as the solidarity of a sports team; and it is disvaluable when it serves injustice or oppression. Like war, again, its value is *instrumental only*. Other things equal, solidarity is *permissible* when and because it is correctly aimed at a just goal and pursued without violating anyone's rights; it is *required* only if it is discernibly the only or best way to alleviate an important injustice or achieve some other morally obligatory end.[2] Such teleological solidarity is most at home in the nonideal theory of promoting justice against an unjust status quo. Its normativity is on this view inherited from the natural duty of justice or from moral responsibility more generally.

Tommie Shelby's liberal theory of solidarity, laid out in *We Who Are Dark*, follows the just war structure characteristic of teleological solidarity. Shelby's aim is to reconcile specifically black solidarity with a liberal orientation that rejects "intrinsic racism"[3] as well as any thick conception of community or shared comprehensive conception of the good. Shelby is especially careful to reject as oppressive any added biological, religious, ideological, sexual, or socioeconomic class norms beyond the thin idea that African Americans bear the stigma of racism in American society. Individual conscience rules: no individual should stick with the group in the face of wrong decisions. He thus rejects what he calls "classical" Black Nationalism and Black Power nationalism in favor of a "pragmatic" version in which black solidarity is adopted only for the sake of justice, and on the causal hypothesis that black fellow-feeling and the shared stigma of racism in American society might spur individuals to sacrifice for one another rather than free ride.[4] Commitment to

---

[2] Virginia Held, "Can a Random Collection of Individuals Be Morally Responsible?," *Journal of Philosophy* 67 (1970); Shelby, *We Who Are Dark*; Scholz, *Political Solidarity*; Anna Stilz, *Liberal Loyalty* (Princeton: Princeton University Press, 2009).

[3] Kwame Anthony Appiah, *In My Father's House: Africa in the Philosophy of Culture* (New York: Oxford University Press, 1992), 14.

[4] Shelby, *We Who Are Dark*, 70.

others notwithstanding, Shelby's account gives a clear answer to the agency problem; the individual is sovereign. When the group's aims diverge from the project of liberal racial justice as the agent understands it, she should stand down or criticize the group's divergence.

With some important nuances, Sally Scholz's feminist political theory also understands solidarity teleologically. Though Scholz emphasizes relationships within solidary groups and between the group members and the broader society—and hence, one's conception of justice is fluid through a process of social criticism and introspection—she also takes the achievement of social justice to be at least normatively, and perhaps conceptually, built into solidarity.[5] Carol Gould similarly builds the pursuit of justice into the concept.[6] Sandra Bartky also defines solidarity in terms of its moral goals: "[t]o stand in solidarity with others is to work actively to eliminate their misery."[7] Each of these authors is concerned to avoid grounding solidarity in shared ascriptive-group membership. The initial risk of intrinsic racism makes Shelby suspicious of solidarity and of calls for it, even as he recognizes its indispensability under current conditions. Similarly, Scholz, Jodi Dean, Chandra Talpade Mohanty, and Allison Weir theorize feminist solidarity without any appeal to antecedent "sisterhood" or even "strategic essentialism," but rather by appeal to interests and struggles as understood through critical analysis.[8] In no case may we ascribe interests or actions to those whose individual voices we cannot hear.[9] Individual conscience is therefore sovereign.

Solidary groups do often characterize themselves in terms of their aims, and their aims in terms of justice as they perceive it. Solidarity is thus *purposive*. But that an action is purposive does not entail that its morality must be assessed teleologically in terms of its actual or intended goals. In the first instance, solidary actions often fail to achieve the justice that they seek, and the strong likelihood of failure is knowable in advance. Nonetheless some fights are worth joining even if defeat is virtually inevitable. From Denmark Vesey's attempted slave uprising to the Warsaw Ghetto to the Arab Spring, surviving the fight—or even just having it—might be a kind of victory in itself, even

---

[5] Scholz, *Political Solidarity*, 189. [6] Gould, "Transnational Solidarities," 156.

[7] Sandra Bartky, *"Sympathy and Solidarity" and Other Essays* (Lanham, MD: Rowman & Littlefield, 2002), 74. The quoted sentence concludes, "…not to arrange one's life so as to share it." Yet, as we shall see, sharing others' fate in some salient way seems essential to solidarity. I expand on this idea in Chapter Six.

[8] See Sally Scholz, "Feminist Political Solidarity," in *Feminist Ethics and Social and Political Philosophy: Theorizing the Non-Ideal*, ed. Lisa Tessman (New York: Springer, 2009); Dean, *Solidarity of Strangers*; Allison Weir, *Identities and Freedom: Feminist Theory between Power and Connection* (New York: Oxford University Press, 2011); Mohanty, *Feminism without Borders*.

[9] See, in this regard, Gayatri Chakravorty Spivak, *A Critique of Postcolonial Reason: Toward a History of the Vanishing Present* (Cambridge, MA: Harvard University Press, 1999), 235.

though *winning* is the stated purpose. Having the fight might even trigger a crackdown that makes matters worse. It does not follow from this that one should not have had the fight at all. This fact sits badly with teleological justification.

On the other hand, solidarity might involve actions that are not couched in terms of justice or might have no real link to any particular group aims. For instance, one might, in solidarity, refuse to speak badly of someone or to sit silently by while others speak badly of her, even if the things people say are true, quite apart from any particular aims that she might have. Or one might refuse someone else's offer to pay for lunch or a drink, for instance if accepting such an invitation risks or expresses—or seems to express—cooptation. Actions undertaken in solidarity are most often purposive, but they are not therefore well understood in teleological terms.

Even when solidarity is aimed at realistically achievable ends, working to promote justice or alleviate others' misery is *neither necessary nor sufficient* for solidarity. First of all, at least some of those who are *not* in solidarity with some group G take themselves to be promoting just treatment for G. The white clergymen to whom Martin Luther King addressed his "Letter from Birmingham City Jail" took themselves to be working in their own way toward justice for African Americans and the realization of civil rights.[10] We can take them at their word as thinking that law-abiding action would be more effective than civil disobedience, and hence that their course of action was the single most effective one available for achieving racial justice. Still, they were not in solidarity. Solidarity required *not* that they work to promote justice in whatever way seemed right to them—doing their part as they saw it—but being *on side*. The fact that the most prominent civil-rights organization was engaging in nonviolent civil disobedience meant that solidarity required participation in or support for its doing so. One could not manifestly oppose civil disobedience—even on grounds that it was actually setting back the cause, and even if that was actually the case—and still be in solidarity. Thus working to promote justice or alleviate misery is not sufficient for solidarity. Going along with the chosen course of action is a necessary condition.

Nor is working to promote justice even necessary for solidarity. For if we suppose that the white clerics are right, and Dr. King is wrong, and civil disobedience really is the less effective way to promote justice, and hence that the participants in the civil rights movement are wrong about what is in their own best interests, this does not change the fact that solidarity lies in supporting what they actually do decide, not what they *should* decide. Thus working to alleviate misery or promote justice is also not a necessary condition of being in solidarity. Perhaps surprisingly, then, one can be in solidarity with

---

[10] King, "Letter."

others while acting in a way that *exacerbates* their misery; the key is to be doing what they ask or supporting their work. Working for justice or to alleviate G's misery is, then, neither necessary nor sufficient for solidarity with G.

To put the previous point in procedural terms, solidarity normally requires an *actual* rather than merely a *hypothetical* procedure. Solidarity depends on what real-live workers do in fact choose, rather than what ideally rational workers with full information *would* choose. Admittedly, such procedures must meet certain requirements in order to legitimately claim to generate *the* choice of *the workers*. Actual procedures might sometimes be infeasible, for instance if the victims of oppression are unable even to articulate demands. I shall address these worries in Chapter Three; for now the key point is that solidarity with G is, in the core case, an actual-procedural notion grounded in the authority of G (or of the individual g_i) to determine its (their) own interests. A supporter s is in solidarity, then, not when s acts on the best account of G's interests, or when s does whatever is most likely to achieve G's interests, or still less when s does what s *believes* to be in G's interests, but when s manifests support for G's action, or does what G asks supporters to do. Thus although solidary action is purposive in the sense that it is instrumental action—action taken as a means to an end—it is not for that reason *teleological* in the sense that its ends justify it.

It may be objected that this focus on doing what G asks captures a kind of solidarity of empathy or support, but not a solidarity of shared fate. The reason the workers of the world should unite is first and foremost that they "have nothing to lose but [their] chains," and only secondarily that there are other workers calling for support; but as I have recast it, only the latter enters the picture.[11] In reply I want first to emphasize that solidarity applies as much to the case of each individual g_i's solidarity with group G as to the case of s's siding with G. Whether some worker is (descriptively) in solidarity with The Workers depends not on whether they are together winning the world, but on how the individual is responding to the group's call to action. Nor does whether that worker *should* (normatively) be in solidarity with The Workers depend on antecedent agreement about what constitutes winning the world or losing their chains. But I cannot make this case fully until I answer the justificatory problem in Chapter Six. Second, shared fate is, if not fully chosen, then at least as much a commitment that people make or a lens through which they explain their social world as it is a fact of life. The Marxian analysis according to which the workers of the world, or indeed even of a single country, share their inexorable fate under capitalism is a highly controversial

[11] I am grateful to John Cumbler and Bob Goodin for raising this concern. See Karl Marx and Friedrich Engels, *The Communist Manifesto*, in *Karl Marx: Selected Writings*, ed. Lawrence H. Simon (Indianapolis: Hackett, 1994), 186.

one that cannot be assumed in the analysis of the concept of solidarity. The sharing of fates has to be explained as part of the theory of solidarity, rather than assumed to be an antecedent fact of social life.[12] It follows that the solidarity of shared fate is part of, rather than prior to, the solidarity of support.

2.1.2 Coalitions and Associations

All that said, it would be possible for the theorist of teleological solidarity to reply that if solidarity requires *hindering* justice simply for the sake of being on side, then so much the worse for solidarity. The natural duty of justice seems more attractive: it keeps its eyes on the prize. The prize is not unity, it is justice. Moreover, at least when aimed at *liberal* justice, teleological approaches insist on individual agency as a bulwark against demands to submerge some members under others—say, women under men, or non-Christians under Christians. If solidarity denies this bulwark, so much the worse for solidarity.

Quite apart from any moral case that can be made for or against individuality and the promotion of justice, there is the more fundamental problem that they impose an unrealistic expectation on real-world social movements and run counter to the moral psychology of participants. Distinguish two "directions of fit" between action and endorsement. Sometimes, perhaps most often, we decide to act in a certain way because we think it is rationally or morally the best thing for us to do, given our current beliefs and motivations. Sometimes, perhaps most often, this is how we decide to act together with others for political aims. For instance, we join a march against the war because we believe the war is wrong and the march just might help stop the war. This orientation to collective action is that of *coalition* or *association*.[13] Coalitions emerge when members' agreement on ends or means is logically or normatively prior to participation. Such coalitions may be characterized by what Scholz describes as mutuality and social criticism, and hence individuals' minds may change in coalition politics. But even if not *temporally* prior, the individual conscience is nonetheless conceptually so. Each associate is always acting according to her own—admittedly evolving—conception of justice; if she were not, she would not so act. Association thus occurs when the agent's conscience drives the bus:

---

[12] See the discussion in Chapter Three and, more fully, Chapter Six. Numerous feminist authors have rightly objected to the rhetoric of "sisterhood" on similar grounds; see Section 2.2 for fuller discussion. Andrea Sangiovanni emphasizes the commitment to share fates as part of the concept of solidarity. See Andrea Sangiovanni, "Solidarity as Joint Action," *Journal of Applied Philosophy* 32, no. 4 (2015), 340–59. I discuss Sangiovanni's view at length in Chapter Three.
[13] I am grateful to Bob Goodin for discussion of this contrast.

one acts because of (logically) antecedent commitments to certain aims or values.

Teleological solidarity need not be *conceptually* linked to the primacy of individual conscience, but the two typically come together. And although the liberal tradition—as I shall discuss in Chapter Four—has the resources to break this tight link, that tradition has a strong tendency to fall back on it and does so as a general rule. Liberalism is deeply committed to the value of individual resistance to accepted norms and expectations. The priority of individual agreement to obligation is thus a hallmark of teleological solidarity and a commonplace of liberalism.

The implications of this basic commitment can be seen in the debate over nonconsensual obligations or duties. Suppose you are asked to be in solidarity with farmworkers who are on strike for better pay and working conditions— for instance, by refusing to purchase produce from the struck farm. You can be nonconsensually morally required to boycott only if doing so is implied by the natural duty of justice.[14] The natural duty of justice requires you to promote and support just institutions.[15] Therefore, you have a nonconsensual moral duty to boycott the produce of the struck farm only if doing so is a necessary condition of promoting or supporting just institutions. We can perhaps weaken this to a feasibility claim: you have a nonconsensual duty to boycott the produce of the struck farm only if doing so is the most feasible and least costly means of discharging your duty to promote and support just institutions. The entailment goes in only one direction, because there may be further considerations that override a *pro tanto* duty to boycott. For instance, there might be an overriding moral constraint that forbids boycotting that farm; or you might have a valid agent-centered option to do what does not bring about the most just results. This might occur because there are many different injustices and we are entitled to select our own areas of focus based on our particular interests or judgment. Or it might occur because nonmoral considerations justify overriding moral demands in a given case. In these cases the natural duty to support just institutions would imply a range of options each of which generated only an imperfect duty.

Even stating this demand opens it up to a significant range of judgment calls: the empirical causal claim that supporting *this particular* group of farmworkers has any chance at all, let alone the best or only chance, of bringing about justice; the normative claim that justice does indeed require

---

[14] See Anna Stilz's discussion of the Kantian foundation of the state, in Stilz, *Liberal Loyalty*, 54. See also Michael Hardimon, "Role Obligations," *Journal of Philosophy* 91, no. 7 (1994); A. John Simmons, "External Justifications and Institutional Roles," ibid. 93, no. 1 (1996). Strictly speaking there may be other natural duties, but—especially in a liberal framework—these duties are not likely to apply in a political context, and are all regulated by the natural duty of justice in any case.

[15] Rawls, *A Theory of Justice, Revised Ed.*, 98–9.

that these farmworkers be better treated, and better treated in the way they demand; and the highly personal claim that joining the boycott in this case will not do any harm to you or your relationships which you have an agent-centered option to reject, or indeed an agent-centered constraint requiring you to reject. Whose judgment calls are these to make? It seems clear that they have to be yours. We can then double or even treble the number of variables by noting that each of these judgment calls is subject to uncertainty. For instance, it may be that you assign an initial probability of only 0.5 to the claim that these farmworkers are in fact unjustly treated—not knowing anything in advance, you treat the claim as equally likely as not. You are empowered then to decide how much to spend on trying to remedy your uncertainty, and again, on which sources to consult—knowing that your choice of sources can affect the likelihood of being convinced one way or the other.[16] And if you are not convinced, then there is a strong liberal presumption in favor of your right to get on with your life. At least as long as you are not the one who needs help, the deck is stacked in your favor because individual conscience wins.

Yet suppose now that it is *objectively true* that all these judgment calls turn out to favor a duty to boycott in this particular case: the farmworkers are right, supporting them is efficacious, etc. Yet suppose you do not recognize this. There are a few familiar moves. One is for others to try to convince you that you face more stringent duties than you and your peers typically recognize, for instance grounded in duties of rescue,[17] duties not to harm or kill unjustifiably,[18] duties following on causal association,[19] or duties to avoid being part of unjust practices[20] or benefiting from injustice.[21] But even the most stringent of these—for instance, Onora O'Neill's negative duty not to kill unjustifiably—are widely regarded as norms that are *unenforceable against individuals*. Proponents of such duties do not aim to hold any civilian publicly accountable for the harms for which he is responsible, or with which he is tainted. Thus in the absence of institutional political change or a marked revision in social norms, the enforcement mechanism for even stringent and demanding personal duties is simply, again, personal conscience. It's a judgment call, and it's *your* call to make.

---

[16] Kai Spiekermann and Arne Weiss, "Objective and Subjective Compliance: A Norm-Based Explanation of 'Moral Wiggle Room'," *Games and Economic Behavior* (forthcoming).

[17] The classic source is Peter Singer, "Famine, Affluence, and Morality," *Philosophy & Public Affairs* 1 (1972).

[18] Onora Nell, "Lifeboat Earth," *Philosophy & Public Affairs* 4 (1975); Thomas W. Pogge, *World Poverty and Human Rights* (Cambridge, MA: Polity, 2000).

[19] Onora O'Neill, *Bounds of Justice* (New York: Cambridge University Press, 2000); Christian Barry and Gerhard Øverland, *The Responsibilities of the Affluent to the Poor: Doing, Allowing, and Enabling Harm* (New York: Cambridge University Press, forthcoming).

[20] Robert E. Goodin, "Inconsequential Duties of Consequential Collective Action," unpublished manuscript, ANU, 2015.

[21] Daniel Butt, "On Benefiting from Injustice," *Canadian Journal of Philosophy* 37, no. 1 (2007).

In short, liberals tend to be reluctant to amplify our duties much beyond what social conventions expect of us. Still less do they hold us accountable in any way for failing to be motivated to act on amplified duties, or especially for failing to be convinced that these are our duties or that they ought to motivate us at all. Each of these challenges just iterates the question of conscience. First, what am I required to do? Second, am I a bad person for *individually* "living high and letting die"? Third, is it really the case that we have such demanding obligations? Fourth, is it realistic or desirable that people change in such a way that they act on these obligations to the exclusion of small luxuries and local relationships? It is crucial that these are *iterated appeals to individual judgment*. Our ethical autopsy in Chapter One suggested that conscience is likely to be too bound by conventional norms and limitations on our ability to appreciate the perspective and plight of others. And more dangerous still, conscience is likely to depoliticize all these issues. Teleological solidarity travels with individual conscience, and it is conscience that drives the bus.

The link between teleological solidarity and individual conscience is thus close to inevitable, and the association between liberalism and the default to conscience is a powerful presumption. For if solidarity is justified by the requirement to *bring about* or *maintain* justice, then in practice, whether we have any duty to act in solidarity depends on what we believe—or can reasonably be expected to believe—about all these normative and empirical matters; and whether we can be held accountable for failing so to act depends on a positive demonstration not just that we were *wrong* but that we were *culpably ignorant* about all these matters. Thus any requirement of teleological solidarity comes down to solidarity with those who are promoting the cause that *the agent* thinks is just, in a way that *the agent* thinks best; and being as engaged as *the agent* thinks she ought. Conscience rules. The problem of solidarity then becomes that of boosting individuals' motivation or ability to participate in a collective action when they could have gotten away with free-riding, and solving the assurance problem that arises when every agent is situated in just this way. In practice, the agent's skepticism about whether the ends and the act in question are really required by justice will be decisive against solidarity. In practice, teleological solidarity is a theory of association or coalition.

What makes solidarity so powerful—for good or ill—is that solidarity *inverts the direction of fit between acceptance and action*: one acts on the aim, and only then—if even then—endorses it. Individual agency must be brought into conformity with collective agency. The hard cases that actually isolate solidarity, then, are those where commitments are not shared. The individual wills the end not because *she* chooses it but because *the group* does. Solidarity, in other words, is essentially *deferential*, at least in the dispositional sense that we would go along even in the face of some disagreement with the group over ends and means. Even if the individual disagreed, she would still choose as she does. Thus her agreement does not explain her choice.

It is this inverted direction of fit that makes solidarity a distinctive form of practical agency. By contrast, teleological solidarity seems not to be a kind of practical agency at all. All that teleological solidarity adds to our standard list of requirements is the sentiment or attitude. Such sentiments might motivate action, but they cannot justify it. Hence when Shelby for instance confronts a genuinely hard case—whether middle-class and elite blacks should leave the suburbs and move to inner cities in order to rebuild black residential communities—his theory implies that those without young children are morally permitted to move if they feel sufficient "special concern" or "loyalty," but those who have young children would be "irresponsible" to do so.[22] The justification for taking any action or none at all in solidarity has "no philosophical solution";[23] it comes down to how strongly motivated one is by the sense of solidarity. Calls to be in solidarity are not, however, requests for sympathy or fellow-feeling. Nor are failures of such fellow-feeling necessarily failures of solidarity. One can participate while resenting it or doubting the wisdom or likability of one's allies. Consequently, sympathy and fellow-feeling are neither necessary nor sufficient for solidarity.

Fundamentally, solidarity is a type of action: working with others for political aims, paradigmatically in contexts where interests and values diverge. Teleological solidarity loses sight of this contextual element, presupposing interests that are completely shared, at least as far as the chosen action is concerned. The liberal coalition, on this view, is an association of people whose worldviews intersect, and who work together to push forward that intersection. But what distinguishes solidarity, which the teleological approach obscures, is that there might not be agreement even on the very issue that is the object of shared struggle.

2.1.3 Agonism and Deference

What do we make, then, of a notion that involves struggle for political aims but is not characterized or justified by those aims, and which demands action but not agreement? Political struggles can be characterized in two ways: *teleologically*, by reference to the goals for which the sides are fighting, and *agonistically*, by reference to the sides that are engaged in the struggle. Usually, one of these takes precedence over the other. In the case of solidarity, agonism takes precedence over teleology: the meaning and justifying features of solidarity depend not on what you hope to achieve, but on which side you are on.

---

[22] Shelby, *We Who Are Dark*, 114–15.   [23] Ibid., 86.

Agonism is not *antagonism*.[24] Typically, political struggle is against other actors. But that is not a logical necessity; the struggle might be to galvanize an apathetic group or unify a fragmented one, in which case the struggle in question is not against any agent but against a phenomenon or mindset. Moreover, one can think highly of one's opponents and not question their motives. One can even invite them in, and hope to find common ground.[25] That said, however, political struggles do tend to be waged against other actors, and so solidarity will most often pit us against individuals or groups who represent divergent positions. This opposition need not be permanent, but it is characteristic of solidarity.

Inasmuch as agonism precedes teleology, solidarity involves the agent's choosing sides without confidence that the chosen side is in the right. All the judgment calls we canvassed earlier—whether the farmworkers are treated unjustly, whether this boycott will help, whether it is possible to win this fight—are no longer the individual's calls to make. A corollary of this point is that if, after joining, the agent disagrees with something the group decides or does, it does not follow that she should switch sides or disengage. We cannot build a notion of solidarity out of the agent's logically and normatively prior knowledge of what justice entails. The solidarity has to survive some amount of disagreement about this. Thus in contrast to the teleological orientation, which presupposes agreement and reduces solidarity to an attitude, the agonistic orientation attains deeper insight by foregrounding the context of divergent interests. This feature of solidarity crucially implies that the individual agent in solidarity practices a kind of *deference*; he stands ready to put aside some range of his own judgments about aims, methods, facts, or values, in favor of someone else's or a group's. In putting aside her own judgments s does not necessarily act *contrary* to them; it's just that she does not act on her own judgments. She might agree with the other's judgment, but her agreement is not the basis for her going along.[26] She might even agree with her opponents more than with her allies. It follows that she would do the same even if she disagreed about ends or means, or if her interests diverged. Acting with a collective counts as solidarity only if it meets this counterfactual test: at least in

---

[24] My usage of these terms differs from that of Chantal Mouffe. Mouffe uses "antagonism" to mean intergroup conflict, whereas "agonism" is that essential feature of politics where we can have a "we" only by definition against a "they." I use "agonism" to mean siding with others in a struggle, and "antagonism" to mean a particular attitude towards others, namely, being disagreeable or conflictual where that is not strictly necessary. So my use of "agonism" should not be taken to imply complete overlap with Mouffe. See Chantal Mouffe, *Agonistics: Thinking the World Politically* (New York: Verso, 2013), 5–7.

[25] Dean, *Solidarity of Strangers*. I am grateful to Linda Radzik and Yujia Song for discussion of this point.

[26] My account here builds on Joseph Raz's "normal justification" of authority. I will have more to say about this in Chapter Four. See Raz, *The Morality of Freedom*, 29. Carol Gould also emphasizes that solidarity involves deference. See Gould, "Transnational Solidarities," 157.

some range of cases, we would stand down if the group determined that our act was not warranted, and we would stand up with the group even if we disagreed.

Teleological solidarity offers an inadequate account of what is both so terrifying and so uplifting about solidarity. In solidarity we act together under conditions of incomplete agreement and uncertainty about what we as individuals can do with the group, and what the group can do together. We join up with others for some reason *other than*, or at least, *in addition to*, the shared goals, while means are undecided and capacities are not just unknown but indeterminate. There is no prior fact of the matter about what the group will be capable of, or how. Consequently, if our decision to side with others is morally significant, for good or ill, it must be taken before goals, means, or capacities are determined and must have its moral worth independent of them. That is to say, in contrast to mere association and the strong presumption of the teleological approach and the liberal tradition, acting together is *logically and normatively prior* to pursuing common ends. We take on common ends because we're acting together, not vice versa.

2.2 LOYALTY SOLIDARITY

If solidarity is not action taken for political ends but action taken on others' terms, then perhaps solidarity is better understood in terms of loyalty. Simon Keller defines "loyalty, and some other concepts in the vicinity," as follows:

> Loyalty is the attitude and associated pattern of conduct that is constituted by an individual's taking something's side, and doing so with a certain sort of motive: namely, a motive that is partly emotional in nature, involves a response to the thing itself, and makes essential reference to a special relationship that the individual takes to exist between herself and the thing to which she is loyal.[27]

Understood in this agonistic and action-oriented sense, perhaps loyalty breaks with mere coalition and hence can account for the distinctive practical agency of solidarity where teleological approaches failed. The agent in loyalty solidarity would take sides independently of one's own particular judgments about the justice of the ends and the means, and hence, independently of individual conscience.[28] The fundamental challenge for a loyalty approach—what will

---

[27] Simon Keller, *The Limits of Loyalty* (New York: Cambridge University Press, 2007), 21.
[28] See Alasdair MacIntyre, "Is Patriotism a Virtue?," *Lindley Lecture* (Lawrence, KS: University of Kansas, 1984); Richard Rorty, "Solidarity or Objectivity?," in *Objectivity, Relativism, and Truth: Philosophical Papers I* (New York: Cambridge University Press, 1991).

keep it from collapsing into teleological solidarity—is therefore to justify taking sides without falling back on an independent evaluation of the rational or moral preferability of one side's aims or tactics. That is, loyalty solidarity needs to be justifiable even if its ends are not. It must explain how to take sides nonconscientiously.

2.2.1 *Non*conscientious Action

What could justify taking sides in a struggle without reference to the justice of ends or means? One initial hypothesis would be affiliation around a substantively shared identity or experience such as "sisterhood" or class or race consciousness. As we noted in Section 2.1, many authors reject such identity-based solidarities on grounds of "essentialism," where a single supposedly shared experience determines the movement's politics and disciplines the members. Given antecedent power imbalances, the "essence" in question normally prioritizes the concerns of the most privileged participants.[29]

Alasdair MacIntyre argues, however, that such liberal or rational objections to loyalty are wrongheaded: it is question-begging to demand a rational justification of solidarity (or specifically, patriotism) because solidarity stands apart from rationally grounded moral systems. According to MacIntyre, "loyalty-exhibiting virtues" such as patriotism and solidarity

> exhibit a peculiar action-generating regard for particular persons, institutions or groups, a regard founded upon a particular historical relationship of association between the person exhibiting the regard and the relevant person, institution or group.[30]

MacIntyre emphasizes that the particular regard characteristic of loyalty-exhibiting virtues is not founded in gratitude or in a general endorsement of the goods provided by the relationship in the abstract. Rather, patriotism is grounded in a particular commitment to

> the nation conceived *as a project*, a project somehow or other brought to birth in the past and carried on so that a morally distinctive community was brought into being which embodied a claim to political autonomy.[31]

Other "loyalty-exhibiting virtues," including loyalty solidarity towards political movements, might either be grounded in their own particular free-standing projects, or be derivative on and justified by the national project.

---

[29] See Section 2.1. See also Dean, *Solidarity of Strangers*, 175; Weir, *Identities and Freedom*, 68–9.
[30] MacIntyre, "Is Patriotism a Virtue?," 4.   [31] Ibid., 13–14.

MacIntyre's critique of rationally founded morality purports to brush aside the *justificatory* questions of whether one *ought* to be in solidarity, and if so, with whom and for what. Instead, solidarity is necessary for (fully) human life, and the designated object of an individual's solidarity is not, at bottom, freely chosen. There is no serious option of "going it alone" or perhaps even of switching one's deepest loyalties. The justificatory problem thus dissolves due to MacIntyre's answer to the *agency* problem: membership in group G is causally necessary for, and partly constitutive of, individual agency, and *that* justifies loyalty to G.

MacIntyre does not mean to imply, however, that individuals should be mere avatars of their groups. An individual can and should develop virtues that enable her to take a critical perspective on the groups of which she is a member. Indeed, perhaps there is this possibility *only* with respect to groups of which she is a member, since only there will her ideals and vocabulary be sufficiently shared with others to permit the kind of sympathetic but critical engagement that is required for a fair assessment.

How, then, should the individual agent act with respect to the group whose shared project makes possible her agency? MacIntyre rejects blind support, instead, supporting values familiar to liberals—freedom, rationality, integrity—but scrubbed of what he regards as liberal atomism, and paying special attention to the social conditions that enable these values to flourish.[32] We should choose liberal democracy, for instance, and institutions that foster integrity, and we should work to bring out the most humane readings of the values embedded in our traditions.[33] MacIntyre denies that patriotism requires undue deference to inhumane and unjust policies on the part of the state. "[W]hatever is exempted from the patriot's criticism[,] the *status quo* of power and government and the policies pursued by those exercising power and government never need be so exempted."[34] No given *status quo* is tantamount to the project as a whole, so no given *status quo* is beyond criticism.

Indeed, sometimes the *status quo* is so bad as to merit outright opposition. MacIntyre proposes that the cause of a particular government might diverge so radically from that of the nation itself that we should align ourselves against the government, in the name of the nation's values. For instance, Nazi "Justice"—call it J_n—runs so radically counter to German "Justice" (J_g) that all good Germans should in fact repudiate Nazism. But they should not do so

---

[32] Alasdair MacIntyre, "Social Structures and Their Threats to Moral Agency," *Philosophy* 74 (1999).

[33] See, similarly, Richard Rorty, *Achieving Our Country* (Cambridge, MA: Harvard University Press, 1998); Michael Walzer, *Interpretation and Social Criticism* (Cambridge, MA: Harvard University Press, 1987).

[34] MacIntyre, "Is Patriotism a Virtue?," 13.

in the name of "Justice *per se*," which either does not exist or does not exercise any hold over the German patriot, but in the name of J_g in particular. In suggesting this escape from Nazism, MacIntyre recognizes that the answer will not appease a liberal. Sometimes, the regime's project will radically diverge from the national project and the character of its divergence will reflect the goodness of the national project in contrast with the regime's. In such cases— J_g over J_n—things work out. Yet he recognizes that so sharp a divergence "may not and often will not" happen.[35] Most often, dissent will be unlikely or, perhaps more pointedly, dissidents will be neither more nor less advocates of the national project per se; patriotism will not, then, take sides. Fair enough; perhaps that is as it should be. But now suppose dissent occurs in this context anyway. Should we be on the left or the right? Each side appeals to an interpretation of the national project that is, by hypothesis, not demonstrably required by the project itself. We must then appeal to some other values or none at all, or not join up with any side. Popular politics under MacIntyre would then be just what a liberal would expect: different people making different independent judgments about normative questions, and working teleologically to achieve their ends. Loyalty solidarity collapses into teleological solidarity.

Worse, now suppose the government is not in a spasm of evil that contravenes the ideals of the national project, but to the contrary, it is in a spasm of *good* that departs from an evil history that has characterized the national project from the beginning. Mark Graber argues that the Civil War- and Reconstruction-era US governments diverged from values that were arguably embedded in a fundamental antebellum Constitutional compromise which allowed white elites of North and South to dominate the nation without either set of elites being able to impose its will unilaterally on the other.[36] Arguably, Reconstruction failed because that elite successfully reasserted the values of the national project of elitist white supremacy over the government's project of racial justice.[37] Now the worry is not that MacIntyre's patriot would have no basis for choice, but that he would have to *oppose* Reconstruction and, even today, retrospectively endorse its failure.

More mundanely, and more frequently, it might just be the case that both sides of a dispute are fighting for reasonably attractive values that they plausibly find embedded in the national project—individual liberty and free markets vs. equality of opportunity and a safety net, or whatever. In these cases patriotism does not determine which side they should be on. Then the

---

[35] Ibid., 15.

[36] Mark A. Graber, *Dred Scott and the Problem of Constitutional Evil* (New York: Cambridge University Press, 2006).

[37] David Lyons, *Confronting Injustice* (New York: Oxford University Press, 2012), 66–74.

question is whether their falling on one side or another of this divide can be determined by an *iteration* of loyalty—that is, "identity politics." MacIntyre insists that we have no alternative but to start from our various identities, roles, and offices, and that even the most rigorous deliberation yields not abstract general moral truth but productive tensions among "socially embodied points of view."[38] Fair enough, but the fact remains that if the national project does not require any particular option, we must do what seems right to us as members of the nation; teleology and conscience return.

If there are moral reasons to join one side, they should not be equally good reasons for joining the other side. We can grant that these reasons are built on a social infrastructure, and we might even grant that they differ from society to society or even family to family. But we still need reasons. Hence loyalty solidarity provides a thesis about the social constitution of agency but this social constitution cannot give Spanish *encomenderos* any *reason* for their position on Indian rights, or white Alabama bus riders in the 1950s any *reason* to support segregation or desegregation. The justificatory questions might be approached somewhat differently than they would for people in different contexts, but they are still recognizably justificatory questions that individuals must solve for themselves. So loyalty solidarity does not shift the agenda the way it purports to.

2.2.2 Solidarity is not Loyalty

MacIntyre's account of loyalty solidarity does not ground an agonistic approach to political struggle. Yet it might be thought that this challenge could be met by some other approach. I therefore want to show that loyalty solidarity suffers from a deeper problem, namely, that loyalty and solidarity are importantly distinct notions, and efforts to assimilate the two generate confusion. Drawing this contrast requires our first refinement of the preliminary definition of solidarity.

Both loyalty and solidarity involve submitting one's own agency to that of a larger group. This is the *deference* criterion, where individual agents are disposed to stick with the group even when the group acts counter to the individual's best judgment. But beyond that the two notions differ in at least three important respects. On Keller's account of loyalty,

(L1) It is the *relationship* with group G that binds person S; hence,
(L2) the relationship binds S *in particular* to G, and
(L3) G itself becomes the *object* of S's obligations.

---

[38] MacIntyre, "Social Structures and Their Threats to Moral Agency," 318.

Solidarity differs in each of these respects:

(S1) It is some general reason *r* that binds *S* to *G*;

(S2) *r* purports to bind *S* under a general description, not due to *S*'s particular features;

(S3) *r*, rather than *G*, is the object of *S*'s obligations.

With loyalty, the relationship itself has normative force. This force therefore applies only to those who are in the relationship or aspire to be. The relationship becomes not only the source and site of obligations but the object of further obligations. Loyalty-given obligations are individual obligations to promote a collective, including by serving the collective's adopted ends. In solidarity, by contrast, it is reason *r* that binds *S*. The relationship may generate felt obligations but it does not itself become the object of moral obligations. Rather, in an important sense solidarity becomes their *subject*: solidarity-given obligations are individual obligations to *constitute* the collective in pursuit of something else. The collective is a product of the obligation. *S* is not (or rather, need not be) a part of *G* in any sense at all until reason *r*, favoring solidarity with *G*, comes to apply to *S*.

Further, while solidarity and loyalty are both deferential, they are so in different ways. Loyalists remain committed to the group even if it is in the wrong, for instance, in the case of loyalty to one's army unit or one's nation in an unjust war. If loyalty is justified in such cases, it will be so insofar as the special ties thereby promoted outweigh or excuse the disvalue of wrongful action. Solidarity's deference criterion, however, derives not from the group but from reason *r*—that is, from whatever justifies the choice of group. It is therefore compatible with solidarity to leave the particular group in the event that the group ceases to merit solidarity, given reason *r*. The deference involved in solidarity is based not merely in the possibility that *S* and *G* disagree, but in the possible divergence between either of their positions and reason *r*. Solidarity is then compatible with either

(S4) *r* picks out *G*, and for that reason *S* sides with *G*; or

(S5) *r* picks out group *H*, and for that reason *S* sides with *H* instead of *G*.

Thus, for example, suppose reason *r* is that one should side with the least well-off.[39] Then in S4 we suppose that *G* is worst-off, and in S5 we suppose that *H* is worst-off. *S*'s prior allegiance with *G* does not determine which side *S* should be on; reason *r* does. Note further that agreement between *S* and *G* plays no role in S4 or S5. Solidarity is deferential in virtue of choosing a side *without reference* to *S*'s views about who is right. Solidarity would have *S* stick with *G*

---

[39] See Chapter Five for a discussion of the content of reason *r*.

despite its being (in *S*'s view) wrong, or leave *G* despite its being right. *S* may then be called upon to act against conscience.

This contrast not only distinguishes solidarity from loyalty, but also gives new insight into teleological solidarity. Three variables are in play: what *S* believes, what *G* chooses, and what *r* requires. Teleological solidarity would side with what *S* believes; loyalty would side with what *G* chooses; but solidarity involves siding neither with *S* nor with *G* but with what *r* requires, and deference becomes a hallmark of commitment to the *reason*, not the group. If this is right, then solidarity is not merely political action on others' terms, but *reason-driven* political action on others' terms.[40]

This tripartite distinction between loyalty, association, and solidarity can be seen in the sixteenth-century case discussed in Chapter One. Sepúlveda, loyal to the Empire, sees it as his obligation to provide ideological cover for the Emperor; this is political action on *relationship-driven* terms. Vitoria, the proto-liberal, sees it as his obligation to find the truth as best he understands it: political action on *his own* terms, albeit conscientious ones. Only Las Casas takes it to be his obligation to stand on the side of the Indians, because they are oppressed, whether or not their behavior is conscionable.

It might be thought that the real difference between Las Casas and Sepúlveda is not solidarity vs. loyalty but loyalty to the Indians vs. loyalty to the Crown. That this is not the case can be seen in Las Casas's reversal on the question of African slavery. Until the trans-Atlantic slave trade got underway in earnest, Las Casas himself kept slaves and thought that the Indians could be saved if they were replaced as laborers by imported Africans. However, once he saw that enslaved Africans were as badly off as the Indians, he saw that—in our terms—reason *r* applied to the two groups equally. If it were loyalty that bound him to the Indians, he could have maintained his support for the use of African slaves. Solidarity, however, requires his reversal and eventual repudiation of the transatlantic slave trade.[41] Nor is this a shift in *conscience*. David Brion Davis observes—understandably by way of criticism—that even after Las Casas came to oppose the Atlantic slave trade, he never concluded that slavery in itself was immoral.[42] Exactly so: it is solidarity, not a revolution in his conscience, which convinces Las Casas of the wrongness of the enslavement of both Africans and Indians. The conscience of Vitoria, on the other hand, never seems to have led him to question the legality or morality of slavery as such, or to have bothered much to find out the conditions under which the slave trade was developing.[43]

---

[40] This structure holds as a conceptual feature of solidarity, whatever the content of *r*—right or wrong, good or bad.

[41] Clayton, *Bartolomé De Las Casas: A Biography*, 426.

[42] Davis, *Inhuman Bondage*, 354–5.

[43] For Vitoria's comments on slavery see "Letter to Fray Bernardino de Vique, OP," in Vitoria, *Political Writings*, 334. He seems to imply that *if* the slave trade had the character that

Solidarity offers a *general* reason *r* for the choice of a particular object group *G*, saying that everyone should in principle be in solidarity with *G*. Solidarity is thus agent-neutral. If *G* does something improvident or immoral while still being selected by *r*, then deference entails sticking with *G* despite wrongness. But if *G* ceases to be picked out by *r*, solidarity requires everyone to shift away from *G*. Once *r* selects *G*, one is then required to incur obligations pursuant to *G*'s aims—obligations to act for *G*.[44]

2.3 CONCLUSION

This chapter has canvassed two general strategies for approaching the concept of solidarity. The first, teleological strategy, understands solidarity as the shared pursuit of political aims such as, paradigmatically, justice. But this mistakes a political action that is explained purposively for one that is justified teleologically. As an extraordinary means of achieving political ends, solidarity then becomes justified insofar as these extraordinary means are required and pursued in a permissible manner. Further, since the justice of the goal and the necessity of extraordinary means are inevitably questions for the agent herself to determine, teleological solidarity cannot handle the deferential aspect of solidarity; the agent her- or himself is the ultimate judge of the moral and strategic challenges that confront the political struggle. Individual conscience must win out. But as we saw in Chapter One, conscience is an unaccountable and unreliable guide to moral behavior. And as I have argued here, in solidarity one chooses sides independently of the ends one pursues, and of one's own assessment of the justice of the cause.

If solidarity does not depend on the justice of the cause and the agent himself is not the final arbiter of that anyway, then solidarity is *agonistic*; it is in the first instance about taking sides, not about getting results. But what could justify such a choice? The second strategy canvassed here, loyalty solidarity, conceptualizes human agency as bound up with or partly constituted by human sociality, such that the question is not whether to be in solidarity but how. Nonetheless, once the specific claims of these approaches are isolated, the views end up leaving us in the same boat as the teleological approach; needing to find moral grounds, answerable to the agent himself, for choosing one side rather than another or rather than no side at all.

---

we now acknowledge it had, then slavery would be wrong. But he doubts that it had this character, and does not seek to find out. To be fair, Pagden and Lawrance date this letter to 1546, the last year of Vitoria's life, by which time he was immobilized by illness. And of course even Las Casas had slaves until 1544.

[44] Again, I do not assume that one is *morally* required to do this.

The takeaway is that solidarity is agonistic and deferential political action. Its justification depends on the identification and defense of a reason r that can justify solidarity without itself asking the agent to assess the justice of the cause. This account will also have to explain why deference is justified, and how far it should be taken. These challenges frame the remainder of the book. But first, we need a fuller, positive solution to the conceptual problem, explaining solidarity as a kind of action and accounting for links between individual and group. This is the burden of Chapter Three.

3

Solidarity in Action

According to Elizabeth Anderson, the abolitionists achieved "the most profound instance of moral progress the world has ever seen."[1] The abolitionists were individuals, but they did not merely act as individuals. Nor were they an ephemeral, corporate, or identity group, but a social movement. Following Charles Tilly and Sidney Tarrow's influential "contentious politics"[2] model of social movements, Anderson ascribes to the abolitionists, *as a movement*, a number of aims, intentions, and actions, including the bootstrapping one of inventing the social movement itself. The abolitionists carried out "a sustained, coordinated campaign that mobilized hundreds of thousands of people."[3] The abolitionists pioneered

> [m]any of [the] activities in the repertoire of contention—the logo, the mailing list, the network of committees, the iconic image vividly illustrating the complaint, the consumer boycott, the nationwide publicity campaign, the report card on representatives....Others, such as petitioning and litigation, had long existed, but were raised to an unprecedented scale and organization by the movement.[4]

Assuming these actions constituted *solidarity*, what made them do so? With whom were the agents in solidarity? And anyway, who were the agents?

In Chapter Two I distinguished between the conceptual, agency, and justificatory problems for a theory of solidarity. The first two chapters made progress toward solving the conceptual problem by distinguishing solidarity from conscientious political action, from teleological collective action, and from loyalty. In the current chapter I need to complete this part of the project

---

[1] Elizabeth Anderson, "Social Movements, Experiments in Living, and Moral Progress: Case Studies from Britain's Abolition of Slavery," *Lindley Lecture* (Lawrence, KS: University of Kansas, 2014), 2.

[2] For a recent statement of this approach see Charles Tilly and Sidney Tarrow, *Contentious Politics*, Second ed. (New York: Oxford University Press, 2015). A useful overview of the Sociology of social movements is Suzanne Staggenborg, *Social Movements* (New York: Oxford University Press, 2008).

[3] Anderson, "Social Movements," 11.   [4] Ibid.

by giving a positive explication of solidarity and a theory of solidary action. The latter will begin the solution to the agency problem.

3.1 WHAT IS SOLIDARITY?

Our revised rough definition of solidarity is *reason-driven political action on others' terms*. So understood, solidarity is *agonistic* and *deferential*: unlike in such relationships as coalitions, associations, alliances, and instances of sympathy or support, the agent in solidarity chooses sides prior to the endorsement of that side's aims, and is disposed to defer to that side's views about what is to be done, how, and why. But in contrast with loyalty, solidarity is agent neutral in the sense that we take sides based on a general reason *r* that applies to everyone, rather than a particular relationship between agent and object. Solidarity is achieved by the act of honoring—not crossing—a picket line, even if one has never heard of the union whose picket line it is. Solidarity can thus also involve switching sides if the applicable reason changes its valence. The ethics of solidarity depends on the content of reason *r*. As far as the concept of solidarity goes, however, reason *r* could be anything.

I do not deny that in core cases, solidarity often involves rich relationships and is aimed at justice. Both the loyalty view and the teleological view have their merits. But as is often the problem with core cases, they are "core" precisely because the moving parts all tend in the same direction. Consider instead a disturbing case that isolates what is distinctive to solidarity. Suppose Wernher von Braun is a Novice Nietzschean who believes that one should side with whoever projects unaccountable power. For this reason he becomes a Nazi in 1937, and then an American in 1945. During his stint with the Nazis he engages in a number of political actions chosen not because he thought they were right or for a paycheck, but because they are directed by the unaccountably powerful. Von Braun engages in political action on others' terms. His primary intention is to act as others do or would, and hence neither his own interests nor the particular ends that he pursues on their behalf are authoritative. According to the current definition, he is in solidarity, first with the Nazis and then with the US.

Yet von Braun switches sides; how can someone who switches sides be said ever to have been in solidarity? Switching sides may reflect either or both of two dispositions, one of which is *essential* to solidarity, and the other of which is fully compatible with it. The essential element is following reason *r* rather than the particular individual or group come what may. Solidarity is agent-neutral in the sense that it purports to bind anyone similarly situated, not just this agent; and it is reason-driven in the sense that it binds the agent to any object that meets the given description, not to this particular object. This is why any Novice Nietzschean would forsake the Nazis by 1945 in favor of one or the other postwar superpower. Following the reason is essential to solidarity.

In a second sense, switching sides is *compatible* with solidarity when it reflects the disposition to, as it were, drop in and out of movements rather than build a relationship over time. Since solidarity is reason-driven rather than relationship-driven, it does not entail any longer-term arrangement or dedication to a particular movement or cause. In core cases, again, long-term dedication is not uncommon: Las Casas and the abolitionists are fighting on behalf of the most oppressed people on earth, so inasmuch as reason r is *support the oppressed*, its implication will be focused on the same group as long as such oppression continues. But in other instances the referent of "oppressed" shifts, and r shifts with it. Thus solidarity does not entail long-standing relationships among particular persons or within a particular group. Instantaneously refusing to cross a picket line constitutes solidarity, and so does crossing the aisle when one's erstwhile side turns against others who better embody reason r.

Nor does mindset matter, except inasmuch as the action done in solidarity must be freely done, in whatever sense everyday intentional actions are normally "free." Coercion contravenes solidarity because the agent does not freely choose or perhaps even intend the action in question.[5] But the mere fact that the agent has doubts does not matter. Indeed it is precisely the lack of certitude that the call to solidarity is designed to overcome. To be sure, merely siding with whoever pays the bills is mercenary, not solidary. But this is why we are characterizing von Braun as a Novice Nietzchean rather than being "ruled by expedience."

It might be thought, however, that von Braun's version of reason r is ineligible to play the role, since supporting unaccountable power does not count as a *moral* view; and insofar as solidarity is a moral category, defined in terms of justice, it is impossible to be in solidarity with someone on grounds that are nonmoral or immoral.[6] I agree that solidarity often involves moral relationships, and that on the whole solidarity with the oppressed in their struggle against oppression is the "core case" of *morally justified* solidarity. But this moral justification is what needs to be explained and defended in the normative theory—starting in Chapter Five below—not defined into the concept itself. Even those authors who define solidarity this way tend to

---

[5] Andrea Sangiovanni notes that there can be background coercion, just not coercion in the solidary act itself. For instance, there can be solidarity in an army unit even if the members of the unit have been conscripted into service and ordered into battle. I agree with this point. See Sangiovanni, "Solidarity as Joint Action," 346.

[6] Gould, "Transnational Solidarities."; Jean Harvey, "Moral Solidarity and Empathetic Understanding: The Moral Value and Scope of the Relationship," *Journal of Social Philosophy* 38, no. 1 (2007).

recognize this, since they distinguish, for instance, "reflective" from "conventional" solidarity,[7] "moral" from (mere) "political" solidarity,[8] and so on. On similar grounds it might be thought that "deference" is appropriate only toward the disadvantaged, and hence solidarity must be in support of their struggle against injustice.[9] The language of deference enters the debate originally through Laurence Thomas's category of "moral deference"[10] which, he argues, should be practiced by members of higher-status or advantaged groups with respect to disadvantaged groups. Jean Harvey cashes this out as involving a kind of empathetic understanding, where one works to understand the world from the perspective of the other.[11] Harvey thinks that the moral relationship of solidarity is built on this empathetic understanding. As Harvey recognizes, though, this is a moralized notion that demands more than solidarity *simpliciter*. Such moral deference may often be the best means of achieving deference in particular circumstances, but the two notions are not synonymous.

On my account deference enters solidarity definitionally as action *on others' terms*; "deference" in effect analyzes out "on others' terms." Acting on others' terms is crucially different from acting *to promote their aims* or *in their behalf*. It is rather a case of acting *on* their behalf in the sense of acting *as if I were they* —acting as their understudy. For this reason deference is a counterfactual or dispositional property of the agent in solidarity. To act on others' terms is, in the first instance, to be disposed to change course if the other indicates that that's what they want. Thinking of the abolitionists, we can imagine a delegation of newly escaped slaves coming to them to say that their tactics are somehow making things worse, and asking them to stand down or change tactics. If the abolitionists are in solidarity with the slaves, then they will do as the escaped slaves ask. Or in the Rosa Parks case, we might imagine a version of the story where Mrs. Parks does give up her seat and, when an outraged bystander seeks to object *in* her behalf, she asks him to stand down; if he is in solidarity with her, then no matter how outraged he is at the injustice, no matter how objectively outrageous the injustice in fact is, he will stand down. Deference is thus *a disposition to act as directed or authorized by another*.

Treating deference as a dispositional property makes it duly responsive to or solicitous of the will of others while remaining amenable to individual initiative. What we want is a concept of siding with others not because they are right but because they are the ones to side with; in doing so the agent in solidarity— the *subject* of solidarity, as I shall call this person or group—restricts the scope

---

[7] Dean, *Solidarity of Strangers*.   [8] Harvey, "Moral Solidarity."

[9] Bartky, *'Sympathy and Solidarity' and Other Essays*; Gould, "Transnational Solidarities."

[10] Laurence Thomas, "Moral Flourishing in an Unjust World," *Moral Education* 22 (1993). For discussion see Chapter Four.

[11] Harvey, "Moral Solidarity."

of her own independent judgment. Yet sometimes the object of solidarity is voiceless, or simply cannot be consulted in time. In such cases we must stand up without consultation; then the subject must take the initiative. For instance, the outraged bus rider—being white in Montgomery, Alabama, in 1955— cannot communicate with Rosa Parks prior to identifying himself as her supporter, for the act of communicating with her in the relevant way instantly identifies him as such. Nor, we may suppose, would she scan the bus for friendly white faces. So he must take the initiative, either by standing up to object to her treatment or by approaching her with a quiet offer. Suppose he does the former, demanding that all persons be served as equals on the bus, and that if she is ejected then all justice-loving people must get off. Mrs. Parks can override this initial action by giving him explicit instructions. If she asks him to stand down—fearing, for instance, that she will be violently assaulted if there is a disturbance—he can either stand down as asked, or stand up for principle. We are supposing he is right about the principle at stake. But if he stands up for principle against Mrs. Parks's wishes, then he is not in solidarity with her. Solidarity entails the deference involved in standing down when asked.

Sometimes there is a larger gap between the moment of initiative and the time when the subject can check in with the object. In such cases, we can distinguish two salient ways of acting for an absent other, only one of which is compatible with solidarity. First, the subject may act as the object's *trustee*. In this event he uses his own best judgment about how to promote the ends of the object. This is the bus rider standing on principle, or action *in* behalf of the other. Solidarity rejects trusteeship and requires acting instead as the object's *surrogate*. Although trustees are controlled by the object's good, the trustee assumes responsibility for independently determining what is best for the object. In contrast, surrogate decision makers are strictly controlled, to the extent possible, by what the object has chosen or would choose, even if the surrogate thinks that the choice is bad for the object.[12] Agents in solidarity must be surrogates but not trustees—unless, of course, they have been explicitly appointed trustees, or perhaps in cases of epistemic remoteness where the object's values and instructions are impossible to discern in the instant, and must be imputed by the subject.[13]

Finally, solidarity is a form of action, but we must understand "action" capaciously. Standardly, actions are events—my walking a picket line is the event where my body moves in a certain pattern in a certain place at a certain time. Yet this is not a necessary condition of action in solidarity. In the first instance, action includes omission; for instance, consumer boycotts

[12] Allen Buchanan and Dan Brock, *Deciding for Others* (New York: Cambridge University Press, 1989), esp. chap. 2.
[13] See Section 7.2.

are instances of acting by omitting from purchasing the boycotted item. Second, action includes accepting obligations, even if the obligation itself does not need constantly to be acted upon. For instance, the agent in solidarity accepts the obligation to honor a picket line, but might need to positively act on this obligation only one day a week. And third, solidarity seems also to include *standing ready* to accept obligations. For instance, suppose there is a merely informational picket outside a hospital. Then solidarity does not require refusing to cross the line. Indeed, it seems to require nothing at all except a readiness to accept obligations, should they be assigned. Solidarity is, then, action, but in a broad sense.

In addition, solidarity may be individual action, corporate action, or the action of unincorporated collectives. And it may be wondered exactly how, for instance, ephemeral collectives can share an intention to accept obligations. It is this challenge of reconciling solidarity with contemporary theories of collective action to which I now turn.

3.2 SOLIDARY COLLECTIVE ACTION

The abolitionists were neither an incorporated group, nor an ephemeral group, nor yet an identity group. No particular members or methods can be taken as essential to the group, since the demography of the movement changed over time and the movement lasted for nearly a century. Nor can any specific aims or values be taken as essential to the group, since these evolved over time in ways that even the most central actors could not predict, and the changes in group ideals drove changes in individual psychology.[14] To be sure, not everything the abolitionists did has to be analyzed as solidarity, and we must be careful in specifying whom they are in solidarity with. But the key here is that some things they did *as a social movement* were instances of collective action in solidarity. And that has to be explained.

An individual can act in solidarity with another individual. For structurally similar reasons, an incorporated group can be in solidarity with another incorporated group: the United Auto Workers participated in the March on Washington in solidarity with the Southern Christian Leadership Conference.[15] And permutations of these are possible, too. But these ontologically more

[14] John Cumbler, *From Abolition to Rights for All* (Philadelphia: University of Pennsylvania Press, 2008), 89.
[15] Corporate agency is now widely regarded as straightforwardly explicable. For the classic account see Peter A. French, "The Corporation as a Moral Person," *American Philosophical Quarterly* 16 (1979). For a recent realist account see Christian List and Philip Pettit, *Group Agency: The Possibility, Design, and Status of Corporate Agents* (New York: Oxford University Press, 2011).

straightforward instances of solidary action cannot explain abolitionism—or civil rights more generally, or the labor movement, and so on. For in these and many other cases, individuals constitute *un*incorporated groups, and agents of all kinds constitute movements, and these entities conceive, intend, value, and act. How is that possible? We can put this challenge schematically as follows. We observe the phenomenon of:

Solidary Collective Action (SCA): (i) the individual s_i together constitute a subject group S, and
(ii) the individual g_i together constitute an object group G, and
(iii) S is in solidarity with G.

What has to be true of the s_i and the g_i, and of the relationship between them, such that SCA comes out true?

In the first instance, solidarity is action, and hence we must characterize groups in such a way that they can take intentional actions. But S and G may be groups of different sorts. Although G takes priority in determining what is to be done, G might also be unable to take action, or not constituted to do so. For instance G could be an ethnic group or some other mere set of individuals characterized in terms of shared features, such as crime victims or future generations. In such cases G's interests must be discovered by S through proxies or through a process of surrogate decision making and individual initiative. Normally, however, G is also able to act, and solidarity entails that G's decisions about what to do are authoritative for S. Thus although G may be an individual, an incorporated group, or not the kind of entity that can take action for itself, the essential challenge for solidarity is how unincorporated groups can choose, act, and defer to others.

In contemporary work on collective action we find two exemplary general approaches: those that collectivize the *content* of the intention, and those that collectivize its *subject*—or in other words, those in which individuals intend joint actions or projects ("I intend that we *J*"), and those in which an irreducibly plural subject does the intending ("We intend to *A*").[16] Recently, Andrea Sangiovanni has proposed a shared-goals account of solidarity that fits within the broad "collective content" school. His account helps us clarify the nature of deference, but, as I shall argue, it nonetheless turns out unsatisfactory; in certain respects it is too strong, in others too weak. Relying on shared goals to fix action, Sangiovanni's account misses the distinctive *asymmetry* of the deference relation. First, if S defers to G, G's intentions are *authoritative*

---

[16] A leading example of the former is Michael Bratman, *Shared Agency* (New York: Oxford University Press, 2014). A leading example of the latter is Margaret Gilbert, *Living Together: Rationality, Sociality, and Obligation* (Lanham, MD: Rowman & Littlefield, 1996). I shall discuss these views in Sections 3.3 and 3.4.

for *S*. Second, consequently, *S* need not share *G*'s goals, whether that entails having no view at all about them or even disapproving of them. I shall propose an alternative account of "Deferential Solidary Action" that, avoids appeal to shared goals and satisfies condition (iii) of SCA. I then turn to two parallel accounts of the nature of groups—one from Margaret Gilbert's "plural subjects" school, and one from Michael Bratman's "plural content" school—to explain the nature of *S* and *G* themselves. In an attempt to remain agnostic across this main fault line in theories of collective action, I will argue that both frameworks, suitably tweaked, can explain group agency in solidarity. The key tweak in each case is that solidary action occurs only when *S* values *G* or *G*'s agency, and acts accordingly.

3.2.1 Sangiovanni's Account

Suppose that you and I are members of the abolitionist movement. To be such it is not enough that we desire or hope for the end of slavery, or talk to each other about how much we desire it. Nor does it suffice simply to show up at an anti-slavery rally. Rather, if we are to be abolitionists there must be something we *do*, together, and perhaps something we *intend* together, that makes us so.

Sangiovanni explicates solidary action principally in terms of shared goals. On his view, "I act in solidarity with you when:

1. You and I each (a) share a goal (b) to overcome some significant adversity;

2. You and I each individually intend to do our part in achieving the shared goal in ways that mesh;

3. You and I are each individually committed (a) to the realisation of the shared goal and (b) to not bypassing each other's will in the achievement of the goal;

4. You and I are disposed (a) to incur significant costs to realise our goal; and (b) to share one another's fates in ways relevant to the shared goal.

5. Facts 1.-4. need *not* be common knowledge."[17]

If it is to be the case that *we* are abolitionists, then, *each* of us must share the goal not only of, say, attending an anti-slavery rally, but more broadly, of abolishing slavery; indeed we must each individually be committed to this goal, and to achieving it together. Further, we must intend to do our part for abolition, even at significant cost.

---

[17] Sangiovanni, "Solidarity as Joint Action," 343. For Bratman's most recent statement of his planning theory see Bratman, *Shared Agency*.

Sangiovanni crucially departs from standard approaches to collective action—emblematically that of Bratman—in rejecting shared *intentions*. The New York anti-slavery society and the West Midlands anti-slavery society are in solidarity because they share goals, but they do not coordinate their plans. There is no shared agency. This shift avoids an element that critics of Bratman have raised as an important challenge, namely, that his account applies only to small groups.[18]

In addition to sharing a larger, urgent goal to which each member is committed, solidary groups must intend to achieve this goal by meshing their plans. "Meshing" requires only mutual compatibility, not that agents pay any attention to the structure of one another's plans. As Sangiovanni puts it, "subplans mesh just in case there is a way for each participant to satisfy their subplans that is compatible with achievement of the shared goal."[19] Although coordinating subplans might be advisable, Sangiovanni argues that it is not strictly required for the action to count as an instance of solidarity, provided "we are not actively undermining our shared goal or each other."[20] In addition, he emphasizes that solidarity requires more than one-off, easy actions such as dropping a coin into a bucket or retweeting. Rather, condition (4) draws a distinction between "interest groups" and solidary groups; if we are not willing to incur "significant costs" and "come to [others'] aid" when they suffer misfortune, then we are not in solidarity with them.[21] It follows that a single group may have both interest-group supporters and solidary supporters; if some participants drop a coin in a cup while others make real sacrifices, only the latter are in solidarity. And finally, by not requiring common knowledge, Sangiovanni enables scaling up to large groups where it is implausible to suppose that each individual knows that each other individual is participating, and each knows that each other one knows, and so on.

Thus whereas I have preliminarily defined solidarity as *reason-driven political action on others' terms*, Sangiovanni's account may be glossed as the *meshed, costly, and fate-sharing pursuit of shared urgent mutual goals*, where "urgent" captures the overcoming of adversity, and "mutual" means that goals are not merely shared but that each is individually committed to them. His account avoids reliance on incorporation as well as identitarian or ascriptive-group criteria. Each individual is acting in solidarity in virtue of sharing commitment to a valued goal the achievement of which would overcome significant adversity. His account also bridges multiple kinds or objects of solidarity. For instance, in addition to the "political solidarity" that is our focus

---

[18] See Bratman, *Shared Agency*, 7; Scott J. Shapiro, "Massively Shared Agency," in *Rational and Social Agency: The Philosophy of Michael Bratman*, ed. Manuel Vargas and Gideon Yaffe (New York: Oxford University Press, 2014), 258; Kutz, *Complicity*, 97.

[19] Sangiovanni, "Solidarity as Joint Action," 345. By "each" I take him to mean "all at once," not "one at a time."

[20] Ibid.   [21] Ibid., 346.

here, "social solidarity" may be understood in terms of the harms of the state of nature, which the state overcomes by establishing a legal order and con-straining private coercion.[22] And "human solidarity" may even be understood in terms of the harms of a highly conflictual world system or one riven by savage inequalities. In addition to being the first rigorous effort to analyze solidarity as joint action, then, Sangiovanni's account has many attractive features and implications.

3.2.2 Evaluating Sangiovanni's Account

Sangiovanni's account is a significant leap forward in understanding solidarity in action-theoretic terms. Yet his account moves uncomfortably back and forth between intentional criteria and objective criteria. This generates diffi-culties of knowledge and commitment on the intentional side, and of success conditions on the objective side.

The core worry has to do with specification in terms of goals. Like all purposive action, solidary action is conceived and individuated in terms of its ends, but it is not principally justified by appeal to goals, nor do we choose sides on the basis of shared goals. To the contrary, when S is in solidarity with G, it is G, not G's ends, that S endorses or values. S is disposed to adopt *whatever* goal G sets for the action or as a political aim. For instance, insofar as they are in solidarity, heterosexual persons who support the right of same-sex couples to marry do so not because they individually want same-sex marriages to be possible, but because the LGBTQ community treats that as an important goal. If alternatively the more radical marriage-skeptical position defended by Claudia Card and others had gained traction, solidarity would not involve commitment to the goal of equal marriage but rejection of *that very same goal* as chimerical or self-defeating.[23] The goal does not drive the bus, the object group does. Sangiovanni might try to accommodate this worry not by revising the shared goals criterion but through his "togetherness" criteria, particularly the requirement that each participant be committed not only to the goal but to "not bypassing each other's will." But this still keeps the cart before the horse. To say "I want to achieve end E together with you" is different from saying "I want to help you pursue your ends, whatever they happen to be." The nonbypassing condition is merely a constraint on means and as such is insufficient to account for the agonistic rather than teleological character of solidarity. We will need to understand the role of asymmetry and authority, to which I shall return below.

---

[22] Ibid., 354.
[23] Claudia Card, "Against Marriage and Motherhood," *Hypatia* 11, no. 3 (1996); Ann Ferguson, "Gay Marriage: An American and Feminist Dilemma," ibid. 22, no. 1 (2007).

Shared goals raise not only intentional problems regarding commitment, but problems with characterizing the satisfaction conditions of the goal, and the nature of the adversity to be overcome. Goals whose realization would overcome adversity are typically well down the road relative to the goals that animate solidary action. Refusing to cross a picket line is acting in solidarity, but holding the line—the goal to which S's refusal contributes—is only a proximate, tactical goal. This tactical goal cannot count as overcoming adversity, because the picket line itself is an *artifact* of the struggle, not its purpose. Yet if we understand the relevant adversity in larger terms, the goal might not be shared, for it is inevitably unknown to some of the participants, and the participants disagree amongst themselves about what the broader goal *is*. For instance, both left-libertarians and Maoists can agree on the proximal goal of "occupying Wall Street," but they disagree on the broader goals of the Revolutionary Communist Party. Worse, among those who share or purport to share distant goals will be people who are not only not in solidarity but locked in pitched battles. Workers and bosses typically both desire a happy and productive workplace, conservatives and progressives a free society. There is no level at which putatively shared goals can be specified that makes the goals informatively definitive of the scope of solidarity.

To be in solidarity is to side with G irrespective of whether one endorses G's goal. This agonism implies the possibility that S is *alienated* from G's ends or even G's chosen means. Further, inasmuch as S defers to G, solidarity is *asymmetric*. These features pose difficulties for Sangiovanni's account.

3.2.2.1 Alienation

Alienation comes in at least three forms. The first is *intentional distance*: S might not care about G's goal. The second is *disapproval*: S might in fact disagree with G's goal. And the third is *personal animus*: S might dislike G. Scott Shapiro describes a case of shared activity featuring all three forms of alienation. Suppose Abel wants his house repainted, so he contracts separately with Baker to scrape the old paint and Charlie to put on a new coat: "Baker and Charlie are both alienated from the project of painting the house. They don't care a wit about painting the house, only in getting their money. Indeed, they may hate Abel and not want him to have a nicely painted house....Yet, they can still paint the house together."[24] Even if we grant that they are painting the house together, Baker and Charlie are not in solidarity with Abel or with each other. Each intends to do his part of the paint job, because that is what Abel contracted with each to do. But in addition to the intention, solidarity seems to require a pro-attitude. This suggestion raises two obvious questions: first, how

---

[24] Shapiro, "Massively Shared Agency," 271.

to analyze "pro-attitudes" in a non-mentalistic theory of agency; and second, what the content of the pro-attitude might be. I propose to cash out the pro-attitude as an instance of *valuing*, as Michael Bratman explains this in his planning theory of agency. Bratman characterizes "valuing x" as having a policy of treating x as justifying in (shared) deliberation about what to do.[25] To say that solidarity entails a pro-attitude toward x is, then, to say that the agent values x.

What, then, must the agent in solidarity value? Shapiro's example gives us three options: Baker and Charlie could value *the money*, Abel *himself*, or Abel's *goal*. Valuing the money, however, is valuing one's own *private* goal rather than the shared goal. That cannot turn employment into solidarity. So we can leave this aside. Sangiovanni would propose that they must value Abel's goal: *getting the house painted*. By contracting with Baker and Charlie, Abel has made his own goal the shared goal. But we saw in the previous subsection that this is not promising. What remains, then, is that Baker and Charlie must value Abel himself. Yet again this could go in two directions. They could value Abel either by valuing his *interests* or by valuing his *agency*. Valuing his interests is compatible with acting as his trustee, for instance by violating the contract in a way that they justifiably believe he would prefer, if he were informed. We have seen that this is insufficient for solidarity. Instead, the better analysis of valuing Abel is valuing his *agency*: treating *because this is Abel's plan* as justifying in deliberation about what to do. Deference to G entails pursuing G's plan *because and insofar as* it is G's plan. It is neither necessary nor sufficient that one endorse G's ends; it is essential that one intend to contribute as G directs and because G says so. One can be wrong about what the group has decided or whether one has so contributed, for instance due to confusion or miscommunication. One can even (secretly, or "under one's breath") hope that the action fails, for instance because then one's preferred course of action will have been vindicated.[26] But one must treat *because it is G's plan* as justifying in deliberation about what to do. This shows that what defeats solidarity in the alienated painters case is neither intentional distance from nor even opposition to Abel's goal—in the *de re* sense of the house's being painted—but only alienation in the *personal animus* sense. Baker and Charlie need not like or trust Abel, but they cannot oppose his being able to achieve what he has set out to do (*de dicto*). They must value Abel's agency.

---

[25] Michael Bratman, "Dynamics of Sociality," *Midwest Studies in Philosophy* 30 (2006): 3. Bratman treats "valuing X" as distinct from "believing X to be valuable." One can believe something to be valuable without valuing it; valuing it requires including it in one's practical reasoning in the sense defined.

[26] I am grateful to RJ Leland for this point.

3.2.2.2 Authority and Asymmetry

Sangiovanni assumes that solidarity is a *symmetric* relation, such that S is in solidarity with G iff G is in solidarity with S. But solidarity is not a symmetric relation; it is deferential. S may be disposed to defer to G even if G is not disposed to defer to S. For instance, Indians struggling against Spanish imperial rule are not disposed to defer to Las Casas, nor are enslaved persons disposed to defer to abolitionists. Solidarity is therefore *asymmetric*; perhaps surprisingly, then, it is *not* the case that S and G are in solidarity with each other, at the same time and on the same issue.[27]

This asymmetry provides some insight into Sangiovanni's nonbypassing condition, which in turn forces a further revision to our rough definition of solidarity. The nonbypassing condition as Sangiovanni states it is that if S and G are in solidarity, then each is "individually committed...to not bypassing each other's will in the achievement of the goal." Nonbypassing is just valuing the other's agency. But if solidarity is asymmetric, then it is not the case that *each* need be so committed; rather, only the one who is in solidarity must be. Dr. King famously used a strategy of creating big media moments in order to engage white support; but this does not mean he had to commit himself to not bypassing the will of white supporters in the pursuit of civil rights. S must be committed to not bypassing G's will, then, but G need not have a symmetric commitment with respect to S.

Yet Sangiovanni might object that, without mutuality here, G could then be secretly scheming to *undermine* S after, or even before, the goal is achieved. If so, then S's solidarity seems to miss its target; S is not a comrade but a tool. I grant that solidarity is incompatible with such subterfuge, but I deny that the remedy is to insist on symmetry. For although G cannot scheme against S, it is also the case that G need not constrain its pursuit of its aims in order to avoid bypassing S. G might meet only a weaker condition of *not* intending *to* bypass S's will. In other words, G need not value S's agency in the full sense; rather, it must merely be the case that G does *not disvalue* S's agency. Solidarity would then require that S's nonbypassing commitment be somehow *consummated* by G. This consummation occurs when G accepts S's support and does not scheme against S. So for instance, white allies for racial justice are in solidarity with black-led organizations because the former are disposed to defer to the

---

[27] They might be in solidarity with each other on different issues, and they might see the issues as at bottom the same, yet not be symmetrically situated on either issue. For instance the SEIU endorses LGBTQ rights as workers' rights, but if the LGBTQ community shifted its view on what constituted their rights, then the SEIU would defer. Meanwhile the LGBTQ community might at the same time be in solidarity with the SEIU on the "fight for $15," but if the SEIU shifted to $14 or $16, then the LGBTQ community would deferentially shift its support to the new number. The two would then be in solidarity with each other, but this would not make their solidarity symmetric because they would be in solidarity on different issues.

latter; and though the reverse is not the case, black-led organizations also do not scheme to throw the white allies under the bus.

It may be objected that asymmetry has awkward implications with respect to the individual g_i who constitute group G. If g_1 is disposed to defer to g_2, then g_2 is not disposed to defer to g_1, and so g_2 is not in solidarity with g_1.[28] The answer to this is that g_1 and g_2 are both in solidarity only if they are in solidarity with G, that is, the group that they form. "We are in solidarity" should then be analyzed not as a collective and symmetric shared commitment—I with you and you with me—but as a relation of joint deference to the group that we constitute together. Thus the asymmetric character of solidarity correctly brings out a crucial feature of the relationship between G and the g_i, and amongst the g_i. In core cases it is likely that G's aims involve promoting the interests of the g_i—for instance, the union is for the workers—but what is essential to the definition of solidarity is that the workers are with the union.

It might be objected that these characteristics misdescribe the relationship among groups that are indeed symmetrically situated with respect to a larger struggle. For instance, it seems as though distinct civil rights groups such as the SCLC and SNCC are in solidarity inasmuch as they are both working for civil rights. Yet neither group is disposed to defer to the other; in our terms, each sees itself as G.[29] This case seems to support Sangiovanni's shared-goals view as against the current deferential view. Since solidarity is action, though, it will be more fruitful to zoom in to particular actions or campaigns, rather than think in terms only of the distant vague goal of civil rights. In any given action or campaign, one group might be in solidarity with the other, whereas the reverse may be true elsewhere, and in still other cases the two might not be in solidarity at all. For instance, in Chicago, SNCC might fall in line with the SCLC, whereas in the sit-in campaign the reverse is true. Further, many individuals are in solidarity with both organizations, siding with SNCC when it issues a call to action, siding with the SCLC when it does. But if we abjure commitment to a shared end, then the question of solidarity does not arise between the two groups *as such*. They work in parallel as part of a movement; perhaps they even see one another as part of a team. But each is in solidarity with the other only when and insofar as it is disposed to defer, and the other consummates this deference.

If these arguments have succeeded, then, thanks to Sangiovanni's account, we may finalize our definition of solidarity to reflect the consummation requirement: solidarity is *reason-driven, consummated, political action on others' terms.*

---

[28] I am grateful to Bob Goodin for this challenge.
[29] I am grateful to Andrea Sangiovanni for this objection.

3.2.3 Deferential Solidary Action

I here want to propose an alternative analysis of solidary action. I will first give the analysis and then explain it. The proposed analysis is as follows.

(DSA) S acts in solidarity with G regarding A if:
1. S defers to G on the question of doing A,
2. because of some reason r which picks out G as the appropriate object of deference regarding A;
3. G consummates S's deference;
4. S values G's agency; and
5. S is disposed to share G's fate with respect to the struggle of which A is a part.

DSA captures the agonistic and deferential character of solidarity. It is asymmetric and avoids the assumption of shared goals. Condition (1) diverges sharply from a shared-goals or teleological orientation, and entails that S acts on G's plan or as G's surrogate. This implies that S is disposed to change course in the event that G changes its plan. Condition (2), on the other hand, diverges from loyalty, and disposes S to change course when G ceases to be the appropriate object of deference. Condition (3) distinguishes solidarity from wary alliances by requiring that G does not undermine solidarity by treating S as a tool. Condition (4) limits S's alienation by requiring that S treat "because this is (or would be) G's plan" as justifying in deliberation about pursuing A.

It may be wondered, however, what has happened to Sangiovanni's condition (4a), which requires "significant costs." DSA does not require significant costs, but condition (5) does require that S be willing to share G's fate with respect to A—for instance, that the white bus rider not sit back down after Rosa Parks is ejected, content to get on with his day once he has made his show of support; rather, he gets off the bus with her, sharing her fate as one who is denied his basic civil right to public accommodation. But this need not be a significant cost; the white bus rider might have been getting off at the next stop anyway, or might find that he enjoys the camaraderie of walking with others, and does not experience a bus boycott as burdensome. What is plausible about Sangiovanni's "significant costs" condition can be fully captured by the notion of shared fate, without implying that the agents are engaged in the extended pursuit of shared goals.

One final note on DSA. Because S values G's agency, DSA provides a first glimpse of the deontological moral argument for solidarity with the least well-off, which I shall develop principally in Chapters Five and Six. By acting in solidarity with them we affirm the value of their agency, quite apart from the goodness or badness of any state of affairs we help to bring about, or fail to bring about. Insofar as it is valuable to affirm the agency of the least well-off, then, this hints at a nonteleological value of solidarity. Thus DSA links the nature of action in solidarity to the moral theory of solidarity that I will defend in Chapter Six.

3.3 SOLIDARY CONGREGATIONS

DSA provides a sufficient condition of *action* in solidarity, but does not explain how individual s_i or g_i become groups S and G, respectively. That is, we have explained condition (iii) of SCA, but not conditions (i) and (ii). The current section addresses those conditions by offering two plausible approaches—one a revision of Margaret Gilbert's plural subjects theory, the other a revision of Scott Shapiro's Bratman-inspired shared agency theory. We will not need to decide between these two approaches; the theory of solidarity can remain agnostic on the key question of the nature of noncorporate social groups. If the discussion succeeds it will show that solidarity is compatible with either approach.

On its face, a plural subject theory, which posits a social atom constituted by, but not reducible to, individual agents, seems well-positioned to explain solidary groups. Margaret Gilbert argues that in everyday practice we constitute social atoms by taking on joint commitments:

> in the basic case of joint commitment, matching expressions of personal readiness *to enter a particular joint commitment* are necessary to create that joint commitment. These expressions must be made openly and it must be common knowledge between the parties that they have occurred.[30]

Social atoms are fundamentally normative social structures, constituted by commitments and cemented by the right that each member has against each other member that he or she participate in the group's action, and the corresponding obligation to do so. No one can be released from such an obligation except severally by each other participant. Joint commitments are holistic in that it might even be the case that no person intends to do what the group intends, or does what the group does. Moreover, the joint commitment may generate dependent individual commitments that are not *personal* commitments.[31] This distinction is on its face particularly valuable in accounting for authority and alienation. Individual s can be (nonmorally) obligated by membership to pursue G's plans, and concomitantly entitled to chastise any member of the social group who fails to do so, whether or not s personally endorses G's plans. This could explain why, as we noted in

---

[30] Margaret Gilbert, "The Structure of the Social Atom," in *Socializing Metaphysics*, ed. Frederick F. Schmitt (Lanham, MD: Rowman & Littlefield, 2003), 54.

[31] See ibid., 50.

Chapter Two, solidarity is experienced as required whether or not it is morally obligatory.

Gilbert's account, however, has difficulty with both the asymmetry of solidarity and its reason-driven character. It is not the case that either *s* or *g* incurs an obligation to the other to continue participation until being released from this social group by each participant. Asymmetry entails that *s* takes on an obligation with respect to *g*, and though *g* consummates *s*'s solidarity, *g* does not symmetrically defer to *s*. Nor need *s*'s solidarity extend beyond the current struggle. As long as the account of joint action floats free of our reasons for joining, it cannot capture solidarity.

Talbot Brewer revises Gilbert's account by distinguishing between groups founded in different kinds of *commissive utterances*. Some commissives, such as "I promise to...," are performatives that generate commitments. Performatives are made true by their utterance, and do not report anything about the person who undertakes them. In contrast, commissives such as "I side with..." and "I am determined to..." are assertions made true or false by the speaker's mental states or dispositions. Brewer holds that these latter commissives bespeak "internalist commitments that can be made known by the commissive utterances."[32] Once made known, such internalist commitments may give rise to externalist ones. For instance, when *s* declares that she stands with *G*, she may give *G* license to expect her support. Beforehand, *s* might have been no less (internalistically) committed to *G*, but now *s* is also externalistically committed. Commissives that report commitments generate what Brewer calls *associations*, whereas performatives create *aggregations*.[33] Unlike aggregations, associations depend on reason-governed commitments, and their normative force—or lack thereof—rests on the underlying reasons in their favor. Brewer argues that many of our most important cooperative activities are associative rather than aggregative.

Brewer distinguishes aggregations and associations on the basis of whether the group in question is built on a prior commitment. But there are two ways that a group can be built on a prior commitment. One is when the commissive reports an internalist commitment and thereby creates an externalist one. But things might also work the other way around: *s* might assert an externalist commitment, and thereby create an internalist one. For instance, solidarity with a union is grounded in a reason, not a performative: one sides with the union against the company because there is some reason for doing so. Yet insofar as one is in solidarity one does not say, "I stand with the Teamsters because I reject the lower wage scale for new hires." The reverse is true: one rejects the lower wage scale because she stands with the Teamsters. She need

---

[32] Talbot M. Brewer, "Two Kinds of Commitments (and Two Kinds of Social Groups)," *Philosophy and Phenomenological Research* LXVI, no. 3 (2003): 559.
[33] Ibid., 566.

have no independent view on the lower wage scale for new hires, no internal commitment to the rightness or wrongness of this wage scale.[34] Agent *s* does not stand with the union *because s believes that their demands are right*, then, but *because theirs is the side to be on*. This reversal of direction runs counter to Brewer's intention with regard to associations. One is not asserting an internalist commitment to the Teamsters or, still less, the particular provisions of their contract. But nor is the assertion just performative, a radical choice independent of principle. Alongside Brewer's "aggregations" and "associations," we might call groups founded in externalist commitments *con*gregations.

Perhaps, then, the best account of solidary groups is as follows. Whereas the inner-circle group *G* might be either a Gilbertian aggregation or an association, *S* is a congregation formed by the internalization of externalist commitments. This model also makes better sense of at least one of Brewer's exemplary commissives, namely, "I stand with...." Brewer presents this commissive as a report of an internalist commitment, but *s* might never have heard of or thought about *G* before standing with it; or *G* might have come into existence just at that moment; or *s* might have always opposed *G* until just now, when suddenly *G* is under attack. So *s* need not be internally committed to standing-with-*G* or to the principle on which *G* makes its stand. "I stand with..." is as much self-discovery as it is self-report. A good example is the emergence into international prominence of the Revolutionary Association of the Women of Afghanistan, in late 2001. People around the world became solicitous of the views of RAWA to determine whether they should support the US invasion, the post-Taliban government, and so on. The worldwide supporters of RAWA were its congregants.

This account of *S* and *G* meshes with our sufficient condition of solidarity. *S* might neither share *G*'s ideals, nor join *G* in Gilbert's sense of creating a mutually obligating plural subject. Yet *S* will nonetheless undertake actions subject to *G*'s directives, acting as *G*'s surrogate and being disposed to share *G*'s fate. Another virtue of understanding *S* in terms of externalist rather than internalist commitments is that it separates *S* from the underlying values themselves. And this is particularly helpful for cases where reason *r* shifts— for instance from *G* against *H* to *F* against *G*. When answering the Teamsters' call for public support on the wage scale, the agent is not forming a Gilbertian social atom, be it an association or an aggregation. The supporter defers to the Teamsters, and the Teamsters consummate this deference. But nor do the Teamsters thereby have any right against the supporter to continue supporting the union until such time as they are mutually released from this obligation. If Teamsters for a Democratic Union should then object to the contract that

---

[34] This point is parallel to the one about same-sex marriage and solidarity with the LGBTQ community in note 27 above.

the union brass has negotiated, the supporter might shift to support TDU for the very same reason that she had previously supported the union brass. By externalizing the values undergirding the group, the theory of congregations accounts for the deferential relationship between S and G, and accounts for alienation and authority as normal parts of group function that do not undermine cohesion.

That said, however, plural-subject theories of group agency remain controversial, and I want to show that the theory of solidarity can remain agnostic on this front. In the next section I shall run a parallel account of solidary groups, this one grounded in shared agency.

3.4 SHARED AGENCY AND SOCIAL MOVEMENTS

In the alienated-painters example discussed earlier, we followed Shapiro in treating Baker and Charlie as individuals painting the house together, for Abel. We might then wonder under what conditions we can treat Baker and Charlie as a *group*—group S, say, as I have been using this variable—in solidarity; and when we could regard a collection of individual g_i as group G. The plural-subjects approach discussed above could understand groups as aggregations, associations, or, I proposed, congregations. The shared agency model, in contrast, suggests that individuals would become groups when they met the appropriate conditions for acting together.

Building on Bratman's idea that plans have a fundamental role in agency, Shapiro proposes five conditions that are jointly sufficient for group G to perform act J:

(i) There is a shared plan for G to J;
(ii) Each member of G intentionally follows her part of the shared plan;
(iii) Members of G resolve their conflicts about J-ing in a peaceful and open manner;
(iv) It is common knowledge that (i), (ii), and (iii); and
(v) J takes place in virtue of (i) and (ii).[35]

According to Shapiro, "shared intentional activity is activity guided by a shared plan."[36] In small groups the plan may be inexplicit because personified in what Shapiro calls the "J-authority" of a particular person whose directives are taken as authoritative.[37] Those who accept J-authority seek to "vertically mesh" their behavior with that of the authority, and following such authority counts as *rational*—because integrated into a planning structure—even if

---

[35] Shapiro, "Massively Shared Agency," 277.   [36] Ibid.
[37] Ibid., 266.

immoral. It is thus rational for von Braun the Novice Nietzschean to follow Nazi authority. In larger groups, J-authority is not personified but manifest in an explicit plan.

"Sharing a plan" occurs when each participant is committed to acting on the plan and engages in the joint activity because of that commitment. Shapiro specifies that "a plan" is an *abstract object*; in effect, there must be some true description of each person's action such that it falls under the plan. Nonetheless, Shapiro brings the plan back down from Plato's heaven by requiring that the plan have been (at least in part) designed for the participants, and that each participant accepts the plan. In the alienated-painters case, Abel devises a plan, and Baker and Charlie follow it, each by intending to do his own part and having no attitude toward the other's part or to the task as a whole. Charlie needs the paint to be scraped before he can do his part, but he does not intend that Baker do this; he has no intentions about Baker at all. He just wants the paint to be scraped so he can do his job and get paid. Our question here is not whether this account suffices for *solidarity*. The question here is whether Shapiro's account is sufficient to form the group S or G. And while I think that it is not the *only* way to account for such groups, it is indeed sufficient for them.

Bratman objects to "Shapiro Shared Agency" on grounds that it is too broad. He gives the example of theatregoers who exit the theatre all at once: though they lack plural intentions, there is a plan that they follow, they accept that plan, each participant plays his or her part, resolves disputes peacefully and openly, and this is all common knowledge.[38] This seems to make too many actions into cases of shared intentional agency, and to miss what is distinctive about efforts to do something *together*. Another way to articulate this worry is that on Shapiro Shared Agency, an individual counts as acting together with others even when those others enter his planning only parametrically, rather than as members of a team. That is, he plans *around* them, not *with* them.

It is true that "Shapiro Shared Agency" demands considerably less than Bratman's account, and less too than solidarity. But for precisely this reason, social movements of the sort with which we began this chapter may fall under Shapiro Shared Agency. In a real sense, the abolitionists—the New York Anti-Slavery Society and the West Midlands Anti-Slavery Society—are acting all together as a social movement. Yet due to lack of coordination or inability to communicate, they have to plan around one another rather than work together day-to-day. Each Society is parametric to the other, yet they are nonetheless a social movement. For our purposes, Bratman's challenge brings out a feature,

---

[38] Michael Bratman, "Rational and Social Agency: Reflections and Replies," in *Rational and Social Agency: The Philosophy of Michael Bratman*, edited by Manuel Vargas and Gideon Yaffe (New York: Oxford University Press, 2014), 294–330.

not a bug: Shapiro Shared Agency explains joint agency even at the macro level of social movements.

3.5 CONCLUSION

I want to close by testing the account. Do our conditions cover cases that look like solidarity, but not cases that do not? In a first case, imagine a set of individuals who find themselves being bullied. Suppose a professor and a majority of students share a particular political conviction, a small minority disagree, and the professor starts using that minority's opinion as a straw man for laughs. The bullied students g_i don't know one another before this, so there is no antecedent group G. Suppose a bystander student s_1—who, like our white Alabama bus rider, is in the majority and so had been laughing along, but now recognizes that her peers are being bullied—desires to act in solidarity with the bullied students. She has three options. She can choose one of the students, g_1, and act in solidarity with that individual, much as our bus rider could act with Rosa Parks. But if s_1 is to act in solidarity with the bullied students as a group, there must first be some group object of her solidarity. She might, then (second), wait for them to aggregate or associate, perhaps verbally or perhaps by reaching a rough impromptu plan that comes together as each, say, stands up and objects or walks out. She would then adopt their tactic—whether she thought it productive or not—because it was their decision about how to respond. But suppose no such group emerged, the students being cowed by the threat of the upcoming final exam. She might, third, take the initiative to stand up *for* them, perhaps by challenging the professor. Her action may then spur the g_i's association. Group G would then be an artifact of the struggle.

In these cases, s_1 (1) attempts to defer to G, in this event by acting as G's surrogate, in the matter of the bullying professor, (2) because the g_i are being bullied. If (3) the g_i consummate her support—whether by welcoming her stand or by asking her not to make a big deal of it—then she joins them in solidarity; but if they instead were to quickly join the majority by laughing at s_1, then they fail to consummate her support and her attempted solidarity fails. But suppose they welcome her stand and quickly form an impromptu plan of action, and s_1 acts on their plan of, say, standing up and walking out; she does so because (4) she values their agency. Finally, (5) s_1 shares g_1's fate in the sense of being exposed to the professor's retaliation. Thus solidarity in the case of individuals and small ephemeral groups meets our criteria for Deferential Solidary Action.

In a larger-scale case, suppose a UAW member, Paul, arrives on the UAW bus at the March on Washington. His membership in the UAW makes him part of an incorporated group, and insofar as he does what the group directs according to its decision structure, he is acting as part of the group. But in this case it is likely that he was not told to come to Washington, but volunteered; hence the question is whether his trip to Washington is taken *as* a member of the UAW. Now we need to appeal to a noncorporate conception of shared agency. But this is straightforward inasmuch as Paul intends to follow the UAW's plan and values the UAW's agency; in turn the UAW is in solidarity with the Southern Christian Leadership Conference insofar as it follows the SCLC's plan and values its agency.

Suppose now that Peter, a different UAW member, very much wanted to march, but was asked to stay home and staff the phone lines. Suppose that he cannot find a replacement but decides to go to the March anyway. Then, he does so as an individual and *not* in solidarity, or at least not as a member of the UAW, since he has shirked his role. That this was his role is easily explained, again, in terms of the union's corporate agency or the plan of action it has devised. His shirking entails that when he shows up at the March contrary to his union's directives, he does not do so *as* a union member; he is not valuing the union's agency. This is a striking conclusion; Peter is (i) a UAW member; (ii) at a march that the UAW is at, (iii) because the UAW is at it, (iv) intermingled with the other UAW members at the March; (v) holding a sign, chanting, and clapping along; but (vi) still not there *as* a UAW member and (vii) *not* acting in solidarity. But I think this is the right result; no doubt some FBI informants also met these criteria. To be in solidarity one must be doing one's part of the group act as determined by G.

Next, consider Elizabeth Anderson's account of the abolitionist movement. The principal difficulty here is that plans are not stable over time. Thus understanding massively shared agency to follow a plan requires that we understand plans to be under continual revision. Congregations seem most useful here, since all the supporters of abolition may be congregants of one or another primary anti-slavery society each of which is, in turn, a congregation committed to the value of the enslaved persons; the congregants leave the work of revising plans to that society, and each society tries to defer to slaves or to act as their surrogate. Shapiro could account for this dynamism in a similar way. Participants become members when they accept roles in a plan; so far so good. But what accounts for the movement's maintaining its character as abolitionist despite continual revisions in its plans, including at the highest level? One hypothesis is that there is a core goal—the abolition of slavery—and this goal remains fixed even as the plan evolves around it.[39] But I think this is inaccurate. Through changes in plans the consistent value is not emancipation per se but the interests of enslaved persons. So the slaves' agency is valued, and

---

[39] This would presumably have to be Sangiovanni's explanation.

the abolitionists' plans are revised by reference to that. A clear example of this is in US abolitionists' support of the election of Abraham Lincoln in 1860 despite the fact that he did not run on an abolitionist platform; and again in Lincoln's own eventual repudiation of "emigration" in favor of "amalgamation" after meeting with free blacks who rejected emigration outright.[40] What is essential for Shapiro is that the plan be stable enough that it can be the object of common knowledge, and that the participants be stable enough that the ones who stay can get on with their meshed subplans despite the revolving door of new and former participants and the slow evolution of the plan itself.

The moral challenge of solidarity is whether deference could ever be justified. I shall argue in Chapter Six that it can. For now, we have been concerned with the ontological question of solidary collective action. This challenge comes down to two facets: the problem of unincorporated collectives that act together in solidarity, and the problem of deference. Deference is action on another's behalf—action such that the agent is an understudy or surrogate decision maker for the object, not a trustee or an independent sympathizer. Our account of Deferential Solidary Action provides a sufficient condition of such activity. As for unincorporated collectives, I have proposed two parallel accounts of collective action, one shared-agency view and one plural-subject view. Either of these approaches might eventually turn out to be inadequate to the explanation of collective action, but I have shown here that, in that event, solidarity will not be the decisive difficulty.

These results complete the reply to the conceptual challenge, *what is solidarity*. The answer is that solidarity is by definition *reason-driven, consummated deferential political action*, and solidarity occurs when the subject (1) defers to the object in a particular context and (4) values the latter's agency, (2) for a reason; (3) the object accepts the subject's deference, and the subject (5) commits to share the object's fate within the relevant context. The challenge now is to discern whether deference can ever be appropriate, and if so, how and why we should identify a particular person or group as our object of deference.

---

[40] Doris Kearns Goodwin, *Team of Rivals* (New York: Simon & Schuster, 2006), 161–2.

4

Autonomy and Deference

Imagine a 2001 debate around the proverbial water cooler regarding whether the US Congress should pass the "USA Patriot" Act.[1] Abe suggests that the Act infringes upon important privacy interests. Bea claims that its built-in safe-guards as well as longstanding legal protections and bureaucratic norms will prevent unreasonable invasions of privacy. Cecil says, "Read the bill. You can't decide this question from an armchair." Abe and Bea skulk back to their cubicles and dial in to AOL.

It is difficult to answer Cecil's charge. The bill is hundreds of pages long. It involves countless cross-references to extant laws and agencies. The implications of the Act can be reasonably followed out only by experts, but no single expert is likely to be able to do this alone, and anyway, experts disagree. Even in retrospect, despite numerous instances of government overreach, it is unclear whether or to what degree these occurred pursuant to the Act, were contrary to the letter of the Act but were—foreseeably or otherwise—made more likely by its provisions, or were straightforward violations of the law that cannot be blamed on the Act. So which of our water-cooler interlocutors is right? They cannot plausibly answer Cecil by saying that they know they are right without having read the Act. But even if they have read the Act they cannot plausibly claim to have understood it and its implications. Cecil's appeal to individual responsibility—to autonomy—*immobilizes* Abe and Bea rather than empowers them.

Similar problems arise on a wide range of issues where we choose sides by reaching conclusions we believe to be rationally well-founded, but without the degree of expertise we would need for anything approaching full information. In such cases of great complexity, from surveillance to financial regulation to international conflicts, individual reasoning about the common good or even about one's own good runs a high risk of being thwarted or misdirected due to the complexity of the empirical or normative issues at stake and of the political

---

[1] *Uniting and Strengthening America by Providing Appropriate Tools Required to Intercept and Obstruct Terrorism (USA Patriot Act)*, 107, H.R.3162.

landscape against which these issues arise, as well as the remoteness of the evidence that might (if properly interpreted) decide the issue. Worse, on display in such public disputes, unintentionally or otherwise, is the entire gamut of fallacies and errors of reasoning. Guarding against these errors and abuses of reasoning in even a single dispute could be a full-time job. It is not something that we can do in general.

One reason that an account of solidarity must make a place for deference is that having a politics at all must make a place for deference. To recapitulate our earlier discussion: roughly, deference is the requirement that the agent be willing to act on others' judgment rather than just his or her own. Deference is tied to agonism. To say that solidarity is *agonistic* is to say that the question *which side are you on* is prior to the question *what is the right thing to do*. But, agonism does not imply loyalty; in solidarity one chooses sides for a reason that applies to people in general, not just to those who are in a certain relationship. I join in solidarity not because I think *I* ought to, but because I think *one* ought to. Personal loyalties and ties might make this easier or harder—for instance if the country or class or family I belong to is involved on one side of the struggle—but solidarity is grounded in a reason. It follows that solidarity is agent-neutral, not agent-relative.

These desiderata now form a rather fine needle to thread: we need to choose an object of solidarity on the basis of a reason that is not itself a substantive moral norm. For if we choose on the basis of *substantive* norms, then it is conscience that does the work. So we must first identify, and then justify, that nonsubstantive norm. The current chapter explicates and defends deference against autonomy. Chapter Five identifies and justifies a nonsubstantive moral norm on the basis of which we might choose sides.

4.1 THE PRINCIPLE OF AUTONOMY

Chapter Two showed that teleological solidarity collapses into a politics of conscience because it insists that the myriad judgment calls that go into a decision about how to act on our natural duty of justice are all down to the agent her- or himself. These judgment calls include empirical ones about whether a certain action is likely to lead to the desired ends, normative ones about whether the current situation is unjust and the target situation more just, and metanormative ones about whether my contrary motivations track genuine agent-centered options. The liberal tradition is associated with a strong commitment to individual autonomy. Indeed, from a liberal perspective, deference on matters of conscience would seem to be a principal reason to *repudiate* solidarity. One reason to be a liberal about solidarity is precisely in order to subordinate it to the agent's best judgment of the morality of ends and means. Philip Soper characterizes this commitment as the Principle of Autonomy (PA):

> PA: Autonomy requires individuals to make their own judgments about the merits of opposing views and about the correct action to take.[2]

The current chapter explicates and refutes PA, but then shows that liberals need not have been committed to it.

4.1.1 Conceptual and Evaluative Interpretations

On its face, PA is a conceptual claim about the necessary conditions of an action's counting as autonomous: only those actions that flow from the agent's real-time, actual judgment count as autonomous. PA is a claim not about the content of our ends but about who has authority over them: if s's act A is to be autonomous then s's reason for A-ing must be that s believes it to be what s has most reason to do right now. Thus if r is pointing a gun at s, then s hands over his wallet autonomously because that is what he has most reason to do right now. So characterized, it is hard to see how an event could violate PA and still count as an action at all.[3] To fail so to act would be to fail to *act* at all. If this is all that PA entails, deference is no threat to autonomy.

Yet this minimalist conceptual interpretation of PA makes "heteronomous action" impossible by definition. And surely heteronomous acts are not impossible. Thus on a more interesting—but still conceptual—reading of PA, actions are autonomous only if they meet some test: the agent's decision to act must not be manipulated or coerced by outside agents, clouded by confusion or irrationality, or unchecked by some kind of internal authorization mechanism. So understood, PA tracks "positive freedom" and compatibilist conceptions of free agency.[4] This substantive conception of autonomy is more useful than the minimalist conception, for now heteronomy is possible and is something to worry about. But deference still poses no problem for autonomy; if s rationally judges that what she has most reason to do right now is act on g's authority, then deference is autonomous. Any time deferring was the all-things-considered most reasonable thing to do, autonomy would require deference rather than following one's own judgment.

In Chapter One I characterized Bartolomé de Las Casas as deferential inasmuch as he went out of his way to generate his own justification for

---

[2] Philip Soper, *The Ethics of Deference* (New York: Cambridge University Press, 2002), 5.

[3] For discussion see Philip Pettit, "Construing Sen on Commitment," in *Rationality and Commitment*, ed. Fabienne Peter and Hans Bernhard Schmid (New York: Oxford University Press, 2007).

[4] See for instance Harry Frankfurt, "Freedom of the Will and the Concept of a Person," *The Journal of Philosophy* 68, no. 1 (1971); Gary Watson, "Free Agency," ibid. 72, no. 8 (1975); Susan Wolf, *Freedom within Reason* (New York: Oxford University Press, 1993), 73.

what *someone else* thought to be most reasonable, even though his own sincere moral commitments entailed that this position was egregiously wrong. Vitoria, in contrast, relied on his own best moral and empirical judgment. His judgment was informed by the plight of others, but he nonetheless interposed himself as the arbiter of their claims. Similarly, in Chapter Two I characterized the conscientious liberal agent as failing to defer because that agent decided it was up to him to discern what his natural duty of justice entailed in a given instance, arrogating to himself empirical, moral, and rational authority. And at the outset of this chapter, Cecil called on Abe and Bea to do the same regarding the USA Patriot Act. To be informative, then, I think the theoretically challenging characterization of PA must reside in this vicinity—it must divide this self-asserting agent from the deferential one, Vitoria from Las Casas. Let us therefore understand PA as a norm of authorization:

> PA_c: s's act A is autonomous only if s's decision to A is grounded in s's judgment that A is the right thing to do in this situation, and there is no t such that t's judgment about A determines s's judgment about A.

So stated, PA_c—with the subscript identifying this as a conceptual principle—distinguishes Vitoria from Las Casas. The site of autonomy is not in the tight link between intention and action, as is the case on the purely formal interpretation. Nor is autonomy situated in the structure of reason or the will, as in the substantive interpretation. Rather, the site of autonomy on this interpretation is outside of volition itself, in prior practical judgment about normative and empirical matters impinging on the question of what it is best for a person in the current situation to do right now. The heteronomous agent, then, authorizes another to adjudicate the reasons that impinge on the agent. I will argue below that "authorization autonomy," which PA_c isolates, is too demanding; it rules most of our political (and much other) action heteronomous.

As a conceptual claim, PA_c says nothing about whether we should care about autonomy. Nothing yet follows about whether one *ought* ever to act heteronomously; all that follows is a sufficient condition of an action's being heteronomous. My job would be easier if I assumed that an act's being heteronomous is no mark against it or no misfortune for the agent who performs it. But I think autonomy is in fact desirable for individuals, and other things equal, autonomous acts are preferable to heteronomous ones. Assuming that this is the case, then, we can restate the Principle of Autonomy as not just a conceptual claim but a *value* claim:

> PA_v: Other things equal, it is desirable that agents act autonomously rather than heteronomously.

PA_v might apply in various domains, including the moral and the prudential. Insofar as the scope of action includes believing or accepting propositions, PA_v could even apply in epistemic contexts. With these conceptual and evaluative statements of the Principle of Autonomy in hand, we can also finally give a more precise, but still preliminary, statement of a norm of deference.

> D_0: One ought sometimes to act on another's decision about what is all things considered the right thing to do in this instance, even if one had a feasible alternative that was preferable by one's own lights.

So stated, D_0 does not *negate* PA_v but indicates that there is a range of circumstances where other things are not equal—where one ought to act heteronomously. My task in the remainder of this chapter is to defend and fix D_0, thereby constraining PA_v. The liberal tradition strongly favors PA_v, and so in this respect my argument will challenge the liberal tradition. But as I shall argue in Section 4.3, liberals *need not* insist on authorization autonomy in all circumstances, and if, as I hope, the moral argument for deference is compelling, liberals will have good reason to accept "authorization heteronomy"—deference—in many real-world cases.

4.1.2 Moral Arguments for Autonomy

It is not hard to discern initial moral arguments in favor of PA_v and against D_0. Such arguments emerge from across the spectrum of normative ethical worldviews on offer today. From virtue-ethical and natural-law perspectives, the rightness or wrongness of an action depends in part on the action's agent-relative features; an action can be fully moral only if it flows from individual conscience or a stable state of character. Action against conscience is then always less than fully rational or moral. Put otherwise, the moral properties of an act-token *a* depend in part on the state of the agent who does *a*, and deference is always an improper state.[5]

Alternatively, PA_v may be defended deontologically as an implication of a commitment to autonomy and equality. Essential to agency here is each person's acting as a co-equal legislator for a kingdom of ends.[6] For this reason, signing away one's authority over which action to take would constitute using oneself as a mere means and treating someone else as a moral dictator. Finally, consequentialists might worry that a nation or group of followers would be capable of mass madness. It is by now a cliché that we should celebrate the lone individual who sees through the madness and stands up to the "smelly little orthodoxies which are now contending for our souls."[7] To be sure, this

---

[5] Aristotle, *Nicomachean Ethics*, trans. Terence Irwin, Second ed. (Indianapolis: Hackett, 1999); Finnis, *Natural Law and Natural Rights*, 126.

[6] Immanuel Kant, *Groundwork for the Metaphysics of Morals* (Peterborough, Ontario: Broadview Press, 2005); Barbara Herman, *The Practice of Moral Judgment* (Cambridge, MA: Harvard University Press, 1993).

[7] George Orwell, *A Collection of Essays* (New York: Mariner Books, 1970), 104.

celebration of the individual may itself be one of those little orthodoxies, a bit of "dead dogma"[8] that is contradicted by a Donald Trump more often than it is confirmed by an Orwell. Nonetheless, there is a powerful idea here: we need the social critic, the gadfly who holds us to our own ideals, helping us stay on-track when we are distracted or fooled.[9] If such a person were to defer, we would be sunk. Thus a consequentialist defense of PA_v holds that the *social* good depends on *individual* autonomy.

For all these reasons, the Principle of Autonomy poses a real challenge to deference, and seems strongly consonant with the liberal tradition. Other things equal, the more autonomy the better.

4.2 FOR DEFERENCE

We now have a clear and controversial—yet on its face highly plausible—evaluative principle of authorization autonomy. This principle is supported from across the spectrum of familiar moral schools of thought. The burden of argument rests on anyone who would restrict PA_v.

The current section bears that burden. I reject both the virtue-ethical and the deontological arguments by showing that PA_v is too demanding; it sets up an ideal that we cannot meet. Yet even if we could, doing so would perversely impede the development of coherent political commitments and effective political organizing. Deference is an essential element of a division of political labor that makes political action possible. This result also defeats the consequentialist defense of PA_v, on the plausible hypotheses that having political commitments and engaging in political action are good overall. Even if we could meet the demands of PA_v, it would be better if we did not. Finally, I offer two positive deontological arguments for D_0. First, deference to certain others can be a form of respect for persons. Second, deference can *enhance* our autonomy diachronically even if it limits autonomy synchronically.

4.2.1 Autonomy and Immobilization

Cecil suggests that it is irresponsible to have a view on the USA Patriot Act unless one has read it; such a view would be heteronomous—relying on someone else's say-so—and hence PA_v implies that Abe and Bea should withhold judgment. But they also have many other projects and responsibilities.

---

[8] John Stuart Mill, *On Liberty*, ed. Elizabeth Rapaport (Indianapolis: Hackett, 1978), 34.
[9] Michael Walzer, *The Company of Critics: Social Criticism and Political Commitment in the Twentieth Century* (New York: Basic Books, 2002).

Moreover, the only basis they have for knowing that the USA Patriot Act is particularly important at all is that someone said so. So we can just push the water-cooler conversation back a step: suppose Abe and Bea disagree about whether the USA Patriot Act is a *particularly important* piece of legislation, worthy of having an opinion on. Cecil scoffs, "Read the other bills. How can you know which are the most important bills unless you read them all?"

Congress passes hundreds of bills each year. Even the "least productive" Congresses pass upwards of 200 bills per year.[10] And this says nothing about state and local government, rules made by executive-branch agencies, appellate court decisions, the behavior of public officials at all levels, and so on. Cecil's advice could hardly be more immobilizing. Making only autonomous judgments about all these issues that affect us is simply incompatible with the project of getting on with life. PA_v sets before us an aspiration that is not just somewhat beyond our grasp; given our current institutions and psychology, there is zero chance that we can come anywhere close to meeting it. Further, assuming that some of our other obligations are themselves unchosen, sometimes we will have to choose between the PA_c-enhancing act of learning more, and the PA_c-reducing act of meeting responsibilities, and it is by no means clear that we should in this case strive for autonomy. For instance, suppose Abe regards himself as having a filial duty to call his mother. Unfortunately, he is only on p. 224 of the USA Patriot Act. He thus cannot yet form an opinion on whether this is a good piece of legislation. Calling his mother would meet a heteronomous obligation, and hence would be a *pro tanto* violation of PA_v. In the end PA_v counsels a backwards rank ordering between these two acts, and implies that Abe should strive to finish reading the Act before coming to an opinion on it. PA_v is incorrect in both of these judgments. PA_v is contrary to any feasible or morally permissible revision in our daily practices.

PA_v is also violated by every single social movement that has ever existed. Social movements do not grow and succeed by pouring resources into developing fully reasoned arguments and double-blind, peer-reviewed studies to rationally convince potential supporters. Rather, movement organizations take advantage of unforeseen opportunities to build support and mobilize their base; for instance, they respond to threats by building coalitions of others who, though broadly like-minded, might know little about the issue in question but respond due to shared social networks or only partly worked-out sympathies.[11] Movements also use "critical events" or "focal moments" such as, often, staged crises, strikes, and direct actions where they might goad the

[10] Drew DeSilver, "In Late Spurt of Activity, Congress Avoids 'Least Productive' Title," *FactTank: News in the Numbers* (2014), http://pewrsr.ch/1y13OnQ.
[11] Nella Van Dyke, "Crossing Movement Boundaries: Factors That Facilitate Coalition Protest by American College Students, 1930–1990," *Social Problems* 50, no. 2 (2003).

state into spectacular repression and gain sympathizers.[12] Or they develop "frames" through which they interpret events for bystanders, recruiting support from among the previously uninvolved population. Recruiting bystanders is especially important for the least empowered groups, the ones with the fewest resources with which to employ in-house intellectuals to explain their plight in detail to bystanders, and to refute victim-blamers.[13]

Neither individuals, as bystanders who might be mobilized, nor organizations, embody PA_C. Yet it does not follow that the appropriate response to this lack of complete expertise is to shut off—to forswear political judgments because we do not know the answer to the fourth assertion made by Climate Denier #27. We might instead be well-advised to choose a side at least provisionally despite knowing that our epistemic situation is influenced by factors that seem to be near-textbook cases of epistemic irresponsibility: social networks, salient frames, preferred experts, and so on. Political action is the site of a complex division of labor, including cognitive labor, which both realizes and relies upon an economy of trust. PA_V must regard these features of our shared political life as regrettable. Maybe in some cosmic sense they are regrettable, but for the kinds of agents we are these phenomena are necessary for any coherent political commitments at all. And not just commitments, but deliberation: if not for reliance on the testimony of others, we would not understand institutions or even our own values well enough to coherently deliberate about them. It is *through* the practice of choosing actions based on judgments that are less than fully informed that we become able to be informed about things that matter to us, and informed about what does indeed matter to us.

PA_V is, then, a principle of *anomie* masquerading as autonomy. The immobilization that it generates might enhance our autonomy in a single instant—if for example we seek to learn more about a particular bill before deciding whether to support it—but this is a very local and synchronic phenomenon. On a broader frame and over time, PA_V offers a counsel of stasis. In the interests of autonomy we would allow our political lives to unfold without so much as a peep out of ourselves.

Let us, however, suppose for the sake of argument that individuals *can*—whether or not they should—autonomously withhold judgment and action until such time as they are fully informed, and that they can be motivated to act on this commitment by trying to inform themselves. Each person would then refuse to take sides prematurely, maintaining neutrality while weighing evidence. This is the ideal to which Cecil calls Abe and Bea.

---

[12] Marshall Ganz, "Resources and Resourcefulness: Strategic Capacity in the Unionization of California Agriculture, 1959–1966," *American Journal of Sociology* 105, no. 4 (2000), 1019.

[13] William A. Gamson, "Bystanders, Public Opinion, and the Media," in *The Blackwell Companion to Social Movements*, ed. David A. Snow, Sarah A. Soule, and Hanspeter Kriesi (Cambridge, MA: Blackwell Publishing, 2003).

Unfortunately, a common characteristic of the sorts of cases we have identified is not only complexity and dispute between two or more reasonable-sounding sides, but also what we might call *conscription*: the disputants force a choice. When I am a bystander to a focal event, often I cannot but take sides; the question is only which side I am on. Our white Alabama bus rider finds himself facing Rosa Parks. He did not ask for this. But here he is. Or suppose John has a routine appointment at his private hospital, "Blue Sword." As he arrives he sees nurses picketing, with signs reading, "On Strike: Boycott Blue Sword!" and "Blue Sword Unfair to Nurses!" No matter what he does, he takes a side: if he walks through for his appointment, he sides with the hospital; if he reschedules or changes physicians, he sides with the nurses. He cannot do neither. He is conscripted. Conscription is not uncommon; it is our normal political condition. Perhaps we rarely see picket lines anymore, but either we avoid purchasing from or investing in an embattled corporation, or we do not. Either we burn fossil fuels for recreation, or we do not. But we cannot avoid moral implication until all the numbers are in. Thus even Cecil cannot avoid taking action before having determined what is genuinely best.

It may be objected that autonomy does not frown on rough-and-ready judgments, but only on closed minds. Autonomy thus requires a readiness to revise our commitments in light of new information. Faced with a good rebuttal, we owe it to ourselves and others to find out whether "our side" has a good answer. There is some truth to this, but I want to make two replies to it. First, it is easier said than done. There is virtually always apparently reliable information available somewhere that would contradict our conclusions, as well as other reliable information that would confirm them. We are only rarely in a position to take the time it demands, and almost never able critically to assess it without reliance on others. Sometimes we must act. Moreover, open-mindedness is not always justifiable; those who maintain a permanently open mind are taken advantage of by others who use this as a weapon. It is not for nothing that first the tobacco industry, then the fossil fuel industry, adopted the tactic of sowing doubt. Under certain circumstances increasingly strident and possibly even violent engagements might be justified.[14] We do not demand of Martin Luther King that he have done the philosophy of language or the philosophy of science required to refute racism before he acts; nor do we take seriously the possibility that some new discovery in these areas would somehow prove the truth of racism. In these areas it is the moral commitment that regulates the metaphysics, not the other way around.[15]

---

[14] For useful discussion see Lyons, *Confronting Injustice*; Kristin Shrader-Frechette, *Environmental Justice* (New York: Oxford University Press, 2002), 197–202. See also Chapter Eight.

[15] See "The Independence of Moral Theory," in John Rawls, *Collected Papers*, ed. Samuel Freeman (Cambridge, MA: Harvard University Press, 1999).

A second reply to the open-mindedness objection is that there is a time and a place for everything. The focal events that compel instantaneous answers to "which side are you on" are only the crisis points of protest cycles or social movement histories. In the normal course of events there are meetings, strategy sessions, social events, and other behind-the-scenes moments that offer opportunities for critical debate and fact-finding. Those who are interested in getting the right answer can become involved when the cameras are not rolling, as well. And if they do then they can often participate in an interactively or relationally autonomous process of building doctrines and strategies, engaging in fact-finding, and so on; groups are in any case more effective when they involve participants in these sorts of processes, since the rigorous debate enhances the accuracy of information and the ideological sophistication of group members and leaders.[16] We should not, however, suppose that even such meetings model rational discourse in anything like the "Introduction to Critical Thinking" way we might hope. Significant issues and decisions can be put on or off the table in ways that no one notices or understands.[17] Yet the key point here is that the agent who seeks to go from bystander to captain in one fell swoop is arrogant rather than autonomous. In the instant, it is deference or nothing.

4.2.2 The Mechanics of Deference

Suppose we are part of a political organization where no one is disposed to defer. In this thoroughly indeferent group, each of us is fully PA_c-compliant. Each of us is, of course, frustrated by *others'* lack of deference, but this just bespeaks a kind of multiplayer prisoners' dilemma. Our willingness and ability to work together thus depends on everyone's either agreeing, or limiting the scope of questions laid on the table. If we cannot reach agreement on ends or means, on causal hypotheses or moral conclusions, we have to part ways or suspend the controversial action; we can build a coalition only on matters where the joint action intersects our antecedent aims, such that each of us has an individual reason for participating.

Such a situation has an attraction to it. It describes a world of nonconformists and free agents, of loose coalitions that congeal around specific causes and then melt away when their work is done. Unfortunately, this is not how change is made. Powerful actors could simply wait out the free agents, or time their controversial moves for moments when people were distracted, or sow disagreement among them with reasonable-sounding arguments, and

---

[16] Ganz, "Resources and Resourcefulness," 1012.

[17] Kathleen Blee, "How Options Disappear: Causality and Emergence in Grassroots Activist Groups," *American Journal of Sociology* 119, no. 3 (2013).

then continue as before. Groups would have to reinvent the wheel, ideologic-ally and organizationally speaking, each time they sought to act. Social move-ments worthy of the name would be impossible: no movement can be expected to achieve a level of theoretic and practical articulation sufficient to convince every member or still less supporter or bystander, individually, of the truth of a fully fleshed out philosophical doctrine or political ideology, *and* of a priority rule for deciding on elements of that doctrine, *and* of a plan of action for implementing the doctrine against a hostile establishment. No movement could survive if everyone insisted on being the final arbiter of each choice that the movement made—on being, if you will, the PA_c-man. And if not everyone can, why should anyone?

Effective movements need to be role-differentiated. Rank-and-file members obviously must defer sometimes; they are inexpert, and occupied by other things. But leadership has its role precisely because it defers sometimes to the rank-and-file, as well as to the target beneficiaries of group action, if those are separate from the rank-and-file. Formal organizations often have paid staffers, people whose job it is to keep the ball rolling. Paid staffers need contributors. Contributors need to be willing to use their money as proxy for the time they might otherwise have spent not just acting and organizing, but monitoring the paid staff. There then emerges agency risk; an organization with trusting contributors is in position to take advantage of them. But every member cannot constantly look over the shoulder of the paid staff. A board or a steering committee can analyze the books periodically; government agencies can require that forms be filed; but for regular members these arrangements just iterate the agency risk and add to the number of people whose judgment must be deferred to.

PA_v thus establishes a strong default *against* group cohesion and, hence, collective action. If social movements worth the name are to be possible, people must be disposed to both join and stay with the group despite lacking a PA_c-rated justification of the group's behavior.

Deference accounts for individual agency not just in solidarity but in politics more generally. Our preliminary deference principle D_0 understands deference as acting on another's decision about what is, all things considered, the right thing to do in this instance. Yet the demand cannot be that we must *always* do this, and that deference must go *all the way down*. Nor is the demand that we must defer to *just anyone*. Deference must therefore be counterfactual or dispositional, and any justification of it will have to be grounded in a structural reason for selecting among potential objects of deference. A more adequate basic principle would then be:

D   Under certain conditions, one ought to be disposed to act on particular other persons' or groups' judgments about what is, all things considered, the right thing to do in this instance.

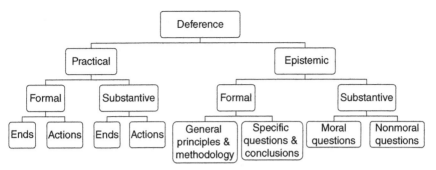

Fig. 4.1. Forms and levels of deference

The judgments in question may be practical (having to do with agency) or intellectual (having to do with knowledge). In each category we can distinguish among two or three sites of deference. (See Fig. 4.1.) First, *formal* deference involves substituting someone else's judgment about ends for my own. Formal *practical* deference substitutes others' judgment about what is good as the rationale or motive of my choices. The substituted judgment need not entail a substituted *good*; the good I pursue might well be my own. What matters is that the *decision* is not my own. Formal *epistemic* deference substitutes another's judgment about what is true. Again, I might agree or disagree; the point is that *my* reasons do not determine my judgment.

Formal deference leaves open two crucial *substantive* questions: what the good, or the true proposition, in question is; and how it is to be pursued or discovered. Call these, respectively, *substantive deference about ends*, and *substantive deference about action*. For instance, I may, on the basis of formal deference, outsource my judgment about the environment to the Sierra Club, such that "the environment" means "whatever the Sierra Club cares about." Now let us suppose that the Sierra Club decides that global warming is the most urgent problem. I practice ends-deference if I accept this specification of the good. Normally, I will then also act-defer about what would constitute behavior rationally aimed at climate-change mitigation. Mere ends-deference is compatible with my still relying on my own judgment about action; for instance, having deferred to the Sierra Club on the view that global warming is the most urgent environmental problem, I might still follow my own best judgment about how to engage this issue. And vice-versa: I might act-defer only after independently determining which end to pursue and discovering the convergence. On the other hand, if I both ends-defer and act-defer, then I also outsource the question of the best methods for achieving the given aim.

Act-deference is quite general, but it is most clearly observable in two types of cases: complexity cases such as those described in the examples above—climate, "homeland security," and so on—and what we might call *nonidentity* cases where I am, for whatever reason, not (fully) a member of the group with which I am in solidarity, or not most affected by the outcome of the struggle.[18] Complexity gives me a reason to defer to certain others in deciding how to act or which policies to support. In a nonidentity case, such as my solidarity with Indigenous peoples seeking self-government, it will at some point cease to be "my place" to assert my own positions as against those of the most-affected groups or persons. I might contribute my own judgments, especially if I have built up a long track record, through thick and thin; and especially if I am in a meeting where a big decision is to be made, rather than at a public event after the decisions have been taken. But in these nonidentity cases my judgments ought always, it seems, to be offered in the recognition that the decision is ultimately others' to make.[19]

Similar forms of deference are inevitable and appropriate regarding epistemic matters. Even if I can explain what it is that climate scientists have proven beyond a reasonable doubt (or how it is that they have done so) such that climate "skeptics" should not be taken seriously, my belief that these scientists have in fact proved it, that all other plausible leads have turned up dry, and that their methodology is valid, simply cannot be founded on my own fully informed judgment, unless perhaps I am myself a climate scientist. It does not follow that I am in no position to say that climate change is real and dangerous and that the "skeptical" alternative explanations such as sun spots or natural cycles are explanatory dead ends.

Yet it might be thought that while opinion leaders may be followed on all these other matters, deference on *moral* issues is incompatible with rational agency: one should never be willing to do what one conscientiously believes to be wrong, simply in deference to others. Political action often presents what appear to be moral dilemmas, such as the use of violence in a just cause, disobedience to legitimate authority, escalating tactics against an opponent who seems to be reasonable, or even choosing sides when every party offers reasonable-sounding moral or empirical arguments for its own position, such as on the minimum wage or hunting. Similarly, political action is often both high-stakes and unsuccessful. Its outcomes are nearly impossible to predict with any certainty. Any moral principle for collective political action must therefore be capable of making hard choices under uncertainty, when every option is morally fraught. But each of us has imperfect moral judgment, and moreover, that moral judgment interacts with our motivational set: those who are afraid may be dissuaded by moral qualms such as a minor risk of violence,

---

[18] For discussion of nonidentity cases see Lawrence A. Blum, "Three Kinds of Race-Related Solidarity," *Journal of Social Philosophy* 38, no. 1 (2007).

[19] See Burke A. Hendrix, *Ownership, Authority, and Self-Determination* (University Park, PA: Penn State University Press, 2008). I do not here commit myself to any "thick" conception of a cultural group; I mean merely to apply the account of group membership presented in Chapter Three.

while those who are arrogant may scoff at "collateral damage" on the way to expected victory. In such cases, persons may be mistaken about the moral properties of a contemplated act, and collective decisions about the advisability of that act may reflect greater moral insight or knowledge than any one person has.[20] Even when well-defined, the dictates of conscience are likely to meet with legitimate grounds for doubt. The idea that individuals are always the best judges of all these things is fantastical; the idea that individuals are normally even *capable* of judging these things for themselves in the sense required by PA_c is not less so.[21]

The defender of PA_v might grant these arguments but reply that deference on moral questions is admissible only subject to a general constraining principle that assures that the individual retains final authority. The question is what such a principle might be. It cannot be that *any* risk of significant harm to *anyone* in the course of a dispute renders the struggle unjustified, or participation in it immoral. This would concede every dispute, in advance, to anyone who can credibly threaten to escalate.

Perhaps, however, it is possible for participants to antecedently decide upon an account of what Mark Wicclair calls the *moral core* of the struggle, a central organizing value that both orients and constrains the choice of tactics and aims.[22] This proposal gets at an important truth, and my eventual account of morally justified deference will follow this basic model. But while political struggle is often fundamentally moral, and solidarity may be built around a kind of moral core, the crucial point here is that this moral core cannot elevate autonomy above other considerations. Whether autonomy should carry the day must itself be open to debate and even deference. Moreover, there may be disagreement about the meaning or content of the moral core, even if there is solidarity among parties. This fact animated the debate between Martin Luther King, Jr., and Malcolm X. For Malcolm X, nonviolence was an arbitrary limitation of legitimate means that amounted to unilateral disarmament. For King, by contrast, nonviolence was essential to the self-purification required if any victory at all was to be possible; it was *violence* that was an arbitrary limitation of legitimate means.[23] We can draw two relevant implications from this debate. First, the supposed moral core of the struggle is itself a moral and political question; to adapt a point from Howard Richards, every concrete case is simultaneously one of tactics, strategy, and the moral core.[24] These issues arise together. It is therefore impossible to hive off a nonnegotiable moral core. Anyway, members of the movement might work together even though they

[20] James Surowiecki, *The Wisdom of Crowds* (New York: Anchor Books, 2005).

[21] Peter S. Cremer, "On Being a Responsible Person," *Southern Journal of Philosophy* 13, no. 1 (1975).

[22] Mark Wicclair, "Conscientious Objection in Medicine," *Bioethics* 14, no. 3 (2000): 214.

[23] Martin Luther King, Jr., *The Trumpet of Conscience* (Boston: Beacon Press, 2011).

[24] Howard Richards, "Deference," *Ethics* 74, no. 2 (1964).

disagree about the moral core, or lack fully formed views about it. Indeed this is the normal case.[25] Thus whether tactics ought ever to contravene the moral core is itself a moral question, and one on which deference might be warranted.

I conclude that deference—including on moral issues—is inevitable if political movements are to be possible or even if persons are to have coherent political commitments at all. It follows that, at least for consequentialist reasons, we are better off admitting deference than trying to exclude the uninformed or remain neutral until we have full information. Returning to Fig. 4.1, these results entail that we might practice a whole variety of forms and levels of deference all at the same time. Such deference is *multilayered*, cascading down the hierarchy of subplans or propositions; at each stage the agent substitutes another's judgment for her or his own, and the categorical distinction between intellectual and practical deference collapses.

Nearly every case of political action involves deference, and deference is most often multilayered. This is inevitable if an effective politics is to be possible; and since an effective politics is at least sometimes desirable, it follows that there are at least some cases where multilayered deference is itself desirable.

4.2.3 Limits of Deference

Suppose that you and I have identified an appropriate object of deference, and they want something that we have *very good reason to believe is bad*, for themselves or others. Should we defer?[26]

To fix ideas, imagine a coal country community faced with the choice of rejecting or accepting mountaintop removal mining. Coal country is a neo-feudal realm where the coal companies act as lords, colluding with governments and financial elites to engineer minimal economic diversity and high rates of poverty. Mountaintop removal is the apotheosis of this neofeudalism, where the geography itself is given over to the lord. Faced with this choice, however, many residents of coal country see no alternative, and accept mountaintop removal as their least-bad option. You and I are confident that accepting it will be worse in the long term, since the coal will be gone within a year anyway, taking the entire community with it. But for good reasons and bad, the community democratically supports mountaintop removal. We appear to have two options: accept the community's judgment and support

[25] For incisive historical analysis along these lines see Michael Dawson, *Blacks in and out of the Left*, The W.E.B. Dubois Lectures (Cambridge, MA: Harvard University Press, 2013).
[26] I am grateful to Christian Barry and John Cumbler for extremely helpful discussion of this problem.

Table 4.1. Deference to bad decisions

	Defer	Don't defer
They are wrong	Respect, but be complicit in [attempted] grave harm	Disrespect, but be innocent of [attempted] grave harm
They are right	Respect, and participate in [attempted] good outcome	Disrespect, and be complicit in [attempted] grave harm

them, thereby supporting mountaintop removal mining; or reject the community's judgment and oppose them.

Part of the difficulty of this case lies in the fact that there are third-party victims of this practice, including people affected by the polluted air and rivers, and future generations near and far. Moreover, we will have to work to determine whether the democratic judgment of the community is based on the subjugation of vulnerable members. I shall discuss harms to third parties in Chapter Eight; here I want to assume away these complications and focus on whether we should defer even in cases where the object of our deference is recruiting us into serious harm *to themselves*. Table 4.1 lays out the moral risks.

I emphasize that we do not have a guarantee that they are wrong, nor do we know whether their preferred policy will win the day or whether our participation will be causally efficacious. Disrespecting the members of the mining community is a guaranteed bad that follows on failure to defer, whereas respecting them is a guaranteed good that follows on deference. But we will have aligned ourselves on the side of a practice that we have very strong reason to believe is bad for them.

Taking into account only the harms to themselves, I think the answer is that we must defer. But this does not decide the manner in which we do so, or the timing of our decision. If we find ourselves in the community after the decision has been made, trying to impose our views on them is worse than disrespectful; the case is closed, and we have no legitimate argument that it should be reopened on our account. But suppose we have been there longer, we are resident there ourselves or at least have built up the trust of the residents, attended meetings, shown good will. In this case we should defer only *after* participating in meetings, discussing the larger situation, amplifying the voices of the least advantaged within the community, pressing for better alternatives and compromises, and so on. If we fail, then at least we tried, and we support the community in its decision. But if we succeed in even a slight improvement of the decision, then we have done considerably more good than if we had stood against the tide as outsiders, aloof from (and unaffected by) the excruciating choices of the community.

I emphasize the limits on this conclusion: we have assumed away any impacts on third parties, and abstracted from the inevitable power relations within the mining community. Our result is thus only a presumption in favor of deference rather than an all-things-considered requirement. Even so, the liberal might find the prospect of supporting mountaintop removal mining to be a giant step beyond the pale. It is to the liberal objection that I now turn.

4.3 LIBERAL DEFERENCE

I have challenged PA_v partly, but not only, on grounds that PA_c sets an impossible standard. PA_c asserts that acting on one's own judgment is a necessary condition of autonomy; PA_v holds that doing so is *prima facie* better than acting heteronomously. What I have shown thus far is that adherence to PA_v is, if not unattainable in *any* circumstances, then at least broadly incompatible with effective political action. Effective political action requires that we engage in a *deferent* manner. Moreover, in conscription cases PA_v demands the impossible, because one or another action is required but neither is autonomous in the sense required. And in nonidentity cases or in the heat of a focal event, PA_v is arrogant, counseling that we fail to defer when the question is not, or anyway no longer, up to us.

Liberalism is at least strongly disposed in favor of PA_v. The liberal tradition celebrates the heroic individual who stands up to social convention or opposes the crowd. John Locke more or less invents modern liberalism with his requirement of individual consent to authority and a right of revolution.[27] John Stuart Mill celebrates this sort of agent.[28] In the oft-quoted words of Justice Louis Brandeis, "Organization can never be a substitute for initiative and for judgment."[29]

A long counter-tradition has challenged liberalism in part by rejecting this ideal of independence as having been built built by and for men of a certain stripe and class.[30] Without challenging this counter-tradition, to which I am broadly sympathetic, I want to argue here, in defense of liberalism, that it need not be committed to the individualist, PA_c-man ideal that has been so close to the hearts of liberals. Indeed despite waxing poetical about individuality,

[27] John Locke, *Two Treatises of Government* (Cambridge: Cambridge University Press, 1988); James Tully, "Political Freedom," *The Journal of Philosophy* 87, no. 10 (1990).

[28] Mill, *On Liberty*.

[29] http://www.brandeis.edu/legacyfund/bio.html, accessed May 28, 2015.

[30] See for some valuable examples Carole Pateman, *The Disorder of Women* (Stanford: Stanford University Press, 1989); Carole Pateman and Charles W. Mills, *Contract and Domination* (Cambridge: Polity, 2007); Barbara Arneil, "Citizens, Wives, Latent Citizens, and Non-Citizens in the Two Treatises: A Legacy of Inclusion, Exclusion, and Assimilation," *Eighteenth-Century Thought* 3 (2007). See also MacIntyre, "Social Structures and Their Threats to Moral Agency"; Walzer, *Interpretation and Social Criticism*.

liberals have shown little interest in actually theorizing or still less designing institutions that enable people to live without deference, not least because the greatest liberty can be liberally justified only if it is equally available to all.[31] It has fallen to illiberals like Ayn Rand to defend PA$_c$-man with any seriousness. I thus want to argue that deference as I have here defended it is compatible with liberalism, and hence the impossibility and unattractiveness of PA$_v$ need pose no deep difficulty for liberals.

The first place to find deference in liberalism is in submission to legitimate authority. Joseph Raz understands authoritative reasons as those that preempt individual judgment in a way that is compatible with our principle (D):

> The fact that an authority requires performance of an action is a reason for its performance which is not to be added to all other relevant reasons when assessing what to do, but should exclude and take the place of some of them.[32]

This is a conceptual claim about the nature of authority: it involves preemption of subjective reasons by authoritative reasons. But such a role for authority immediately forces the moral question of what could ever justify us in accepting authority of this sort. Raz morally defends preemptive authority on grounds of what he calls "the dependence thesis":

> All authoritative directives should be based on reasons which already independently apply to the subjects of the directives and are relevant to their action in the circumstances covered by the directive.[33]

Authority is "normally" justified when, and to the extent that, accepting authoritative directives makes an agent more likely than she would otherwise be to comply with reasons that already apply to her.[34]

A key question for our purposes, then, is what it means to assert that some reasons *apply to* an agent.[35] If this is understood subjectively, then Raz's account will justify deference only so far as the agent is independently motivated to defer; if the agent is not so motivated, then the reasons will not "apply to her" because they will make no contact with her antecedent motivational state. Yet it is not clear how disastrous this is. It's true that in a broad range of cases of deference—including the most urgent cases of conscription—we are asked to take on aims or commitments that we do not already endorse, nor have any reason to, except for having been asked. But the very fact of being asked influences our motivational set and our range of beliefs. For instance, suppose a Euro-American tourist in Quebec comes upon a roadblock set up by First Nations activists, and they ask for the tourist's support. Deference would

---

[31] Rawls, *A Theory of Justice, Revised Ed.*
[32] Raz, *The Morality of Freedom*, 46. Emphasis suppressed.
[33] Ibid., 47. Emphasis suppressed.   [34] Ibid., 53.
[35] On this issue I have benefited from discussion with Chad Lee-Stronach and Frank Jackson.

not involve the tourist's acting on any reasons she or he subjectively had already. The tourist might have had no idea that there were any First Nations in the vicinity. Yet the very fact of being given the new information by the First Nations activists can activate the relevant reasons in the tourist's belief system. The tourist *now* recognizes that the reasons apply to her, and so she defers. Similarly, thinking back to Abe and Bea, they now have a response to Cecil's immobilizing injunction: they have reason to be engaged citizens, and hence reason to defer to trusted opinion leaders on matters of national importance.

Raz's account is all the more congenial if authoritative directives can be based on reasons that *objectively* apply to the agent. In this event, if we have a morally compelling argument for determining the object of deference—that is, for determining to whom we ought to defer—then this argument will show that the relevant reasons apply to us objectively. Then, whether the tourist recognizes it or not, if there is an undefeated reason to defer to First Nations activists in this circumstance, and this reason objectively applies to the tourist, then the tourist ought so to defer.

If Raz's account of authority—or something like it—is successful, then deference is not incompatible with liberalism. But we can say more. Liberals can endorse a free-standing argument in favor of accepting the better judgment of opinion leaders and experts.[36] In many cases where solidarity is invoked, those who invoke it are plainly in a better position than their audience to know details of the situation: it is workers in a particular factory who know the working conditions in that factory; it is victims of spousal abuse who know what sorts of measures tend to exacerbate the problem and which ones make it worse; it is people who have been to prison who are familiar with conditions there; and so on. We do not need to accept a standpoint epistemology to recognize that certain ranges of experience are particularly valuable for gaining insight into specific situations. Indeed it would be a bizarre and arrogant misapplication of aspirations to objectivity to suppose that an outsider with no particular information would be in position to adjudicate the assertions of an agent with this kind of direct experience of the phenomenon under protest. To treat testimony this way would be straightforwardly to perpetrate an epistemic injustice.[37] Thus if our account of the appropriate object of deference—see Chapter Five—tends to pick out people with this kind of direct experience in particular spheres, then liberals ought to defer.

A third argument for liberal deference is that a policy of deference can *enhance* rather than stunt our autonomy. This is most evident over time; by accepting others' directives in the near term we become able collectively to

---

[36] For rigorous analysis, see David Estlund, *Democratic Authority: A Philosophical Framework* (Princeton: Princeton University Press, 2009).

[37] Miranda Fricker, *Epistemic Injustice: Power and the Ethics of Knowing* (New York: Oxford University Press, 2009).

affect our common life in ways that we could not do alone. Given basic realities about how political change happens, deference in individual cases enables us to join with others in ways that we otherwise could not, and thereby be effective instead of quietist. It also exposes us to a greater range of viewpoints, and tests hypotheses we would otherwise not have come up with on our own, let alone tested in real life. So the impact of deference on autonomy is not exclusively negative. This is evident in Abe and Bea's replies to Cecil; it is deference that empowers them, autonomy that silences them.

The final liberal argument for deference is a moral one. Recall the contrast between Las Casas and Vitoria. Each author tries to get inside the head of Indians confronted with Spaniards who both proselytize and murder. Vitoria recognizes that Indians would not immediately see the truth of what the Spaniards claim about religion, but he is unable to treat the Indians as fully independent of his own judgments of reasonableness. He cannot appreciate that they have good reasons to simply ignore or shun Christian missionaries as a class. Hence the Indians' refusal to listen becomes, to Vitoria's mind, an international affront and provocation for war. Las Casas, in contrast, appreciates that the Indians inhabit a vastly different social and theological world, such that European religion and mores might be totally useless to them for an indefinite time. What Las Casas recognizes, but Vitoria does not, may be cashed out as a version of the separateness of persons.[38] Deference is a means of recognizing that the other is not just a slightly reduced version of the self, but rather, someone else altogether. And this recognition of the separateness of persons is a core moral commitment of liberalism.

4.4 CONCLUSION

I have argued that deference is an ineliminable feature of political life. Deference is compatible with plausible interpretations of autonomy but rules out one particularly strong notion of autonomy, and recommends that we accept some range of "heteronomy" in the relevant respect. But the strong form of autonomy is incompatible with our having any meaningful politics at all. The moral principle of deference recommends that we do in fact defer in at least a certain range of cases. Chapter Five presents this range of cases.

---

[38] Rawls, *A Theory of Justice, Revised Ed*; Marcia W. Baron, Philip Pettit, and Michael Slote, *Three Methods of Ethics* (Cambridge, MA: Blackwell Publishing, 1997), 13–14. I am grateful to Duncan Ivison for this observation.

5

The Dilemma of Deference

On July 9, 2005, a broad swath of Palestinian organizations issued a "Call for Boycott, Divestment, and Sanctions."[1] The ensuing "BDS" movement has been the most visible and divisive popular effort to alter the status quo between Israel and the Palestinians and end Israel's occupation of the West Bank and Gaza. It has in particular sown divisions among those who self-describe as sympathetic to the Palestinian cause, many of whom are uneasy about singling out Israel for treatment on a par with apartheid-era South Africa. Yet its divisiveness does not change the fact that BDS is a core case of a popular call for solidarity. An account of solidarity will be simply inadequate if it cannot offer guidance on this case. If the current theory is to reach a verdict on BDS, it will have to discern the structural moral reason that grounds solidarity, and determine what that reason implies in this case. The current theory of solidarity is deferential, as opposed to conscientious, so it cannot counsel us to choose a side based on what we think is right or effective. Instead it must discern a reason that will determine to which side we should defer, and how far we should do so.

If we defer only after making a substantive judgment to the effect that the cause is *just*, then deference is merely a shallow sheen over autonomous moral judgment, and conscience has come in through the back door.[2] Yet if conscience does not play this role, we seem to need a nonmoral reason to defer, which makes it hard to see how there could be a moral theory of solidarity at all. This is the dilemma of deference. If deferential solidarity is to be justified, then, we need a reason that does not fall back on our own substantive judgment.

The current chapter canvasses three strategies for overcoming the dilemma and identifying an acceptable basis for deference. The first is *epistemic*: we identify the genuine experts in a field by appeal to autonomously knowable

---

[1] "Palestinian Civil Society Call for BDS" http://www.bdsmovement.net/call. Accessed May 30, 2015.
[2] See Soper's discussion of whether the two accounts of authority might collapse into one, at Soper, *The Ethics of Deference*, 48–50.

criteria of expertise, and we defer to such experts on grounds of those criteria. The second is *relational*: we build on extant relationships, working within them to promote their morally most attractive elements. The third is *structural*: we identify the objects of deference by appeal to their position in a social structure or relative to certain others. I shall defend a structural criterion, and specifically propose that we ought to defer to those who are, relative to a given struggle, *least well-off*. In turn I understand "least well-off" in nonwelfarist terms: to be least well-off is to be treated (most) *inequitably*, not to have less of any particular psychic or social good or basket of such goods. This proposal opens further serious questions, including the moral status of the demand for deference; what to do when those who are least well-off attack other victims of (lesser) inequity; and what to do when they sincerely want something that will be bad for them. The chapter discusses these questions briefly, but they can be fully addressed only in later chapters.

5.1 EPISTEMIC DEFERENCE

In the previous chapter I defended the basic deference principle (D), which disposes us to act on particular others' judgment in particular kinds of circumstances, *if* we can identify the appropriate object of deference.[3] Epistemic deference would fill in the object variable with an appeal to expertise:

D_E In some conditions, one ought to be disposed to act on expert judgments about what is all things considered the best solution to a given problem.

An epistemic criterion of deference seems particularly appropriate given that Raz's "normal justification" strategy for practical authority, to which I appealed, presents such authority as a special case of theoretical authority.[4] We defer to theoretical authorities not because they simply tell us what to do, but because of their "easy access to the evidence and [their] better ability to grasp its significance."[5] It might be possible to recognize strategic and moral experts as well as experts on particular areas of intellectual inquiry. In fact we seem to do this all the time, seeking out trusted friends for their advice on how to make moral choices, and elevating to leadership roles those who are able to conceptualize strategic situations more effectively.

Suppose, then, that our friend Cecil hears the call for BDS. He does not know whether BDS is likely to hasten the just ending of the Occupation. Determined not to be a mere follower like Abe and Bea, Cecil researches BDS and the nature of social change. He discovers empirically sophisticated

---

[3] See Section 4.2.2.   [4] Raz, *The Morality of Freedom*, 29.   [5] Ibid., 52–3.

arguments about how social change happens, but one article implies that BDS is likely to be ineffective,[6] while the other implies that BDS can succeed if it gains widespread solidarity.[7] Unable to decide between these divergent conclusions, Cecil may then try to weigh the evidence for himself. But as we saw in Chapter Four, this kind of evidence-gathering and assessment is more than a full-time job, even on just one issue, let alone every issue.

Cecil faces a choice. He can ignore the call for solidarity on grounds of irresolvable confusion, or find some other method of determining which experts seem most credible or which arguments to accept. If he ignores the call in cases of expert disagreement he dooms himself to ignoring the call in every case, since few social issues are the object of anything like scholarly unanimity. Yet even if there were no scholarly debate, the problem remains that scholarly unanimity is not intellectually or morally reliable. Policy driven by expert consensus on intelligence,[8] eugenics,[9] differences between genders and races,[10] and economics[11] has often been catastrophic, most often reflecting the social positions and biases of researchers and research subjects in addition to the standard range of human errors and imprecision. Thus scholarly consensus must itself be critically evaluated.

Epistemic deference is therefore not a viable strategy for solidarity. Experts often turn out to be wrong, even on propositions that enjoy near-unanimous acceptance. Further, the matters on which they are wrong are often politically salient, either because the experts are rushing to catch up with events such as emergencies or unforeseen policy issues, or because their consensus reflects a bias held by the powerful at the expense of a social out-group. Strategic and moral expertise are hardly easier to find than intellectual expertise.[12] At their best, meritocratic systems are highly imperfect at identifying merit; most often, the meritocratic sheen covers status hierarchies and measurement biases.

Expertise, be it scholarly, moral, or strategic, cannot resolve the problem of which side to be on. There is no purely intellectual tool for doing so. This result

---

[6] Joseph E. Yi and Joe Phillips, "The BDS Campaign against Israel: Lessons from South Africa," *PS, Political Science & Politics* 48, no. 2 (2015).

[7] Marty Branagan, "Nonviolent Resistance to Nazi Germany: What Occurred and What Could Have Occurred," *Social Alternatives* 33, no. 4 (2014).

[8] Stephen Jay Gould, *The Mismeasure of Man* (New York: Norton, 1981).

[9] Buchanan, "Institutions, Beliefs and Ethics: Eugenics as a Case Study."

[10] Anne Fausto-Sterling, *Myths of Gender: Biological Theories About Women and Men* (New York: Basic Books, 1985); Naomi Zack, *Philosophy of Science and Race* (New York: Routledge, 2002).

[11] See the trenchant comments on the economics profession in Thomas Piketty, *Capital in the Twenty-First Century*, trans. Arthur Goldhammer (Cambridge, MA: Harvard University Press, 2014); Paul Krugman, "How Did Economists Get It So Wrong?," *New York Times Magazine*, September 2, 2009.

[12] On the unreliability—at best—of meritocratic evaluations in the US military, see Thomas E. Ricks, *The Generals* (New York: Penguin, 2012).

may seem highly disturbing. Should we not at least try to get the best information we can, and go by that, making rough-and-ready judgments that we are willing to revise as new information comes to light? The problem with this fallback is that it has all the vices that undermined appeals to conscience in Chapters One and Two. Our judgment calls about who seems reliable, about which claims seem probable, are as subject to bias as our judgment calls about what sorts of behavior seem right or wrong. The burgeoning literature on epistemic injustice has shown that we accord greater credibility to testimony from members of powerful groups than from less powerful groups, and that persons of high social rank are accorded undue "status trust."[13] Again, there is no purely epistemological solution to this problem; rather it is a moral and political problem about epistemology. It must therefore be addressed as a moral and political problem.

The point is not that there is no place for expertise of any sort in political action. Intra-group meritocratic practices might identify expert strategic thinkers on a trial-and-error basis, and, having identified such strategists, the group might call upon them to devise or talk through plans for longer-term success. Within groups, inclusive practices can ensure that all perspectives are heard and new thinking is brought to the fore. When new information seems to challenge the party line it can be engaged with seriously so that the group maintains the most rigorous feasible dedication to truth. In any case these sorts of practices are strategically wise, as it is good for the group to both know the truth and be publicly credible. Similarly, groups might identify, again imperfectly, members who are particularly wise in moral matters, and consult them when the group is at risk of overlooking important interests. Expert communicators can be called upon to develop a coherent message. And so on. Expertise does have a role. But expertise cannot determine which side to join. Experts can be found on both sides of most salient questions. On the other hand, when experts all seem to be on the same side, it might be because they are in the grip of a dead dogma. Thus D_E fails as a basis for selecting an object of deference. Expertise has a role in solidarity, but it is posterior to deference.

5.2 RELATIONSHIP DEFERENCE

A second proposal for discerning the object of deference is to build on extant relationships. Relationships do matter, but their role in solidarity is ultimately constrained and governed by a *structural* determinant of deference. Structure

---

[13] Allen Buchanan, "Trust in Managed Care Organizations," *Kennedy Institute of Ethics Journal* 10 (2000); Fricker, *Epistemic Injustice*; José Medina, *The Epistemology of Resistance* (New York: Oxford University Press, 2012).

and relationship both matter. But structure plays a fundamental role that relationships cannot; that is, relationships are inadequate on their own. Or so I shall argue in this section.

In relationships we are committed to particular other persons and to the aims, if any, of the relationship. In solidarity, the relationship is prior to and regulative of at least any *particular* aims we might choose. This allows us to specify our deference principle for relationships:

> D_R In some conditions, one ought to act so as to maintain and foster reciprocal egalitarian relationships by acting on the judgment of particular other participants in relationship.

It is essential to distinguish D_R from the principle of loyalty solidarity that I rejected in Chapter Two. Here the key is that we develop our politics in conversation with others, where the ongoing conversation takes priority over the conclusions that we reach in any particular case. As Allison Weir puts it, we do not naturally or inevitably find ourselves identified with anyone or any issue in particular; rather, we interpret a range of apparently distinct issues as linked in a particular way—say, as feminist issues—and then, finding those affected negatively by these issues, we invest in "holding together" as a "we."[14] Jodi Dean describes a process of dialogue that might begin with identity politics but over time develop an increasingly sophisticated analysis of the issues that brought the group together in the first place; as the analysis deepens, the particular opponent whose spur might have brought the group together drops out of the picture, replaced by a commitment to dialogue that is at least as rigorous in evaluating our own practices as it is those of the erstwhile enemies. By this point there is no longer an enemy, except the ignorance that previously bound us all.[15]

Since good relationships are built on mutuality and equality rather than hierarchy, we should expect to defer sometimes and other times be deferred to. To be invested in holding together seems to require that we have at least four dispositions:

Shared Aims: We ought to pursue goals agreed upon through compromise or narrow focus, rather than goals that divide the membership.

Priority: I should be willing to defer when the stakes are much higher for you than for me in a particular case, and vice versa.

Respect: I should be sensitive to the burdens I place on you, working to hold down the cost to you of working with me, rather than take your support for granted.

Reciprocity: Sometimes I defer to you, sometimes, you to me.

---

[14] Weir, *Identities and Freedom*, 70–1. Another valuable discussion of relationships in solidarity is Scholz, "Feminist Political Solidarity." See also María Lugones, *Peregrinajes/Pilgrimages* (Lanham, MD: Rowman & Littlefield, 2002). I shall return to Lugones in Chapter Six.

[15] Dean, *Solidarity of Strangers*.

The Shared Aims principle implies that the relationship carries independent weight against any particular cause to which we might dedicate ourselves. Thus if we can equally choose a consensus cause in place of a divisive cause, or a narrower cause on which we agree as opposed to a broader one about which we disagree, we should choose the former, not because of its intrinsic importance but because it builds cohesion rather than causes division.

Inevitably, we sometimes disagree. When we do, we ought to follow the Priority principle, because if the effects of a given policy hit you much harder than they do me, I should defer to your greater vulnerability and investment. Yet even if I do prioritize your plight in this case, you should follow Respect and Reciprocity, remembering our roles will one day be reversed. Each of these dispositions tends to enhance group cohesion and trust, thereby making the group both more effective and more internally egalitarian and supportive.

Schematically, relationship deference might work through a process such as that laid out in Figure 5.1. If *A*'s initial call for solidarity is taken up without doubts (as it is by *B* in 10), then deference is straightforward; the struggle becomes shared. But if *B* is doubtful, *A*'s call may require some negotiation. *B* could just decline; but at (15), *B* instead aims to maintain the relationship, asking for either more information about the case to explain why the action is warranted, or an account of the importance, to *A*, of this particular project. Hence the Priority principle becomes a backup for the initially unsuccessful request. *A* could refuse to respond, simply repeating the demand, but respect for *B* would lead *A* to respond by taking a long view about the significance of this particular struggle, as at (20) and (25), in light of the importance of the ongoing relationship with *B*. At (21), *B* bows out but commits to the continued relationship by indicating a willingness to be on board next time. Here the breadth of divergence on Shared Aims overrides even Priority, but this difference need not be permanent. At (26), *B* defers to *A*'s second request; at (27), however, *B* could again just say no, but instead requests details as to what precisely is demanded, thereby invoking the Respect principle. *A* could reply (as at (35)) by insisting that *B* in particular is needed, or (as at (30)) by providing a role for *B* that is less demanding, either because it gels better with *B*'s preferences or because *B* does not have qualms about it. Either move is an instance of respect. Finally, *B* may either accept the demand (as at (31) and (36)), or repudiate it (as at (32) and (37)). Notwithstanding B's doubts, and a potential decline of *A*'s trust in *B*, the relationship can survive every permutation except (32) and (37).[16] Through dialogue, *A* and *B* negotiate a role for *B* that is more amenable, bearing in mind that the struggle is long, that people are different, and that, at some point, roles will be reversed.

---

[16] We'll return to (18) and its consequences later in this section and in Section 5.3.3.

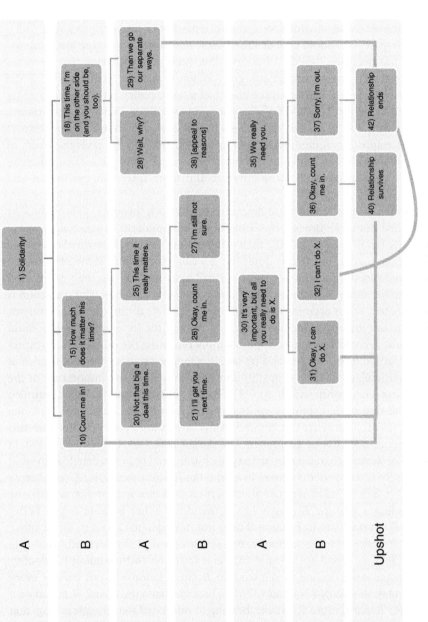

Fig. 5.1. A process of relationship deference

This process is deferential because at no point does B presume to independently assess the importance of this particular struggle. To do so would return to the conscience-driven model where B's agreement on substance is a precondition of B's willing participation. Yet B does insist that her perspective be taken seriously at the outset, in the dialogue involved in the selection of ends. The Priority principle enables A to override B's qualms by appeal to the severity of the impact on A, rather than on the nature of the issue itself. But A has reason to avoid overplaying the Priority principle since over time it will become implausible that every single issue is a life-or-death situation. A can step up the demand (as at (25) and (35)), but if the relationship is to remain equal and mutual then A will have to use these moves only sparingly, and must eventually reciprocate.

The dialogue might, of course, continue. Rather than merely rupture the relationship, B's reply in (32) or (37)—and even or especially B's objection in (18)—might spur A to reconsider the tactic. For even if some idea gained some degree of deference and agreement in a group setting, that setting might be excessively extreme due to in-group dynamics, and the failure to gain the participation of others with whom A is usually in solidarity may serve as a kind of negative feedback that moderates group demands, heading off excessive group polarization.[17] Thus relationship deference can both generate and moderate mass action, and it can both magnify and moderate the power of small groups.

In relationship deference, then, our ends are chosen in dialogue with others or at least *through* the group. We decide upon ends together. Hence the group is prior to any particular aims, and the justice of the ends—by the individual participant's lights—cannot be taken for granted. Relationship deference is a form of agonism, as defined in Chapter Two. B might disagree with the action—might think it ill-advised or immoral or otherwise inapt. But that does not automatically count as a reason for B not to do it. Rather, provided B is interested in maintaining the relationship, such doubts serve to initiate a critical dialogue the purpose of which is as much to maintain the relationship as it is to accomplish any particular action.

Relationship deference thus seems to capture some important elements of solidarity. I want to emphasize that relationships are an indispensable part of the process of deference when we are engaged with the same group over time. Yet relationship deference is not self-sufficient; it requires appeal to social structures.

First of all, a relational criterion of deference is predicated on the existence of a relationship; people the world over whom one will never meet are, in the first instance, beyond the scope of such a criterion.[18] One of the ways that

[17] Cass R. Sunstein, "The Law of Group Polarization," *Journal of Political Philosophy* 10, no. 2 (2002).

[18] Gould, "Transnational Solidarities."

social structures exclude and subordinate is by preventing people from meeting in their daily lives, or at least, from meeting in a setting where any kind of
equal or mutual relationship could be formed. Such structures can also work
by preventing the formation of "networks of solidarity" and by smashing them
when they do emerge.[19] Social structures might also have the effect that
would-be speakers are unable to communicate in a shared language, or to
fill in the background understanding that will make struggles seem meaningful
to distant others.

A relational account also requires reciprocity, and hence in answering A's
call, B legitimately expects that it will eventually be A's turn to defer to B.
Reciprocity might be an ideal to aspire to, and a characteristic of egalitarian
relationships, but if A and B are in unequal structural locations—e.g. one is
much better off than the other—the former's prerogative seems to dissipate.
Discussing Clare Weber's account of solidarity between women in the US and
Nicaragua, Sally Scholz argues,

> The relationship with others formed through political solidarity asks one not only
> to understand the needs of another but also to act in a way that allows that other
> to understand one's own needs. In other words, mutuality, rather than charity, is
> the hallmark of the relation.... Although the power differences between the
> U.S. feminist activists and the Nicaraguan feminist activists proved to be a
> constant challenge, the 'feminist praxis of dialogue and exchange' did, according
> to the accounts [Weber] cites, transform participants and result in concrete social
> change for both activist groups.[20]

Scholz is surely right that charity cannot be the basis of solidary relationships.
Yet nor does what she describes seem to be aptly described as "mutuality"; as
Scholz notes, it was the US women, in particular, who had to broaden and
redefine their initial interests in order to both raise more money for their work
in Nicaragua and address the needs that the Nicaraguan women articulated,
specifically to extend the scope of their concerns to labor conditions and not
just violence against women.[21] And it was the US women who had to work
doubly hard to overcome their antecedent privilege. What goes without saying
in Scholz's account is that recognition and accommodation are structurally
asymmetric.[22] Imagine if the US activists had demanded accommodations
from the Nicaraguan activists, either at the outset or as a matter of reciprocity;
this would have been hubris rather than equality. A similar point can be made
about the United Farmworkers grape boycott. The UFW built solidarity with

---

[19] Ibid.; Dawson, *Blacks in and out of the Left.*

[20] Scholz, "Feminist Political Solidarity," 213. Citing Clare Weber, *Visions of Solidarity*
(Lanham, MD: Lexington Books, 2006), 87, 137.

[21] Scholz, "Feminist Political Solidarity," 215–18.

[22] For similar points, see Gould, "Transnational Solidarities"; Harvey, "Moral Solidarity and
Empathetic Understanding."

consumers by linking the injustice in the fields with the pesticides on grapes in the supermarket.[23] In choosing this strategy the UFW expanded its appeal but took the risk of diluting its message. The politics of this decision would have been quite different if, instead of arising from a strategic decision within the union, it had come from consumers independently worried about pesticides who turned to the farmworkers and proposed that they shift their focus so as better to help the consumers. The higher-status group is not symmetrically situated relative to the lower-status group in determining how to push an agenda, even if the agenda is shared. And relationships of solidarity are defective if they fail to acknowledge these asymmetries by foregrounding the agenda of the worst-off. Thus while mutuality and equality are attractive features of a relationship, including solidarity relationships, they must be regulated by attention to social structure.

A further limitation on relationship deference is that it is not always the case that relationships should be continued, or that strengthening them is preferable to taking actions that weaken relationships or threaten to break them off altogether. Returning to the dialogue represented in Figure 5.1, suppose that A's call to action involves struggle against C, and C is worse-off than A in this case. In this event, A's call to action should not be supported, even if B has no relationship with C and has a longstanding relationship with A. Joining in a relationship with the more powerful against the less powerful looks more like bullying than like an attractive form of solidarity. B's reply should be, not (10) or (15), but

(18): This time I'm on the other side, and you should be too.

The Priority principle thus applies not just within the relationship but outside it as well: if third-parties are much more vulnerable than any of us in the relationship, then the moral quality of our relationship depends on our attention to those outsiders. The same goes for Shared Aims and Respect: if our aims abut those of third-parties who are no better off, we are well-advised, where possible, to narrow our agenda so as to complement rather than conflict with theirs; or better yet, to proactively reach out to them in hopes of joining forces. These principles are then prior to the relational deference that they structure. Relationship deference is attractive *when and because* it dovetails with these structural principles, and is unattractive or neutral otherwise.

This point addresses the worry that a relationship between B and C might "sandwich" A, if in social-status terms $B>A>C$: for instance if, among the majority "Up" population, those who support the civil rights of "Downs" tend to be better off than opponents of civil rights. Then B sides with C against A.

---

[23] Ellen O'Loughlin, "Questioning Sour Grapes: Ecofeminism and the United Farmworkers Grape Boycott," in *Ecofeminism*, ed. Greta Gaard (Philadelphia, PA: Temple University Press, 1988).

Scholz notes that the "participation of the privileged" generates difficulties because the privileged can participate with "authenticity" only if in doing so they chip away at the structure of their privilege.[24] This is challenging enough in general, and the challenge is sharpened still when B is in solidarity with C against A. B must exercise its solidarity such that it not only chips away at B's privilege relative to C, but also does not further empower B relative to A. The key is that the driver of such social criticism cannot be internal to the relationship between B and C, but must inhere in the social structure that includes A as well. B's solidarity with C must not be a vehicle for B's further aggrandizement—be it economic or self-congratulatory—over A.

Structure thus serves as a check on relationships, expanding the scope of our principles of Shared Aims, Priority, and Respect. This is particularly important when the call to action comes from a source that we have never heard of before, or that is in conflict with those we love and care about. Let's return to John from Chapter Four, who arrives at Blue Sword hospital to find nurses picketing and demanding a boycott. Suppose that, beside the nurses, a number of Blue Sword executives, including John's spouse, are leafleting about the nurses' union's interference with hardworking nurses who want to do their jobs and not have some third party speak for them or take dues out of their pay. John's relationship to his spouse is (by hypothesis) much stronger than his relationship to the nurses' union. It is (by hypothesis) more equal, more enduring, and more productive. It is the kind of relationship that John should spend his time strengthening and improving. Yet not only are these facts not decisive in determining which side John should be on, they are not even relevant. John's relationship to his spouse will surely have a motivational impact on him, but it is morally inert in determining to whom he should defer. The appropriate object of deference is determined *structurally*, not relationally.

Taken by themselves, even our strongest and most enduring relationships therefore do not determine the appropriate object of solidarity and do not generate a good case for deference. Indeed, this claim has been a hallmark of feminist theory and activism. As Weir argues, the struggle to develop feminist solidarity as against patriarchy requires feminists to identify shared interests that cut across relationships of subordination. But the shared interests are fundamentally *structural*; identifying them requires not just recognition but a *politics*, and the relationships that feminists build in order to struggle against patriarchy are founded on this structural analysis, not on shared qualitative features. As Weir emphasizes, though we might build an identity or relationship out of a feminist analysis of oppression and

---

[24] Scholz, *Political Solidarity*, 162.

domination, that relationship does not preexist the structural analysis.[25] Moreover, if as we develop this analysis we find that others are structurally worse-off than we are, in the same domain, it is inappropriate to insist that *our* issues be dealt with first, or even that they be coequal with those of others who are oppressed in more invidious ways. Obviously, shared struggles are motivationally easier for everyone, and positive relationships enhance our interest in the struggle and give us strength rather than sap it. But this is no less true of relationships among fat-cat bankers or white supremacists than of anyone else's relationships. It is structures that determine whether the enhanced interest and strength provided by affirmative relationships are good things or bad.

I've argued that both epistemic and relationship deference fail as accounts of whom to defer to. Epistemic and relational considerations are indispensable within organizations, at strategy meetings, and throughout solidarity; organizations should be guided by the truth as best they understand it, and we should foster relationships where possible. But the overarching and regulative criterion is structural. In making this case I have intimated or assumed that the appropriate object of deference is the *least well-off* or the most vulnerable. That is, attention to relative vulnerability regulates relationships such that relationships go awry if they tend to harm the least well-off. Similarly, expertise matters within a group but, since many groups have "in-house" experts, think-tanks, and so on, the identification of experts cannot determine whom to defer to. Nor can we rely on the experts' testimony about whom they are trying to help; as Rawls notes, it is a "convention" of democracy that all parties claim to be motivated by "the common interest," and specifically, concern for the least well-off.[26] The identification of experts to trust and of relationships to foster must therefore be driven by something that is prior to both. And that is, I shall argue, something structural.

5.3 STRUCTURAL DEFERENCE

We already have in hand a negative argument for structural deference: unless regulated by structural considerations, epistemic and relational deference are unacceptable. In this section I must develop a positive account. I'll understand the principle of structural deference as follows:

D_S In some circumstances Z, one ought to be disposed to act on the judgment of those who are least well-off relative to Z about what is all things considered the right thing to do in Z.

---

[25] Weir, *Identities and Freedom*, 66–7.   [26] Rawls, *A Theory of Justice, Revised Ed.*, 278.

A positive defense of D_S will require at least a rough account of Z and what it means to be least well-off relative to Z.

5.3.1 Prioritarianism

The initial, obvious objection to D_S is that it seems to be a Prioritarian principle, and Prioritarianism is false. Prioritarianism is the view that we should not endorse equality but rather prioritize the welfare of the least well-off.[27] Cashed out as an alternative to egalitarianism, Prioritarianism has the implication that, for instance, if Don has $10 and Emily has $20, and we can either give Don $2 (to buy a coffee) or give Emily $2000 (to pay for a week of college), but we cannot do both, we should buy Don the coffee.

T. M. Scanlon argues that priority for the worse-off is required only in cases where the worse-off have an antecedent claim to equal benefit, and only in cases where the benefit afforded them is relevant to a "particular aspect of their well-being." Since we do not have "an overall duty to bring about improvements in others' well-being," it is not the case that we owe a blanket priority to the worst-off.[28] I think this is importantly correct, yet rather than an objection to D_S I think it helps define the scope of D_S—that is, the scope of the "structures" to which D_S makes essential reference. Scanlon's objection assumes that there is a single, absolute worst-off group that is given *blanket* priority. Yet D_S refers to particular circumstances Z. We would need to articulate Z such that, for instance, D_S could take a stand on the Palestinian civil society call for BDS without having to consult the people of Niger or Togo first.[29] If we can do this, D_S would meet Scanlon's "particular aspect" condition, and avoid any implication of "blanket priority." Thus if there is no all-purpose worst-off group, there is no blanket priority. The question will then be how to individuate sets of circumstances. I shall address this in Section 5.3.4; but in order to do so I must first explain what it means to be worst-off in political contexts and to defer to the person or group that is worst-off.

---

[27] The *locus classicus* of this view is Derek Parfit, "Equality or Priority?," in *The Lindley Lecture* (Lawrence, KS: University of Kansas, 1991).

[28] T. M. Scanlon, *What We Owe to Each Other* (Cambridge, MA: Harvard University Press, 1998), 226–7.

[29] According to two prominent rankings of human development and of happiness, Niger finishes last in Human Development (187th out of 187), while Togo is the world's unhappiest country (158th out of 158). The State of Palestine ranks 107th in HDI, and the Palestinian Territories finish 108th happiest. Khalid Malik, "Human Development Report 2014: Sustaining Human Progress," in *Human Development Reports* (New York: United Nations Development Programme, hereafter *UNHDR*); John Helliwell, Richard Layard, and Jeffrey Sachs, "World Happiness Report 2015" (New York: Sustainable Development Solutions Network, 2015).

5.3.2 Equity as Political Well-being

Scanlon's critique of Prioritarianism also seems to assume an ordinal and intrinsically apolitical scale of well-being, namely, welfare. But the context of political struggle requires a specifically *political* account of well-being—one that plots people's status relative to a political context and has both the moral significance and the epistemic accessibility to command the respect of every-day people. In this section I want to propose such an account.

Welfarist conceptions locate prudential well-being in subjective welfare or happiness.[30] This approach might be right as a pure theory of prudential well-being, but from a political perspective it misses the responsibility of agents for their own conceptions of the good, and suffers from difficulties of interpersonal comparison and adaptive preferences.[31] These are particularly worrisome problems for solidarity, since we do not want to be compelled to fight for others' expensive tastes. Just imagine a person who loudly refuses to accept opera tickets when the ballet is sold out. We might empathize with him, but he is no Rosa Parks. Primary Social Goods,[32] Central Human Capabilities,[33] and Human Development[34] overcome these problems, but they are not especially useful for us as individuals or members of social movements because these conceptions require high-level data-gathering and analytical capacities. Both capabilities and primary goods are accounts of political well-being *for governments*, but only derivatively if at all for individuals or activist groups. Individuals and activist organizations are simply not in position to discern or compare one another's lifetime baskets of primary goods. We can do somewhat better at assessing snapshot human functionings such as adequate nutrition, literacy, and basic health. But we cannot truly know how others live unless we know them very well; and even then we are often systematically biased and uninformed regarding one another's actual functionings (and even regarding our own[35]). Harder still is discerning capabilities, since the whole point of the capability/functioning distinction is to respect the free choice of individuals to refrain from attaining functionings that they are genuinely free to achieve if they want. If we are uninformed and biased in assessing others'

---

[30] See for instance L. W. Sumner, *Welfare, Happiness, and Ethics* (Oxford: Clarendon Press, 1996). For methodological discussion in a social-scientific context see Helliwell et al., "World Happiness Report 2015," 13–20.

[31] For discussion see chapter two of Martha C. Nussbaum, *Women and Human Development: The Capabilities Approach* (New York: Cambridge University Press, 2000).

[32] See John Rawls, *A Theory of Justice, Revised Ed.*

[33] See Martha C. Nussbaum, *Frontiers of Justice* (Cambridge, MA: Harvard University Press, 2006).

[34] Malik, *UNHDR* 2014.

[35] For example, see the valuable discussion of "time-pressure illusion" in Robert E. Goodin, James Mahmud Rice, Antti Parpo, and Lina Eriksson, *Discretionary Time: A New Theory of Freedom* (New York: Cambridge University Press, 2009), chap. 6.

LIVERPOOL JOHN MOORES UNIVERSITY
LEARNING SERVICES

functionings, we are all the more so in assessing their freely unrealized capabilities to function. This is particularly salient in a political context because one familiar reason for failures of solidarity tends to be, not the denial that others are functioning suboptimally, but the ascription of this deficit to their free choice—that is, victim-blaming. We impute to others the unrealized capability; and what evidence can be given that they lack that capability? It is not evidence that can easily be imparted, and anyway often the truth is complicated.[36] Moreover even if individuals taken one at a time might have this unrealized capability, a class of individuals might lack it, and the fact of being badly off might lie in the collective experience of subordination rather than the individual inability to escape.[37] What Sen would call the informational basis of well-being judgments has to be observable if individuals and social movement organizations are to be able to use them. It also has to be sensitive to short-term changes in well-being; even if it is true that those who fall into poverty have a reasonable chance of doing considerably better later in life, they might still have temporary grievances that cannot be compensated by the prospect of future benefit. In such cases, lifetime packages of goods are not only unobservable, they are irrelevant. Neither welfarist nor familiar mixed views of well-being can serve as a criterion of political well-being for the purposes of discerning in real time who is better or worse off.

If D_S is to give content to a standing duty to support the least well-off, then the sense in which they are least well-off must be one that commands our respect no matter where or when it is invoked. This would be an appropriate foundation for a deontological theory of solidarity. I believe that the primary consideration of *equity* fits the bill. The hypothesis is that we should choose the object of deference on the basis that that person or group suffers (the greatest) inequity relative to the structure of the political conflict. It is in virtue of being treated inequitably that a person is badly off for political purposes.

Equity is a structural notion. Whether one suffers inequity is independent of one's personal relationship to anyone else and of one's subjective or objective well-being. One is inequitably treated independent of the quality of the reasons one gives or of the moral judgments one makes. Thus if we should defer to the least well-off then we should put aside loyalties, relationships, and even conscientious disagreement and focus on the social structure in order to determine to whom we ought to defer.

To support this argument I must give an analysis of equity and a normative theory that is founded in that analysis. Those are my principal projects for Chapter Six. First, however, I explain the structure of deference, assuming an

---

[36] For this reason Sen, despite his emphasis on heterogeneity and freedom, nonetheless retreats to achieved functionings across populations as proxy for capabilities.

[37] G. A. Cohen, "The Structure of Proletarian Unfreedom," in John Roemer, ed., *Analytical Marxism* (New York: Cambridge University Press, 1986), 237–59.

account of equity and of its role in justifying solidarity. Nonetheless, we need at least a rough sketch of what equity entails, and why it is a viable account of well-being for political purposes.

Equity is a complex moralized notion of what it is to fare well in a political society. It is a core notion of justice, linked to the idea of each person's being treated as neither more nor less than anyone else. So understood, equity is often gestured at imprecisely as a synonym for justice or for specifically economic or distributive considerations in contrast with other forms of justice.[38] But equity is not centrally about equal *distribution*. To be denied equity is not to *get less* but to be *treated as lesser*. Following Larry May, I understand equity as *fundamental* or *formal fairness*: a bare minimum of equal treatment.[39] Someone might be the victim of injustice in the sense that they receive less than their fair distributive share according to some theory of justice. But they might nonetheless be treated equitably because they haven't been victimized in a way that denies their equal status. On the other hand, they might *not* be the victim of distributive injustice more broadly, yet they might nonetheless be treated inequitably: even a wealthy person might be disappeared by the police, or have his assets forfeited under mere suspicion of involvement with illegal activity. So while equity is a core notion of justice it does not always inevitably travel with justice more broadly.

This idea that justice has a distinctive core is a widely held Kantian view. Like May, Anna Stilz isolates the most fundamental justice norms—equality and independence—from the rest of justice. In her view, whereas the remainder of justice, including property rights and distributive shares, is indeterminate until all are living under government, the core is determinate and knowable even in a state of nature. These core equal-status elements forbid assertions of natural authority, and justify compelling entry into civil society.[40] Only equity is authoritative even in a State of Nature. Because of the association with Kantianism, I shall refer to this core notion of equal status as *Kantian equity*. The idea, then, is that to suffer inequity is to be badly off in a distinctively political way, and inequities are uniquely outrageous because they manifest the lesser status of some than others. Whatever else we owe to others, we owe them a duty not to treat them inequitably; and insofar as there is a natural duty of justice it may be roughly cashed out, not primarily in teleological terms as the duty to help bring about

---

[38] Julian Le Grand, "Equity as an Economic Objective," in *Applied Philosophy: Morals and Metaphysics in Contemporary Debate*, ed. Brenda Almond and Donald Hill (New York: Routledge, 1991); David Schlosberg, *Defining Environmental Justice: Theories, Movements, and Nature* (New York: Oxford University Press, 2007). Equity as I explicate it here covers the most important aspects of Schlosberg's "recogniton" and "participation." He denies that equity includes these, but that is because he thinks of equity as synonymous with just distribution. See Schlosberg, 20–5.

[39] Larry May, *Global Justice and Due Process* (New York: Cambridge University Press, 2011), 48.

[40] Stilz, *Liberal Loyalty*, chap. 2.

justice, but in terms of basic respect as the duty not to stand by while another is treated as a second-class citizen.

Building on this last aspect of equity is the Aristotelian notion of "being an equitable person."[41] An equitable person is disposed to share the fate of the other, such that if A is denied just treatment then, insofar as B is equitable, B will be disposed to refuse just treatment until A can get it as well. I shall have more to say in the next chapter about these and other aspects of equity, and about how equity grounds a duty of solidarity. In the remainder of the current chapter I want to explore the implications of D_S where we defer to those who are inequitably treated in a given struggle.

5.3.3 Deferring on the Basis of Equity

Let us return to the relationship-deference conversation laid out in Figure 5.1— where A asks for B's solidarity—and specifically to the relationship-breaking response (18). B here rejects A's call to action in favor of A's opponent, C, but does so not by making a *substantive* (conscientious) judgment that A is wrong. When (18) is compatible with deference it is so because it is instead *agonistic*: predicated on which side the reason supports, rather than its substance as judged by B. If I have been right about epistemic and relationship deference then the appropriate basis for this judgment is neither the expertise of the source nor the relationship between B and the source, but rather the *structural location* of the source. C ought to be heeded as opposed to A because, in this context, C is in the relevant sense least well-off; C is most inequitably treated. Hence B might change sides and thereby abrogate what A thought was a firm relationship.

It might be thought that B's shift would violate the trust that has built up between A and B, and thus that structural deference is an untrustworthy attitude. Worse, knowing in advance that B might switch sides when the chips are down could inhibit successful organizing by A due to a worry that B will not be on-side when needed. The tendency for a structure-based deference to undermine trust, and therefore relationships altogether, therefore might seem to defeat structural deference right from the start.[42] But there is trust, and then there is trust. A might trust B because A knows that B will always take A's side. But this is "trust" in the morally shallow sense of principal–agent relationships, where the agent's job is to do the principal's bidding. This is the sense in which Don Corleone can "trust" his *consigliere* Tom Hagen. But a morally richer notion of trust involves A's being confident that B will give good advice—that B will be on the side of A's doing what, all

---

[41] Aristotle, *Nicomachean Ethics* v.10.1137b–1138a.
[42] I am grateful to Linda Radzik for raising this concern.

things considered, A ought to do.[43] The reason B is trustworthy here is precisely because B is guided by the promotion of the aims of the least well-off, and consequently, B's advice that A not antagonize C epitomizes that trustworthiness.[44]

Notice that, if B is trustworthy in this richer sense, B can appeal only to a very specific kind of reason for rejecting A's call: not that B disagrees, but that A is antagonizing someone with whom A ought to be in solidarity. Insofar as A knows that B is trustworthy in this way, and also knows that C is in relevant respects worse-off than A, A should plan in advance to avoid antagonizing C, and indeed, to work alongside C. Thus (18) is not merely the solidary and deferential response but the trustworthy response; A should not want B's support *come what may*, but only insofar as A's actions are worthy of it. To be trustworthy rather than a sycophant is precisely to be prepared to tell A when A has gone awry.

To be sure, (18) is highly schematic. If A and B have a standing relationship, then a statement with the content of (18) will no doubt be delivered by citing the plight of C and with efforts to build a coalition that includes A, B, and C. A would reply not by simply turning away but with (28) to keep the conversation going and be well-advised, rather than to charge forward at full steam no matter who suffers. Or, seeing the conflict brewing, B might raise the issue in advance in order to encourage A to stand down or shift tactics so that the break never comes. These are indeed instances of A and B working to preserve a relationship, but what's essential is that the relationship is guided by attention to the structural location of A and B relative to C. The structure regulates the relationship and makes the relationship a good one rather than an invidious one.

It might be objected, however, that in at least one crucial respect equity is in no better shape than welfare, primary goods, or capabilities: namely, that we cannot tell who is treated inequitably, or still less, who is treated *most* inequitably, in a given situation; or that even if we could tell it would bring back all the epistemic injustice and conscientious judgment-calls that have bedeviled previous attempts. I deal with this objection in Section 5.4. But first I must return to the individuation of circumstance zones.

5.3.4 Individuating Circumstance Zones

We noted above that D_S is context-relative; it is in virtue of being treated inequitably in Z that some individual g or group G counts as an appropriate

[43] Judith Jarvis Thomson, *Goodness and Advice*, ed. Amy Gutmann, University Center for Human Values Series (Princeton: Princeton University Press, 2001).
[44] This judgment can only be fully supported after I've made the freestanding moral argument for deference to the least well-off in Chapter Six.

object of solidarity and their inequitable treatment is decisive. It is for this reason that we do not need to check with the citizens of Niger before coming to conclusions about BDS. But this requires us to be able to say when a particular person's or group's interests are bound up in Z. We cannot defer on that question because that is the question that determines whether and to whom we ought to defer. The question, then, is how we can individuate and identify circumstance zones.

The practical payoff, for the theory of solidarity, of answering this question is twofold. First, it allows us to distinguish the object of solidarity G from everyone else, and to link individual g_i to group G. My aim is to do this without appeal to any prepolitical or ascriptive group criteria, such that what makes a given individual the object of solidarity is solely the inequity with which they are treated, not their prior membership in some group. To be sure, it is possible that the inequitable treatment will be based on ascriptive-group membership, as in the case of racist or patriarchal systems; but it is the inequity that drives the solidarity claim, not the ascriptive characteristics.[45] Second, it allows us to distinguish in particular between the subjects S of solidarity and the objects G—so that S's action is driven by G's decision. We saw in Chapter Three that each group was constructed by action, but since they act together we need still to distinguish between them.

Unfortunately, it is impossible to completely solve this problem in theory, and some amount of individual initiative in identifying who is affected by a given phenomenon is inevitable. I will appeal to democratic theory to help with the construction of object groups in distinct circumstance zones, but both here and in the next section on the epistemology of inequity, all I can do is indicate methods for making better judgments over time.

Democratic theorists have long grappled with the perennial question, *If the people should rule, who are (or is) the people?* One influential account is the "all affected interests" (AI) principle, which ascribes rights to participate to anyone who is materially affected by the decision to be made.[46] A second influential account is the "common world" (CW) principle, which ascribes rights to participate only to those who share their fate in some whole-life way.[47] A third account tries to discern a pre-political or freestanding account of "the People" such that democratic polities meet certain eligibility conditions

---

[45] See, similarly, Weir, *Identities and Freedom*. Shelby ties black solidarity to the shared stigma of racism, but his suspicions about cultural nationalism and other claims are grounded precisely in the fact that these membership criteria move away from the injustice and appeal to ascriptive, cultural, religious, and other characteristics. See Shelby, *We Who Are Dark*.

[46] Gould, "Transnational Solidarities."; David Owen, "Constituting the Polity, Constituting the Demos: On the Place of the All Affected Interests Principle in Democratic Theory and in Resolving the Democratic Boundary Problem," *Ethics & Global Politics* 5, no. 3 (2012).

[47] Thomas Christiano, *The Constitution of Equality* (New York: Oxford University Press, 2010), 81.

for self-rule. Such conditions might include a degree of self-consciousness, self-construction, or political organization.[48]

Without getting too deep into the details of these principles, we can observe that each provides some rough guidance for us. CW suggests that those whose whole lives are affected by a given form of inequitable treatment have a privileged status from the perspective of structural deference. It is those who live and have children in Love Canal—more so than those who just passed through one time—whose interests should, other things equal, be decisive in determining our response to that disaster. It is sweatshop workers whose interests should drive our action on low-wage factories. But CW must be checked against AI because harms and inequities are not always fixed in place, but move. If it is true that "an injustice anywhere is a threat to justice everywhere,"[49] then we will often find that others who are not *immediately* vulnerable can plausibly claim to be vulnerable down the line. For instance, if those who live in Love Canal knuckle under, then other polluters elsewhere will have an easier time getting away with murder. We therefore can use AI to broaden the scope of, or correct, CW. In extreme cases we might even shift our focus as a result of this corrective: for instance, if a "Buy American" campaign turns out to victimize sweatshop workers overseas, then the latter become part of the struggle at hand, and have a role in determining how to proceed.

Finally, an aggregation procedure such as that used to define "the People" is necessary to move from what each of the g_i wants or suffers to what G as a group wants or suffers. It is in virtue of *organizing* that the difficulties that any g_i faces become politicized. For instance, if someone in Love Canal has two health problems only one of which is shared with other residents or is linked to toxic waste, then the second health problem does not have the political character that generates a claim of inequitable treatment and hence solidarity. It is also in virtue of organizing that the interests of the g_i become politicized. Any individual might prioritize an irrelevant alternative benefit in place of a benefit to which she is entitled by equity. For instance, forced to choose between pursuing a legitimate claim and getting a better job, she might go to the job interview instead. It is in virtue of aggregating that we can focus on which, among the things the group members want, is the thing that they are entitled to or that they are accepting in exchange for what they are entitled to. They might all accept better jobs in place of payment for past harms; but if so then the aggregating procedure is what determines that this is their collective choice rather than a mere set of individual choices.

---

[48] Paulina Ochoa Espejo, *The Time of Popular Sovereignty: Process and the Democratic State* (University Park, PA: Pennsylvania State University Press, 2011); Margaret Moore, *A Political Theory of Territory* (New York: Oxford University Press, 2015), chap. 3; Stilz, *Liberal Loyalty*.

[49] King, "Letter."

These three grounds for identifying whose interests, and which interests of theirs, are at stake, can give us only a rough-and-ready means of identifying circumstance zones. I suspect that is all that is possible in theory. Yet even if we become increasingly sophisticated at identifying the effects of various practices and policies, there remains the further question of identifying who, within a circumstance zone, is in fact treated inequitably.

5.4 THE EPISTEMOLOGY OF INEQUITY

How do we identify who are the worst-off and what they want us to do? Again, there is no guaranteed, quick and easy way to get the right answer in every case. Even so, we have methods that, though inevitably imperfect, are nonetheless sufficient for the rough-and-ready judgments that are the inevitable ground of politics.

5.4.1 Is Inequity Perceptible?

Robert Audi argues that moral properties are perceptible, noninferential properties that we discern, along with their grounds, in core cases of moral wrongness or rightness. We need not see *that* something is wrong (*de dicto*, inferential) in order to see *wrongness* (*de re*, perceptual).[50] Could inequity be like this?

The initial problem with thinking of inequity as a perceptible property is that it is precisely in the deepest cases of inequity that we blind ourselves to the plight of others. Michele Moody-Adams explicates the phenomenon of *affected ignorance*, where the beneficiary of some inequity builds a fortress of denial as a screen against occurrent knowledge of unjust social relations.[51] Elizabeth Anderson describes the case of John Newton, a captain of a slave ship under whose torturous and brutal regime 28 percent of the human cargo died, yet who believed himself to be in "communion with God" and who, when he vowed to live less sinfully, did so by "giving up swearing, and…lead[ing] his crew in prayer services every day."[52] Anderson remarks on the "uneasy wonder" with which "we look upon Newton's moral obliviousness."[53]

---

[50] Robert Audi, *Moral Perception* (Princeton, NJ: Princeton University Press, 2015).

[51] Michele M. Moody-Adams, "Culture, Responsibility, and Affected Ignorance," *Ethics* 104, no. 2 (1994).

[52] Anderson, "Social Movements," 1. John Newton eventually became an abolitionist some 30 years after leaving the slave trade, and went on to write "Amazing Grace."

[53] Ibid., 2. Emphasis in original.

Despite its facial plausibility, then, the thesis that inequity is perceptible seems to confront unending examples of Newtonesque affected ignorance. Yet it does not follow that it is impossible to see inequity, but only that it also possible *not* to see it. What perceptual skills does the abolitionist have that the slave captain lacks? Or vice versa: what is it that the slave captain knows how to hide from himself, but that the abolitionist does not? One is tempted to reply—with Antonio de Montesinos[54] and, later, Kant—the *humanity* of the victims. David Wiggins cashes this out in terms of solidarity itself, a basic recognition of one another as fellow members of the "party of humankind."[55] Such recognition noninferentially acquaints us with the "special power of primitive prohibition" that rules out certain violations and appalls us at the thought that we could be compelled so to violate others.[56]

Each of us is nonetheless capable of violating others in these ways; the risk that we will do so must be reined in by our asking, or being asked, specific kinds of questions, and getting particular kinds of pushback.[57] This suggests that learning to recognize one another and urging others along the path of such recognition is a *process*, and specifically that it can be developed through *mechanical procedures* that get under our rationalizations, rendering inequities visible and forcing our recognition of others.

Along these lines Larry May argues that *visibility* is the institutional bedrock of equity.[58] The fundamental *Magna Carta* rights of *habeas corpus*, non-refoulement, the right to have the charges against one read publicly, and the right to a jury trial are essential backstops of equity precisely because they ensure that the accused is visible. But not only do they ensure visibility, they do so by requiring certain mechanical procedures—they constitute a kind of "checklist" that ensures we stop and attend to someone rather than plough forward.[59] It remains possible to misuse a checklist, as it is to abuse the criminal justice system. Nonetheless, the skill involved in "seeing" inequity and recognizing one another lies in pausing to notice and ask, or indeed, in mechanistically forcing oneself to do so. If John Newton had been required to log each hostage by name, and been accountable for ensuring that each individual who had embarked in Africa debarked upright in America, the 28 percent mortality rate would have been impossible—and with that Newton would have to have attended to nutrition, clean water, sanitation, and eventually, morale, and so on. That alone would not have ended slavery, obviously,

---

[54] See Chapter One.

[55] David Wiggins, "Solidarity and the Root of the Ethical," *Lindley Lecture* (Lawrence, KS: University of Kansas, 2008), 10, citing Hume.

[56] Ibid., 12, 14.

[57] Ibid., 13. Barbara Herman also emphasizes particularity in her account of the compelling power of humanity in others. See Herman, *The Practice of Moral Judgment*.

[58] May, *Global Justice and Due Process*, 10–11.

[59] Atul Gawande, *The Checklist Manifesto* (New York: Picador, 2011).

though if we iterate the thought experiment we immediately see that the "social death" of chattel slavery is incompatible with these practices of visibility. Inequity may not be visible *simpliciter*, but it is clearly the kind of thing one can train oneself to see and remedy, not least by practicing certain formal skills of attending and accounting.

5.4.2 Heuristics

These mechanistic "checklist" procedures teach us to see inequity. Yet political struggles must link such inequities to broader, structural or macro-level ones, in order to determine which genuine complaints are morally the most urgent. I argued earlier that epistemic deference is unhelpful because experts disagree on most of the controversial questions that become the subject of political dispute. Nonetheless, our society is not so opaque to us that we are unaware of basic structural features. For instance, it would be bizarre to try to deny that race, religion, and gender have been longstanding organizing structures in western societies, and that European-descended Christian males have been on top of these structures. No elaborate theory of society is needed. Similarly, that wealth and income are vehicles of advantage is not something it is possible to be sincerely confused about.

To be sure, none of these categories—race, religion, gender, wealth—or their combination gives a full story of advantage or disadvantage for any given individual. Yet the patent reality that certain groups have enjoyed historical advantages relative to other groups makes it possible to use these categories as proxies or heuristics for assessing inequity in practice. On issues disproportionately affecting women we can cultivate the habit of asking where the women are, what they are saying, what their priorities are; on racial issues, where the nonwhites are. This is not to say that everyone with such ascriptive characteristics will be saying the same thing or have the same priorities, but only that if their voices are silent then something is wrong. In some cases the absence of these voices is due to the literal absence of the relevant people;[60] in other cases it is their absence from debates about the issues affecting them that gives pause, as when abortion policy is debated by a panel of men, and so on. Knowing the history of advantage and disadvantage enables us to look for the "missing" people, to ask why they are missing, and to find out what others who meet the relevant descriptions are doing about the issue at hand. The point is not to start an "Oppression

---

[60] Amartya Sen, "More Than 100 Million Women Are Missing," *New York Review of Books*, December 20, 1990; Norman Daniels, *Just Health* (New York: Cambridge University Press, 2008); Justin Wolfers, David Leonhardt, and Kevin Quealy, "1.5 Million Missing Black Men," *The New York Times*, April 20, 2015.

Olympics," but to get us asking the questions that move us toward seeing inequities, and knowing what those on the bottom are doing about them.[61] Structural deference commits us to the proposition that those on top are always answerable to those on the bottom. Listening for when those on the bottom demand answers is, then, always a skill to cultivate when learning to see and acknowledge inequity.

Moreover, this can be iterated: within the group of disadvantaged there may be those who are silenced or subject to coercion, intimidation, and so on. The skill of looking and listening for the voices of those on the bottom can thus be practiced within social movement organizations, too, with special efforts made to ensure that societal advantage does not get reproduced, and to counteract it when it does. These organizational equity skills are closely related to those of relationship deference, but again, the structure regulates the relationship. For instance, if the terms of a relationship are predicated on the silencing of those on the bottom; or if those in charge insist that attending to intragroup inequities would divert our attention from the struggle; then maintaining the relationship is in tension with fostering equity. Equity should win. This does not mean that we must always pick a fight claiming to be standing up for those on the bottom; rather, it means we should inform those on the bottom that we recognize their situation and ask them how, if at all, they want to address it.

5.4.3 Counterfactual Deference and the Role of Conscience

Some victims of inequity live in undemocratic societies. Solidarity with these agents may be harder, but it is all the more urgent for that. They may speak through proxies, but their calls for support might be hard to disentangle from "scrambling" signals sent by their rulers in the form of propaganda or cooptation.

Because the regime's victims may be unable to alert outsiders of their situation or ask for help, it is possible that outsiders should take the initiative. For instance, King Christian X of Denmark rejected the Nazis' rule that all Jews had to wear yellow stars by threatening to wear the yellow star himself.[62] I assume that he did this on his own initiative, and not because any Jews asked him to. Such cases show us the proper role of individual conscience in solidarity. Conscience plays a role that is doubly circumscribed. First, the question of conscience is not *is this right*, or *what is to be done*, but rather, *how can I act on behalf of the victim?* The outsider

---

[61] Medina, *The Epistemology of Resistance.*
[62] http://www.holocaustcenter.org/holocaust-badges. Accessed May 31, 2015.

in solidarity seeks to fight alongside the victim even if the victim is perforce missing; to the extent possible, the agent in solidarity seeks to be the victim's hands and voice. But second, unlike a conscience-driven politics, in solidarity it is essential that the supporter have tried to learn what the victims want, and remain attuned to their voices in case they object to the putative act of solidarity. So suppose that the Jews of Denmark for some reason organized to ask the King to stand down from his position and allow them to wear yellow stars. In this event it would no longer be an act of solidarity for the King to maintain his resistance. Though again, this is iterated: if the community leadership wanted him to stop but those on the bottom did not, the situation would be different.

This investigation of the epistemology of inequity leaves us with several general strategies to pursue and skill sets to develop as we seek to learn to identify the victims of inequity and pursue structural deference. What is essential is that we do not rely on "untrained" conscience or expert datasets, nor do we seek to foster relationships that we think are healthy. Rather we can undertake specific courses of training and formal procedures to enhance our capacity to see inequity and discern who is worst-off in this sense. So trained, our conscience and reasoning play an indispensable role.

5.5 CONCLUSION: BDS—AN INITIAL REPLY

We began this chapter with the example of the Palestinian Civil Society Call for Boycott, Divestment, and Sanctions. Though divisive—or indeed, precisely because it is divisive—this is precisely the kind of issue that a theory of solidarity must be able to address, and hence if we have no answer on that issue we have, in effect, no theory of solidarity. In the current chapter we have covered enough ground for a preliminary answer. The Palestinian civil-society organizations that issued the call for BDS were laboring under military rule from the Israeli side and corrupt and coopted rule from the Palestinian side. The organizations ran the gamut of civil society, in particular including not just men but women's groups, not just Islamist but secular groups, not just intellectual but grassroots groups. They did not call for violence, and hence did not victimize Israelis in anything like the way they themselves were victimized by the Occupation.

It would be astonishing to deny that the members of Palestinian civil society suffer inequity. Therefore the initial response from the current theory is that solidarity requires taking their side in this struggle. It does not do so on grounds that BDS is likely to work, or on grounds that BDS is morally attractive. Both of these may yet be false. It does so because the call is issued by those who are on the bottom of a grave inequity, and the call does not on its face constitute an inequity that would simply shift the status of victim onto the other side by treating them inequitably.

This is, however, a preliminary answer. We will have to return to this case with a more careful analysis once we have in hand the full theory of the ethics of solidarity. That is the challenge of the next three chapters, and I return to BDS finally in Chapter Eight.

6

Solidarity as Equity

6.1 INTRODUCTION

In his *Letter from Birmingham City Jail*, Martin Luther King, Jr., lodges a soft-spoken yet scathing critique of the "white moderate," in whom King claims to be "gravely disappointed."[1] This white moderate, embodied in the clergymen to whom he addresses the *Letter*, is presented as a "great[er] stumbling block in [the Negro's] stride toward freedom" than the "White Citizen's Counciler or the Ku Klux Klanner." For the white moderate "constantly says: 'I agree with you in the goal you seek, but I cannot agree with your methods of direct action'."[2]

In a way, this whole book is a working-out of Dr. King's idea: that the worst thing to be, in a political context, is a "white moderate." If it is easy to know this in hindsight, the conscientious agent nonetheless shrinks from this knowledge in the heat of the moment. Solidarity is backbone.

More specifically, our hope rests in deference to those who are treated inequitably as they engage in strategic planning, voice their call to action, and press for justice. Yet even if the reader will grant my argument, from Chapter Five, regarding how to choose our object of deference should we be animated by this hope or just want to be politically engaged, that argument as yet does not say anything about whether doing so is ever the all-things-considered right thing to do, and if so whether it is a moral option or obligation. Chapter Five argued for deference specifically to *victims of inequity*. But even if this is the best account of deference it does not yet follow that we ever have any positive reason to defer to them, when we might otherwise have exercised our own judgment. In that event structural deference would lose out in any contest against the conscientious exercise of individual judgment. I will argue, however, that structural deference to—that is, solidarity with—those who are treated inequitably partly constitutes equity. Equity solves the justificatory

---

[1] King, "Letter," 295.   [2] Ibid.

problem for solidarity, explaining when and why solidarity is justified. The upshot is that solidarity is sometimes intrinsically valuable, not (just) instrumentally valuable; and it is a perfect duty, not a moral option or even an imperfect duty. These are the core claims of the current chapter.

I began the task of defining equity in Chapter Five. Here I shall explicate three senses of equity, each of which supports the thesis that equity is not only morally important but an "ultimate value"—that is, that equity is valuable irrespective of any further values it supports or brings about.[3] A sound argument to the effect that an act is equitable, or partly constitutes equity, thus provides a strong *pro tanto* reason to perform that act. As an ultimate value equity is not (merely) instrumentally valuable, but intrinsically valuable. And since solidarity with the least well-off partly constitutes equitable treatment of that person or group, it follows that solidarity itself is not merely instrumentally but intrinsically valuable. Solidarity can of course be instrumentally valuable when it helps to bring about equitable or just institutions, or has other salutary effects. This instrumental thesis animates teleological arguments for solidarity, discussed in Chapter Two. But what is distinctive about solidarity as opposed to mere coalitions and alliances—and hence, crucial to the justification of deontological solidarity—is that such solidarity partly constitutes equitable treatment and is therefore intrinsically valuable. If the argument here succeeds then we will have made a major departure from teleological solidarity, and more importantly, we will have given a normative foundation to a wide range of arguments that have tried to articulate solidarity without showing whether or why calls for solidarity are morally compelling. What follows from my argument, should it succeed, is that there is a *pro tanto* agent-neutral perfect duty to be in solidarity with victims of inequity, and that this duty is nonvoluntary. Solidarity is no more optional than it is optional to treat people equitably. Nor is solidarity reserved for extraordinary political moments. Solidarity is equity for everyday life.

If solidarity is a political principle of how one ought to treat people rather than what goals one should pursue, then solidarity with those who suffer inequitable treatment is about treating people equitably. Solidarity with those who suffer inequity is desirable because it embodies three aspects or senses of equity. First, "Kantian" equity is fundamental fairness, or according equal status to each person as a person. Second, "Aristotelian" equity is the correction of universal justice by attending to particularity. And finally, Aristotle's notion of "being an equitable person" is the tendency to step back from the maximum that one can demand, in consideration of whether others are also getting what they are entitled to.

---

[3] Raz, *The Morality of Freedom*, 178.

6.2 KANTIAN EQUITY

I introduced Kantian equity in Chapter Five, following Larry May and Anna Stilz in discerning a core of justice that does not always travel with justice more broadly. May expands on this idea in his theory of international criminal law. Characterizing equity in this sense as getting "quite minimally what one deserves in a context of rules that apply to all," May fleshes it out in terms of Magna Carta rights such as Habeas Corpus, due process of law, trial by jury, and non-refoulement.[4] These Magna Carta rights assure that each is treated as having full status as a person. These rights are the ground from which legal cases can be made, and hence the state may not make them the object of legal struggles themselves. There is no burden on the detainee to prove that he has a right to due process; rather his having a right to due process is the condition under which it is permissible to put any burdens on him in the first place.[5] For Stilz, equity norms are the most basic and only "natural" or prepolitical elements of justice. Basic security of person and possessions is essentially connected to the equal status of each as a person and hence serves as the ground for compelling entry into civil society. The rest of justice, in contrast, is indeterminate until all are living under government.[6]

Aaron James has recently developed a conception of Kantian equity—he calls it deontological equity—grounded in the contractualist ideal of being treated in a way that one could not reasonably reject. Deontological equity is a demand of each person's giving to each other person "what we owe to each other." Consequently, "Equity is not 'just another worthy value'; it is of decisive significance for action."[7] James's theory of equity is contractualist inasmuch as it proceeds from a consideration of what each could or could not reasonably reject under specified choice conditions. The contractualist framing of equity brings out a crucial element with which solidarity is also concerned, namely that we are accountable directly to one another for our actions. It is not enough to be able to derive an abstract justification for action one way or the other; rather, what is essential is that we be able to confront the person whose interests are most directly at stake. The idea that one's justification to another would be such as to give them no reasonable basis for complaint captures this idea. Contractualism also plays up another point that is significant in solidarity: the appeal to agreement as justification of action. Here the justification functions provenancially, by appeal to pedigree, not by appeal to the substantive moral content of the act in question. Such appeal to pedigree is most needed when there is disagreement about the moral quality of an act. The procedure serves the epistemic function of indicating

---

[4] May, *Global Justice and Due Process*, 48.
[5] Ibid., 100–3.   [6] Stilz, *Liberal Loyalty*, chap. 2.
[7] Aaron James, *Fairness in Practice* (New York: Oxford University Press, 2012), 136.

whether an act is wrong by indicating whether someone could reasonably object to it.

In practice, the contractualist approach works back and forth between substance and procedure in the following way: to determine whether some act *a* is wrong, I ask whether anyone has a reasonable objection to it. To determine who might *object*, I follow out the consequences of the act and see whom it affects; to determine whether their objection is *reasonable*, I apply some conception of harm. I assume, of course, that *I* am reasonable, that I can identify the range of people affected by *a*, that I can know the grounds of their objections, and that I am right about whether their objection is reasonable. Yet as we noted in Chapter Five, the (continuing) history of "affected ignorance" and victim-blaming should chasten us in these generous assumptions about our own moral competence. It is arrogant to suppose that I can know enough about others, and about their experience under shared social institutions, to know the full range of their potential objections. And it is more arrogant still to make myself the arbiter of the reasonableness of these objections, since *I* might turn out to be the unreasonable one.

The problem is twofold. First, contractualism envisions a merely *hypothetical* consent procedure whose participants are persons in general. Yet the compelling force of demands for equity arises from the *actual* demands of *particular* speakers.[8] Contractualism thus breaks down as a theory of wrongness just at the moment when, having identified a likely objector, and having imagined what seems to me to be their best objection, I cannot discern whether that objection is reasonable because I don't know enough about how the act affects them—or worse, I deny that it is reasonable because it doesn't seem so from where I sit. As Jean Hampton notes, contractualism is a theory about who matters and how they matter; and it is a theory about which sorts of objections *can* be reasonable.[9] But it does not guide us in determining when those persons *are in fact* objecting, or when their objections are in fact reasonable. For that we need an actual-procedural theory, not a hypothetical one. We need, in short, to hear from the people involved. It is of the essence of an appeal to equity not just that other persons could hypothetically accept their treatment, but that their voices have carried *prima facie* equal weight in decisions, that their interests have been weighted equally and their equality is manifest to them. And their actual voices are most needed precisely when it is not clear whether the act in question does treat them equitably. Even if it turns out that their objection is (by the lights of the theory) unreasonable, it would be shocking to rule it out of court as if from the umpire's chair.

---

[8] For valuable reflection see David Wiggins, "Solidarity and the Root of the Ethical."
[9] Jean Hampton, "Feminist Contractarianism," in *A Mind of One's Own*, ed. Louise M. Antony and Charlotte E. Witt (Boulder: Westview Press, 2001).

Translating actual objections into hypothetical ones is often a source of great moral insight. But in other cases it gives no added purchase on moral problems, and may in fact obscure them, because having translated the objection into an object of critical reflection, we flub the critical reflection. Our reasoning in such cases is liable to be beset by the sorts of biases and epistemic injustices that devalue some people as agents. This devaluing will be especially acute if such people are not even explicitly asked their opinion, but instead have putatively reasonable opinions ascribed to them.

That said, though, steadfastly remaining at the "actual" level by simply asking people their opinion is often not enough either: their explicit state-ments may be devalued in the face of disagreements with higher-status speakers; they may face various forms of duress or internalized oppressions preventing them from speaking their mind; or they might simply be wrong about the way something affects them. Thus although it is a nonstarter for the contractualist to hypothesize others' putatively reasonable objections without asking them, there is also no guarantee that asking them will provide the required information. Even if we have a conversation with particular persons making actual objections, then, contractualism needs to be supplemented with a non-hypothetical ethics and politics of critical engagement with others.

A number of authors have developed accounts of such a politics. In a classic essay, María Lugones advocates what she calls "'world'-traveling."[10] She insists that each person inhabits his or her own "world" of experiences and perspectives, and each person's "world" is coequally real. In order to respect another person as an equal, I must not only—or not even—try to help her, or try to see the world from her perspective, but affirm that the world as she perceives it is as real as the world as I perceive it. Importantly, though, this ontological plurality is, as it were, political, not metaphysical. Lugones does not require that we be philosophically committed to a pluralistic ontology; rather, we need to be committed to this as moral and political agents. This is politically demanding. It is one thing for me to say, "I see where you're coming from"; it's another thing entirely to refrain from adding a "but" clause after that. To affirm another's "reasonableness" is exculpatory—it forgives them their objection. To affirm their *correctness*, however, is justificatory—it insists that their objection be accepted or at least that it get a clear answer and inform further deliberation.[11] In affirming the objector's correctness I thus put myself on the line with them until the objection is given a full hearing. Lugones calls this risking of one's own position "playfulness," and she calls for a "playful" approach to politics. But the term "playful" should not be taken to imply that it

---

[10] Lugones, *Peregrinajes/Pilgrimages*, 26–7.

[11] I borrow this distinction, out of context, from John McDowell, *Mind and World* (Cambridge, MA: Harvard University Press, 1994), 8.

is easy or fun. To the contrary, it is disorienting.[12] When I hear an objection from someone I have hitherto barely noticed, and what they tell me is that the things I do, perhaps the ways I self-identify, partly constitute an oppressive system; it is, to say the least, disorienting for me to ontologically commit myself to the truth of their claims. But suppose I am a white Canadian confronting survivors of residential schools,[13] or a white US citizen asked by African Americans why I should be able to inherit good housing stock or its resale value from my parents;[14] then *how dare I* presume to decide, as if from the umpire's chair, whether their objection is reasonable? The problem is not that I will find them unreasonable, though I might; the problem is that there is a way *I* am supposed to find them. It is not my place to do this.

Lugones here enables those of us who find ourselves in positions of privilege to see beyond the glow of our good intentions. When a well-meaning but privileged person sees himself through the eyes or "world" of those who are treated inequitably, the friendliness of his intentions can no longer be introspected, but can only be read off his behavior. From that perspective, the oppressive relationship and the behavior that supports it come into view. Through others' eyes, the privileged person sees himself as inhabiting and supporting relations of oppression, notwithstanding his intentions to the contrary. Lugones's strategy here prises apart *participation in oppressing others* from *personal malevolence*; we can do the one without being the other. This enables—but also forces—the privileged person to see his social position as it really is.[15]

Although explained purposively as working to overcome interlocking oppressions, Lugones's account is nonteleological. The process of working together as equals, made possible by playfulness and "world"-traveling, realizes in microcosm the non-oppressive alternative world that the participants are trying to build on the macro level. Solidarity then is a form of legislation for a kingdom of ends. While achieving a more just society is a standing hope and explains our action, the value of the practice is principally found in the community of equals that we thereby embody.

My claim here is that, if not the precise details, then at least the basic shift from a merely exculpatory "umpire's chair" acceptance of the other's reasonableness, to a justificatory affirmation of the other's correctness—political not metaphysical— is required for equity in practice. In doing this we are not only working to (teleologically) *bring about* the end of oppression; rather, we *constitutively embody*

---

[12] Ami Harbin, "The Disorientations of Acting against Injustice," *Journal of Social Philosophy* 45 (2014), 162–81.

[13] Harbin, "Disorientations."   [14] Shelby, *We Who Are Dark*, 145.

[15] For a more structural and macro-level analysis that nonetheless aligns instructively with Lugones's, see Iris Marion Young, "Responsibility and Global Justice: A Social Connection Model," *Social Philosophy & Policy* 23, no. 1 (2006). David Owen valuably bridges these two levels of analysis. See David S. Owen, "Othering Obama: How Whiteness Is Used to Undermine Authority," *Altre Modernità/Other Modernities*, no. 3 (2010).

a non-oppressive alternative world—even if, as is likely, our joint efforts ultimately fail, in part or in whole. As Elizabeth Anderson suggests, social movements are "experiments in living," both in the sense that the movement itself can embody new ways of relating, and in the sense that the goal it seeks to bring about is no sure thing.[16] While a more just society is a standing hope, the value of the practice is principally found in constituting a community of equals.

In unjust societies Kantian equity also expresses atonement for the mistreatment that some people have experienced. As Linda Radzik argues, when wrongs have been committed against *G*, then even if I am not responsible for those wrongs, my silence or standing-by communicates—whether I intend it to or not—agreement with or ambivalence about the mistreatment.[17] This fact cuts to the heart of Dr. King's "white moderates." A teleological account would have to interpret King as making the causal claim that his strategy was more effective than that of the white moderate. But people can respectfully disagree about strategy; such a disagreement would merit evidence-based discussion, not the scathing charge that the quietist approach is more blameworthy than active segregationism. Indeed we can easily imagine such a charge's being received, by people who were confident in their own reasonableness, as *unreasonable*. But this is not what Dr. King means. He means that quietism is an outrage against the idea that equal treatment is owed to blacks. Quietism expresses agreement with or ambivalence about mistreatment, or expresses that it doesn't matter all that much. Good intentions divorced from action are totally useless in countervailing the expressive content of quietist behavior.

To answer *G*'s call for solidarity is to repudiate the wrong and make atonement for it. Moreover, by hearing out those who have suffered inequity and taking their side, solidarity expresses that this treatment is inequitable, and hence wrongful, and rejects the assertion that such inequity is tolerable. It therefore raises up the victims, affirming their equal status. This spurs reconciliation and the repair of relationships that inequity strains or breaks. In doing so *S* need not accept guilt or liability for the inequity; rather, *S* may be a bystander or third party, yet still be committed to repudiating the imputation of a lower status to the victim.[18]

Radzik's account supports the view that *deference* in particular, or indeed Lugones's notion of playfulness, is essential to equity. Merely acting in the interests of another—*for* them, according to a (by hypothesis) true judgment about what is best for them—fails to treat them as fully equal and capable of understanding their own predicament.[19] If *S*'s actions are to embody respect

---

[16] Anderson, "Social Movements." See also Cumbler, *From Abolition to Rights for All.*

[17] Linda Radzik, "Moral Bystanders and the Virtue of Forgiveness," in *Forgiveness in Perspective*, ed. Christopher R. Allers and Marieke Smit (New York: Rodopi, 2010).

[18] Linda Radzik, *Making Amends: Atonement in Morality, Law, and Politics* (New York: Oxford University Press, 2009).

[19] See also Baron, Pettit, and Slote, *Three Methods of Ethics*, 13–14.

for the other as fundamentally equal, then G's judgment must itself be respected as determinative of the appropriate action in this situation. This distinguishes solidarity from charity—where the "donors choose," as it were— and also from justice more broadly construed. Insofar as what's at stake is not the most just distribution of social goods but the fundamental equal status and separateness of persons as persons, then S's response to G's call to action must be to affirm G's judgment. S's doing so does not (merely) causally contribute to Kantian equity but constitutes it. Hence deference is not merely instrumentally valuable but intrinsically valuable as partly constitutive of equity.

As a principle of Kantian equity, then, solidarity embodies respect for the coequal full humanity or personhood of those who issue the call to action. If S hears G's call for help in alleviating an inequitable social structure, S is put in the position of either affirming or denying G's basic equality by, respectively, either answering the call or gainsaying it. There is no third option. Structural deference to those who suffer inequity thus cuts through epistemic and other biases that give undue weight to the testimonies and interests of those who occupy positions of power. In these respects, deontological solidarity answers Allen Buchanan's call for a "social moral epistemology."[20] In fraught contexts we must determine how to approach political controversies. The answer I have given here is that if there is disagreement about whether anyone has a reasonable basis for objection, one ought to side with those who are least well-off. It will not do to sit on the sidelines pending further study; we do not have this luxury when disputes impinge on us unbidden. When the rights of social out-groups are at risk, sitting on the sidelines is tantamount to siding with the attackers, allowing their assertion of the lower status of the out-group to go unchallenged. Solidarity does not merely refuse to agree with this assertion of lower status, but actively repudiates it. One thereby acts on the equal status of all as persons, countermanding the assertion, by the perpetrators, that the victims somehow merit this mistreatment or that the rights of the victims can be sacrificed in the interests of "preventive self-defense" or "emergency exceptionalism."[21]

Buchanan might, however, object that solidarity goes too far, that a social moral epistemology based on deference is just the problem. The better solution is to undermine undue deference to putative experts. In the case of eugenics he suggests practices such as enhanced peer review, disclosure of funding sources, credentialing, and an affirmative responsibility on the part of scientists to uncover phonies.[22] We could add, following Stephen Jay Gould, that scientists should take affirmative steps to combat "publication

---

[20] Buchanan, "Trust in Managed Care Organizations."; "Institutions, Beliefs and Ethics: Eugenics as a Case Study."
[21] Buchanan, "Institutions, Beliefs and Ethics: Eugenics as a Case Study," 26.
[22] Ibid., 39–42.

bias" and "Cordelia's Dilemma."[23] It should be clear, however, that the deference I have defended is a world away from the undue deference to elites that Buchanan decries, and from the attraction to a good narrative that Gould worries about. Further, as Buchanan admits, the proposals he lays out do not come close to guaranteeing the prevention of practices such as coercive negative eugenics, but only "point the way toward consideration of construct- ive proposals for avoiding" moral errors on that scale.[24] Buchanan's and Gould's proposals are also fundamentally elite-directed: it is credentialed scientists who can practice enhanced peer review and publish their negative results. This is not a criticism of these proposals; they could indeed have salutary effects in preventing the publication of fraudulent works, and correcting results that do not withstand scrutiny. Yet it remains the case that a politically and economically powerful class with only scholarly opposition can do and impose whatever it wants. The Iraq war and global warming are clear examples: despite the widespread agreement of the vast majority of genuinely credentialed experts in foreign policy and climate science, respectively, that the Iraq war was a mistake and that global warming is both real and danger- ous, these clashes of elites—intellectual vs. crony-capitalist—neither prevented the war nor spurred timely climate action. Political action requires a politics. Buchanan's proposals for a politically situated ethical theory are well taken and important; a theory of solidarity contributes to that agenda. But what is needed, also, is a politically situated *political* theory: one that teaches ordinary citizens how to listen for and hear the demands of social out-groups, and to struggle alongside them. Deontological solidarity does just that. Structural deference to the victims of inequity thus has no quarrel with Buchanan's call for a social moral epistemology that avoids undue deference to putative experts. To the contrary, it is through deference to the least well-off that nonexperts effectively and politically counteract deference to elites.

We are now in position to explain why Martin Luther King's "white moderate" is worse than the White Citizen's Counciler or the Ku Klux Klanner. The signal characteristic of the white moderate is to *see* the inequity of segregation and white supremacy, to *agree* that these are wrongful, but not to repudiate them through solidarity. Deontological Solidarity—political action on the terms of those who suffer inequity—is the repudiation of inequity, whether or not the effort to achieve justice succeeds. Solidarity partly constitutes equity. Because equity is an ultimate value, solidarity is intrinsically valuable. Further, because treating others equitably is a perfect duty, solidarity,

---

[23] Stephen Jay Gould, "Cordelia's Dilemma," in *Dinosaur in a Haystack: Reflections in Natural History* (Cambridge, MA: Harvard University Press, 2011), 125–6. "Publication bias" is a bias in favor of positive results as opposed to negative results; "Cordelia's Dilemma" is the situation where no answer to a question can be given without changing the presuppositions under which the question is asked.

[24] Buchanan, "Institutions, Beliefs and Ethics: Eugenics as a Case Study," 42.

too, is a perfect duty. Through solidarity we atone for standing by or benefiting while others were treated unjustly. Dr. King's claim that the white moderate is worse than the rabid segregationist is then tantamount to a claim that the white moderate does not care about treating people equitably, but only thinks that he cares, basking in the glow of his good intentions. The rabid segregationist, in contrast, does care about equity, but wants to reserve it for white folks. Dr. King's idea is thus echoed in Harry Frankfurt's observation that the bullshitter is more an enemy of truth than is the liar, since, unlike the liar, the bullshitter doesn't care at all about the truth.[25] To borrow Frankfurt's technical term, then, Dr. King is calling bullshit on the white moderate.

6.3 ARISTOTELIAN EQUITY

Ann Cudd describes a double bind facing women's labor. Women do considerably more housework than men, even in families where both partners work for pay. If, as is generally the case, household care labor is not commodified, then capitalism piggybacks on patriarchy to impose on women a disproportionate share of the unremunerated work of childrearing and household management which are essential to the functioning of the economy.[26] On the other hand, if this labor were all commodified then it would be underprovided because it would be impossible for those who perform this work to internalize the positive externalities.[27] I assume that the law itself is not treating women in a Kantian-inequitable manner here; the gender injustice is in the social structures that the law does not itself enshrine. Nonetheless, this double bind generates, for the law, a dilemma of the sort that Martha Minow calls "recreating difference both by ignoring it and by noticing it."[28] If the state tried to intervene to equalize housework, it would thereby treat women and men differently, recreating difference. But if it does not so intervene, then it thereby engenders the differential treatment of men and women. There is no general legislative solution to this dilemma.

But then suppose women organize to solve this problem in a context-specific way, for instance by arguing that family members who can show that they have been performing unpaid or untaxable household labor should accrue Social Security benefits for that labor, at a level equal to that accrued by

[25] Harry Frankfurt, "On Bullshit," in *The Importance of What We Care About* (New York: Cambridge University Press, 1988).

[26] Jennifer L. Hook, "Gender Inequality in the Welfare State: Sex Segregation in Housework, 1965–2003," *American Journal of Sociology* 115, no. 5 (2010).

[27] Ann E. Cudd and Nancy Holmstrom, *Capitalism, for and Against: A Feminist Debate* (Cambridge; New York: Cambridge University Press, 2011), 110–11.

[28] Martha Minow, "Justice Engendered," *Harvard Law Review* 101, no. 1 (1987): 17–22.

the 75th percentile of wage earners who were paying into the system.[29] This is a highly specific solution to a highly specific problem. Taken out of context, such a rule would be arbitrary and unfair. The contribution-based social insurance scheme requires workers to have paid into the system through payroll taxes, and we can grant that the very principle of contribution-based social insurance is not unjust. The women who have organized for reform of this system are proposing that those who pay into a pool should subsidize those who did not pay in. Out of context, this is an unfair misallocation of a contribution-based insurance pool; but even in context, it looks like moral hazard, since it subsidizes the socially undesirable choice to practice a gendered division of household labor.

Even so, it seems that this effort could, and perhaps should, be supported by the agent in solidarity. We have a plausible claim of unfairness on each side. Yet I want to suggest that the agent in solidarity ought to support household caregivers' access to these Social Security benefits. But why?

One answer is that these just rules promulgate injustice when mechanically applied to the particular case. These rules are legally just, in other words, but inequitable in a sense that Aristotle explicates. It is this sense of equity I now want to develop, showing that solidarity embodies not only Kantian equity but Aristotelian equity. Aristotelian equity carves out a role for conscience—duly governed—in solidarity. And Aristotelian equity also shows that solidarity is not a principle solely for *nonideal* theory, but for ideal theory as well. We have reason to be in solidarity even in a just society.

Aristotle understands equity as the *correction of general justice by attending to particulars*.[30] He raises the problem of equity in his discussion of legal justice. Legal justice is the system of general principles to which the legislature aspires in all the laws it promulgates.[31] But law is inevitably subject to two problems of particularity: some cases are uncontemplated by the legislature; others, though contemplated, cannot be handled under the best framing of the general rule.[32] Equity, then, requires judges to solve these two problems of particularity on a case-by-case basis. As Martha Nussbaum writes, "Equity is putting law into the condition to which it aspires in the first place."[33]

---

[29] Goodin et al. mention an "early study" that found, "if all married men divorced their wives and hired them back as housekeepers, National Income would double." Robert E. Goodin et al., *Discretionary Time: A New Measure of Freedom*, 10, citing Colin Clark, "The Economics of Housework," *Bulletin of the Oxford University Institute of Economics & Statistics* 20 (1958), 205–11.

[30] Aristotle, *Nicomachean Ethics*. v.10, 1137a–b.

[31] Martha Nussbaum, "Equity and Mercy," in *Punishment: A Reader*, ed. A. John Simmons, et al. (Princeton: Princeton University Press, 1995), 155; Allan Beever, "Aristotle on Equity, Law, and Justice," *Legal Theory* 10 (2004): 41.

[32] Nussbaum, "Equity and Mercy," 155; Beever, "Aristotle on Equity, Law, and Justice," 42; Aristotle, *Nicomachean Ethics*. v.10.1137b.

[33] Nussbaum, "Equity and Mercy," 155.

Allan Beever adds an important specification. Not only generality but stability is essential to legal justice. Hence excessive fluidity is a legal vice. It would be possible to continually fine-tune laws with a series of minor improvements, but the legislature ought to desist for the sake of stability. Thus the legislature has an affirmative reason not to try to fine-tune the law when hard or uncontemplated cases arise. Instead, "judges are permitted to depart from a literal interpretation of legislation when it is clear that such [literalism] would produce a result that the legislators would not have intended."[34]

The role of discretion in legal justice is most familiar in the context of criminal justice and consequently in the role of judges and prosecutors. But if legal justice is the justice of the legislature in general, then the same problem of particularity will arise in any domain where the legislature makes general rules, many of which can anyway end up before judges or mediators despite not being subject to criminal sanction. Family law, estates, employment law, contracts, and other sites where the law structures relationships can all be distorted by the rigorous application of legally valid general rules, whether or not those rules are just in themselves. Cudd's case regarding uncommodified household labor is an example of this.

Consider two more such examples, where, crucially, we do not need to posit social injustice in order for the inequity to arise. So in considering these cases, suppose that our society is in fact distributively and legally just: for ease of reference, imagine Rawls's theory of justice is true and realized, and we live in a society characterized only by difference-principle inequalities constrained by equal basic liberties and fair equality of opportunity. That is, the society is characterized by inequalities in socioeconomic status and other primary goods, but only insofar as and because these inequalities enhance the overall life chances of the least well-off cohort.[35] Because these inequalities exist, however, the realized value, to the bearer, of the equal basic liberties differs across the population, and so does the actual range of opportunities, including opportunities for offices and positions and for the social determinants of health. Consider health in particular. Norman Daniels remarks that health gradients have been stubborn elements of even the most successful health-care systems in the world. Because the social determinants of health are so

---

[34] Beever, "Aristotle on Equity, Law, and Justice," 42.
[35] Rawls, *A Theory of Justice, Revised Ed.* Other theories should be interchangeable here. Consider the capabilities approach. The society may have attained a level of universal sufficiency according to a reasonable and democratically ratified list of basic human capabilities, and yet there may remain persons whose attainment of some capability—though still above the putative sufficiency threshold—is generally lower than others', and who organize for improvement or equality in provision of that capability. For instance, there might be an achievement gap in schools, despite universal literacy; or, to track the example in the text, there might be stubborn health gradients despite universal health insurance and effective public health schemes. See Martha Nussbaum, *Frontiers of Justice*; Sridhar Venkatapuram, *Health Justice: An Argument from the Capabilities Approach* (Cambridge: Polity, 2011).

multifarious, ranging from instantaneous doctor–patient interactions to the generalized level of stress in a segment of the population, health inequalities track socioeconomic status, professional status, and minority status in all countries, including the most equal ones with the best health outcomes. Rich people live longer, healthier lives, even in the most egalitarian countries.[36] Now again suppose that those on the bottom of these health inequalities protested their relatively worse position. By hypothesis, the health gradients in question are not unjust. Even though there are health inequalities, we can be confident—because the difference principle is satisfied—that these inequalities in fact make everyone, even the less healthy, better off. Nonetheless, those on the bottom of the health gradients organize for changed health policy. Like the household caregivers who organized for Social Security, these agents are demanding more than the difference principle grants them as a matter of justice, and so those on the upside of the health gradients could claim unfairness if the struggle succeeds. Yet it seems at least plausible that one ought to support the struggle: the ineliminability of health gradients may show only that we have not tried hard enough or been creative enough, and, we might think, we owe it to others, as equals, to try harder. Yet in supporting the struggle, we do not revise our general theory of justice, and we might not even change the law; we might instead adopt rough-and-ready policies and practices to try to fix the problem in a way that meets the approval of those on the bottom of the health inequalities. Siding with them in this struggle is an instance of Aristotelian equity. In doing so we take a second look at outcomes—even outcomes of just institutions—to correct for unintended consequences and stubborn inequalities; and we insist that everyone have their day in (literal or figurative) court.

Yet I want to suggest also that precisely because we are at a kind of frontier of justice, where the best we have been able to do is not good enough and that fact generates a conflict of inequities between, as it were, those who are already paying enough and those who are not getting enough, this application of Aristotelian equity is open to conscience in a way that Kantian inequities are not. No one has a claim of being treated as lesser here, but they have a claim of getting less than their fair share. They demand correction of a system that general rules of justice seem to say is already correct. Whereas Kantian inequities overcome conscience, Aristotelian inequities guide conscience and spur creativity. The activists' organizing demands our attention and good faith in addressing the issue; their satisfaction constitutes success. In this way

---

[36] Daniels, *Just Health*, 83–9. To be sure, even the most socioeconomically egalitarian countries today do not meet Rawls's criteria of justice, but this is the best evidence we have. On the divergence between wealth and income stratification in societies as we know them and anything approaching egalitarian systems, see Piketty, *Capital in the Twenty-First Century*, chap. 7.

Aristotelian equity sets our aims and our criterion of success. But since—by hypothesis—there is no Kantian inequity here, deference does not correct inequity, and hence does not itself constitute equity. We may thus apply our conscientious best judgment to the case at hand. Guided by the demand and assessed by the goal, our participation is within these constraints a matter of conscience.

Labor law provides yet another example where Aristotelian equity can correct general legislation even when the legislation is not unjust. Labor law is structured by the assumption that owners of a firm are *ipso facto* constituted as a corporate body, while employees are not. It might have been otherwise; owners might have been prevented from limiting their liability or from negotiating with employees *en bloc*; then, each shareholder would have to sign every employment or procurement contract as an individual, and pay insurance premiums out of pocket for every liability scenario in the workplace.[37] Yet as long as it is not otherwise, labor law enshrines an asymmetry between employer and employee. Workers can achieve corporate status only by organizing, while employers get it automatically. It is this asymmetry that makes "right-to-work" laws seem reasonable.[38] We can imagine a parallel "right-to-manage" law allowing every shareholder to benefit from workers' productivity without having to participate in paying any employee with whom he had not signed an individual contract. The absurdity of such a law is evident. This asymmetry between labor and management is arguably legally just; it reflects a reasonable but contingent way of organizing economic activity. So let's assume that it characterizes the by-hypothesis-just society that we are imagining in this section. At the level of legislation, one or another way of organizing the workplace has to be selected, and any way that is chosen will have some asymmetric effects. Thus the disadvantage faced by workers due to this particular asymmetry does not show that the law is unjust.

We can nonetheless imagine workers agitating for a rule change making it easier to organize—for instance, allowing unions to be certified on the basis of card-checks rather than an election. Out of context, card-check certification of unions seems dubious—there is no anonymity for the worker who is skeptical, and there is no democratic vote where each side has an equal shot at winning. The card-check rule compensates for an asymmetry that *in the abstract* is not unjust, but disadvantages workers in context.[39] In context, then, supporting card-check certification is consonant with Aristotelian equity. Even so, we

[37] Christopher Kutz proposes eliminating limitation of liability and requiring shareholders to take out liability insurance. See Kutz, *Complicity*, 240.

[38] A so-called "right to work" law requires unions, where they exist, to represent all workers whether or not those workers pay dues or "fair share fees." Such laws thus turn union benefits into a commons.

[39] For explanation and defense of the "card-check" rule, see Human Rights Watch, "The Employee Free Choice Act: A Human Rights Imperative," (New York: Human Rights Watch,

have again a site where conscience—guided by the concerns of the workers, and using their goals as a benchmark of success—may play the role of helping us find the position on this issue that seems most right to us. In public deliberation, the workers' demands and goals set the terms of the debate, but do not determine which answer should seem most right to us.[40]

Aristotelian inequity is thus compatible with legally just systems even outside the special case of criminal justice. Such inequities tend to have both direct and indirect effects. Direct effects are those that embody the inequity itself: unions have to spend excess resources on organizing drives and on fighting "right-to-work," women are more likely to be poor when elderly, poor people suffer worse health. Further, indirect effects are caused by the direct effects: unions get outspent in political campaigns and lobbying because their resources are dedicated to organizing or fighting to prevent decertification efforts; women become stuck in bad marriages for fear of future poverty; poor people with worse health cannot work as much or as productively, and become even poorer. The indirect effects eventually become Kantian inequities, but even the direct effects are instances of unfairness and asymmetry. Taken by themselves they do not rise to the level of injustices, or at least, are not evidently correctable by general legal rules without just shifting the burden onto a different party. Yet the demand for correction of inequity nonetheless compels us: either we honor the picket line or we cross it. It is not morally neutral which we do, but the natural duty of justice does not offer any guidance and an untrained conscience is a poor guide in political conflict. Solidarity solves this problem. When people on the bottoms of these Aristotelian inequities organize for these struggles, (i) their call compels engagement; (ii) solidarity with them requires that their goals regulate our intervention in the issue; and (iii) their satisfaction constitutes the benchmark of success. These three conditions constitute our duty of equity. But within the parameters set by equity—and again, assuming that the society is otherwise just—our own best conscientious judgment may be our guide. For an ordinary citizen, the principal means of acting on Aristotelian equity is by hearing, and listening to, others who find themselves disadvantaged by the application of general rules, and taking on their struggle. Solidarity is Aristotelian equity as practiced by ordinary citizens.

We noted in Chapter Two that teleological solidarity seems made for non-ideal theory; such solidarity is the essential tool through which the powerless struggle for social change, catalyzing the transition from an unjust status quo to a just future. But though I welcome the various critiques of ideal theory that

2009). For critique see Richard A. Epstein, "The Ominous Employee Free Choice Act," *Regulation* 2009.

[40] I am grateful to Yarran Hominh for suggesting the link between Aristotelian equity and *conscientiae*, and to John Cumbler for pressing me to rethink this section.

have emerged in recent years, I think it is a mistake to treat solidarity as exclusively a matter of nonideal theory. To do so is to assume that solidarity becomes irrelevant, if not misguided, once justice is achieved. Solidarity as Aristotelian equity breaks this link between solidarity and the nonideal. Solidarity remains valuable even when social justice is achieved. Inequities can persist in just societies, and when they do they are morally outrageous in just the same way that they are in unjust societies. Equity goes beyond justice and has a resolution that is more precise than that of justice. Aristotelian inequity occurs when an institution fails to treat people equally, or denies them a fair hearing, or treats their interests as of lesser importance than those of others for no compelling reason. Such inequities are bound to occur even under just institutions, if only because laws are made for the general case but each person's circumstances are unique. Hence inasmuch as solidarity is equity, solidarity has a place in ideal theory.

6.4 BEING AN EQUITABLE PERSON

Aristotle describes the equitable person as one "who chooses and does [equitable] acts, and is no stickler for his rights in a bad sense but tends to take less than his share though he has the law on his side."[41] Beever comments, "the equitable or decent man is one who accepts less than the law will give him… one who sometimes declines to enforce his legal rights."[42]

On its face this tendency to desist from demanding one's due might seem to be the opposite of solidarity, insofar as solidarity is about demanding recognition and implementation of one's rights. But to the contrary, being an equitable person is of the essence of solidarity—of political action on others' terms—because it is the willingness to share others' fate.[43] Sharing fate is being an equitable person in two respects. First, deference—the disposition to stay on side even if asked to do what one thinks to be wrong or inadvisable—characterizes the equitable person. Even if s has good reason to believe that his own plan is morally or prudentially superior to G's, and hence, that s has rationality or morality on his side, still, s should stand down from insisting on his own plan, and accept G's plan. There are, of course, limits to this, as we discussed in Chapter Five and will do again in Chapter Seven. If G's plan ends up oppressing F, or even s himself, G forfeits its right to s's deference; Aristotle

---

[41] Aristotle, *Nicomachean Ethics*. v.10.1137b–1138a.

[42] Beever, "Aristotle on Equity, Law, and Justice," 44.

[43] See Condition 5 of the explication of solidary action in Section 3.2.3. Despite partial overlap, my analysis of "sharing fate" diverges from Sangiovanni's; mine is closer to Marcia Baron's Kantian analysis. See Baron, Pettit, and Slote, *Three Methods of Ethics*, 15; Sangiovanni, "Solidarity as Joint Action," 347.

might call it "slavish"[44] for *s* to go along. But within that endogenous limit, the equitable person is one who is willing to participate even when quite convinced that *G*'s plan is ineffectual or morally problematic. Some battles are worth losing. And anyway, sometimes one is surprised.

The second respect in which sharing others' fate embodies being an equitable person is one of the most morally distinctive elements of solidarity. Solidarity involves refusing benefits to which one is entitled, if those benefits are not available to another. Suppose A and B are victims of a given injustice and act in solidarity against it. But then B finds herself—not by maneuvering or any other untoward means—in a position to gain just treatment for herself but not to gain such treatment for A. That is, B is at risk of being peeled off. A principle of *justice* would not condemn B for accepting this; to the contrary, she is owed just treatment and has a right to seize it when she can. But this would be an inequitable thing for B to do; in doing so she would abandon A to his fate.

It might be objected that justice would indeed condemn B for being peeled off, since B's natural duty of justice requires her to contribute to the creation of just institutions, and the escape valve makes those harder to achieve. But this depends on an empirical hypothesis that is by no means obviously true. B might think she can achieve more by being within the corridors of power than outside them. Or she might think she has done her share and it is now someone else's turn to step up. Or she might think that full justice will be unachievable anyway, and she does not want to sacrifice herself to a lost cause—she is, after all, morally entitled to just treatment. So without solidarity, the natural duty of justice cannot reliably get B to refuse the offered selective benefit. Insofar as B is an equitable person, however, she will in this respect refuse justice until it is achievable for all.

S is an equitable person, in Aristotle's sense, insofar as she shares the fate of *G*. She does this both on the front end—joining in the action even if she thinks it's not the best or safest idea—and the back end, refusing benefits to which she is otherwise entitled but which are denied to *G*. In each respect *s* is acting politically *on G's terms*—and hence, pursuant to our definition of solidarity. Thus political action on others' terms constitutes being an equitable person, which entails sharing others' fate. Deontological solidarity thus encapsulates all elements of our definition of solidarity.

This result brings us back to the case of Rosa Parks. We noted in Chapter Two that solidarity represents itself as making a compulsory demand. We now see that in doing so—at least provided that we are in solidarity with those who are treated inequitably—this representation is accurate, and the demand is a moral one. Solidarity makes upon us a compulsory moral

---

[44] See Nussbaum, "Equity and Mercy," 159, citing Aristotle, *Nicomachean Ethics*, 1126a8.

demand. The white bus rider who witnesses Mrs. Parks's arrest and removal is legally entitled to continue riding: he has paid his fare for his share of a publicly provided service. He has a right to receive it. Justice would support him in continuing to ride the bus. But if he is an equitable person then he will refuse to accept this service while it is denied to Mrs. Parks. No other response constitutes solidarity, and no other response can claim to respect Rosa Parks as an equal. Only solidarity explicitly affirms and acts on the basic equality of Rosa Parks, repudiating her unequal treatment as something for which no equitable person can stand.

6.5 EJECTING PEOPLE FROM BUSES

We have now completed the argument for a perfect duty of solidarity with the victims of Kantian inequity, and of solidarity-governed conscientious support of victims of Aristotelian equity. Before finishing the chapter, though, I want to show how the account can be applied to some hard cases, avoid collapsing into reliance upon independent conscientious judgment, and address an objection from overinclusion.

It might be worried that the sovereign conscience will inevitably return through one of two potential back doors. The first is in the case where those who are least well-off in a struggle claim an inequity that is so attenuated, or is incurred through such needless voluntary provocation, that we want to let them lie in the bed that they made. The second is where the objects of solidarity, though victims of inequity, themselves engage in inequitable treatment of others.

Joel Feinberg's famous "ride on the bus" presents us with a range of scenarios, each slightly more offensive than the one before, asking when the offense warrants banning the behavior (or removing the offending parties from the bus), despite the fact that no nonconsenting party is harmed.[45] Suppose we determine that the break comes between the following two scenarios:

> *Story 6.* A group of passengers enters the bus and shares a seating com-
> partment with you. They spread a table cloth over their laps and proceed
> to eat a picnic lunch that consists of live insects, fish heads, and pickled
> sex organs of lamb, veal, and pork, smothered in garlic and onions. Their
> table manners leave almost everything to be desired.[46]

---

[45] Joel Feinberg, *Offense to Others, The Moral Limits of the Criminal Law* (New York: Oxford University Press, 1987), 10.
[46] Ibid., 11.

Story 7. Things get worse and worse. The itinerant picnickers practice gluttony in the ancient Roman manner, gorging until satiation and then vomiting on to their table cloth. Their practice, however, is a novel departure from the ancient custom in that they eat their own and one another's vomit along with the remaining food.[47]

Since Story 6 describes behavior that, we stipulate, ought to be tolerated, let us suppose that the driver comes to eject them. The driver thereby treats them wrongly. The picnickers protest their treatment, invoking Rosa Parks, and ask for the support of other bus riders. Intuitively, solidarity here seems not required; at most it seems supererogatory. But can our theory track—or give good reasons for overruling—this intuition? Our question is whether this is a Kantian inequity, such that we must defer; an Aristotelian inequity, such that we may appeal to our solidarity-governed conscience; whether, to the contrary, the picnickers are treating anyone else inequitably; or whether there is no inequity here at all.

One potential response is to say that these passengers, though doing something that is strictly speaking within their moral rights, are nonetheless freely doing something that they should know to be offensive, and that they are free to do privately elsewhere. Society depends on a generalized deference to the feelings of others; if the picnickers are equitable people they will not be "sticklers for their rights" in this case. Moreover, the driver's action restricts only the time, place, or manner, rather than content of their behavior, and so is no inequity. These things may indeed be true, but if we fall back on them, we are relying on our independent judgment about the case and about the appropriate behavior of those who call for our solidarity, bringing back the sovereign conscience and undermining deontological solidarity. Nor may we appeal to community standards of decency, because that criterion has just the kind of track record of oppression that we must resist.

The epistemology of inequity I proposed in Chapter Five suggested a checklist procedure for training ourselves to recognize inequities in our midst. Such a checklist could initially use heuristics to identify suspect classifications of those on the bottom of undeniable social hierarchies. Feinberg's picnickers (*qua* picnickers) would not fall into any such category. Second, the checklist would require us to determine whether the person on the "up" side of the struggle is pursuing aims that are given by a legitimate role. If his role were unjust then no role-given directives could merit coercive enforcement, even if specific commands were not in themselves illegitimate.[48] In such a case we

---

[47] Ibid.

[48] Michael Hardimon holds that putative role obligations flowing from unjust roles are "void *ab initio.*" I suspect this is too strong, but my claim here is weaker: if *A*'s role is unjust, then no commands flowing from *A*'s role may be coercively enforced against *B*. See Hardimon, "Role Obligations," 350.

would have to side with the picnickers. But we can assume here that the role of bus driver is not inherently unjust. Inasmuch, however, as there is a clash of in-themselves legitimate claims—the driver's claim to an orderly and pleasant bus, and the picnickers' claim to do something that (by hypothesis) should not be forbidden—we seem to find ourselves in a case of Aristotelian inequity. We may deploy our conscience, guided by the picnickers' demand and assessed by their goal. Hence we can intervene by speaking up in favor of the picnickers' right to eat, but agreeing that their behavior is offensive and suggesting alternative solutions. For instance, perhaps the picnickers could move to a spot where there are no other passengers around, or could try to be quieter and less demonstrative. If they accept this resolution then we should support them.

This result—that we should be in limited solidarity with the picnickers—seems right to me, given the assumption that Story 6 describes behavior that ought to be tolerated. But it might be objected that solidarity with the picnickers is *at most* supererogatory, and our conscience should certainly not be governed by deference to them. The objection is, then, that deonto-logical solidarity is overinclusive: too many things seem to evoke this putative obligation.

Rather than just clash intuitions here, let us continue with the checklist. Its next item might require place-switching, asking whether we would accept this treatment in the picnickers' shoes, or whether they are being targeted on the basis of anything other than their voluntary behavior. This question cannot be answered a priori. In our ignorance and revulsion, we risk assuming too much. As described, the case permits a process of Relationship Deference as present-ed in Chapter Five: "I could be on your side, but what are you asking me to stand for? How important is it to you?" This might elicit the needed informa-tion. If they are just out for a picnic, they admit that their behavior is not a matter of principle and they would be acting inequitably if they ignored the feelings of others and were sticklers for their rights. Still governed by their demand for solidarity, we can appeal to them to stand down, let the bus get us all where we're going, and have their picnic elsewhere.

But suppose that, upon intervention, they reveal that their "picnic" is actually the observance of a minority religion that requires particular ritual actions at particular times of day; they could not have done this at home because they need to get to a government building at a certain time; they would prefer to come at a different time and keep their rituals private, but the government burdens them by refusing to keep its offices open late. In this religious version of Story 6, the picnickers can plausibly claim to be victims of inequity, and hence demand our solidarity. Indeed, this version reshapes the checklist right from the beginning, since membership in a minority religion is indeed a suspect classification. Now, Story 6 evokes Kantian equity and solidarity is required.

But we are not out of the woods yet. Suppose the religious-minority picnickers were in fact acting as described in Story 7, which we have stipulated to be beyond the limits of required state toleration. We now face a conflict of morally valid claims: *qua* religious minority, their treatment is inequitable; but *qua* beyond-the-pale offense-givers, they treat others wrongly as well. So described, the case seems a straightforward instance of Aristotelian, but not Kantian, inequity. If a religious minority were being straightforwardly prevented from practicing a (victimless) ritual, this would be a Kantian inequity; but what if it is prevented from practicing a ritual that treats others wrongly? There seem to be three types of cases: (i) cases such as the one we have described, where the treatment of others is beyond-the-pale offensive, but not itself inequitable in the Kantian sense; (ii) cases where the religious minority, though a victim of inequity, treats others in a way that constitutes Kantian inequity; and (iii) cases where, within the scope of its own power, it engages in systematic oppression of others. I will discuss the ethics of solidarity in depth in Chapter Seven, but I must offer at least a framework solution here. Take the cases in order.

Cases of type (i) are Aristotelian inequities, and can be dealt with as such; we deploy conscience in a way that is governed by solidarity. The minority group is still entitled to solidarity, but not to full deference. In cases of type (ii), it would be inequitable both to refuse the demand, and to go along with it. Groups that themselves engage in Kantian inequities lose their entitlement to solidarity. Yet nor can their plight be ignored. An example might help. Suppose that our religious picnickers are acting as described in Story 7, and in doing so they violate reasonable public health codes enacted to protect immune-suppressed transplant recipients. These at-risk persons protest in fear for their lives.

In treating others inequitably, the religious minority loses its entitlement to solidarity. Yet in being prevented from practicing their religion, they merit solidarity. As bystanders we should make clear that our support for the minority is unwavering, but only within the bounds of others' equitable treatment. This is a version of response (18) from Chapter Five. But they may legitimately then complain that their religious freedom is being sacrificed to others' health. This retort returns us to the situation of Aristotelian inequity just described, though in a slightly more complicated form. Governed by *both* sides' demands, we search for common ground and a mutually acceptable resolution to the dispute.

Finally, what about a religious minority that is treated inequitably more broadly, but also, within its own power centers, systematically oppresses others? We can put in this category the Aztecs whose human sacrifice Las Casas accepted and Vitoria rejected; or even, here, the "Islamic State" militants drawn from the ranks of Sunnis who are brutally oppressed in Iraq and Syria but who themselves perpetrate horrific acts of oppression.[49] Obviously, we

---

[49] I am grateful to John Cumbler for pressing me to address the ISIS case.

cannot side with ISIS against its victims. But from the position of citizens of the OECD countries that are fighting ISIS, we cannot in good faith oppose ISIS without at the same time challenging the imperialist and arms-saturated world system that benefits us but which reliably generates ISIS and similar extremist groups as its byproducts. This is a case where ISIS is "sandwiched" between us and the objects of our solidarity.[50] While we side with the victims of ISIS, then, we must challenge the imperialist system, even if that system is, ironically, the very thing that puts us in position to help the victims of ISIS. We must not use the victims of ISIS as an excuse to practice more of the violent repression that leaves young Sunni men open to ISIS's siren song. Reform of the world system must work in tandem with work to defend the victims. This way we can, I believe, avoid Vitoria's mistake of using the image of the victim as justification for a war that only asserted imperial power.[51]

6.6 CONCLUSION

Viewing solidarity as equity completes the solution to the three key problems in the theory of solidarity which we laid out in Chapter Two. First, solidarity differs from mere coalition or association because solidarity is action on others' terms. The agent in solidarity acts deferentially and subjects his conscientious judgment to the decision of the group. The coalescence precedes the selection of aims. Second, the agent in solidarity is not fully autonomous in the sense of reserving to herself the right to authorize all her own decisions. Her judgments about aims and means, and her best judgment about moral or prudential rationality, are not always the best principles for action. Third, the value of solidarity is not found in its outcomes but in the way it treats people. Solidarity with those who suffer inequity is a perfect duty, and is intrinsically valuable when and because it constitutes equitable treatment.

Three crucial points bear emphasizing. First, solidarity is not a teleological principle but a deontological one in the sense that it is justified by how it treats people rather than the consequences it helps bring about. For this reason the central case of solidarity in an unjust society is that called forth by Kantian equity. Kantian equity—equity as fundamental fairness—explains when and why solidarity is called for and why deference in particular is required. It does not require any antecedent relationship between the agent and the group. It does not require that the agent seek to enter such a relationship in any rich

---

[50] See Section 5.2.

[51] I believe this conclusion is in the spirit of Gayatri Chakravorty Spivak's critique of the imperialist or orientalist model wherein "white men are saving brown women from brown men." Vitoria, in contrast, falls into just this trap. See Spivak, *A Critique of Postcolonial Reason*, 284.

sense other than the fundamental relationship of being moral equals worthy of equal status and respect as persons.

Second, solidarity need be no less obligatory or justified simply because distributive justice has already been achieved. In this case, however, deference eases its grip somewhat and allows conscience some wiggle room. The achievement of justice in general might—or rather, inevitably will—leave Aristotelian inequities in place, but in such cases we may use our judgment in pushing the agenda of the victims of those inequities.

Finally, solidarity is not merely instrumentally valuable but has *intrinsic* value. Treating people equitably, raising them up as equals, repudiating injustices done to them, and atoning for being a beneficiary of or bystander to such injustices, are ultimate values in Joseph Raz's sense that, on their own and quite apart from any other benefit, they give us reasons for action. Solidarity constitutes equity, and equity is partly constitutive of these ultimate values. Consequently, solidarity as equity is intrinsically valuable whether or not it brings about justice. Yet though it is deontological, it is also agent-neutral, since the requirement to treat others equitably is not grounded in particular features of individual agents.

Since equity is a core concept of justice and of being a just person, the teleological approach is right to draw an essential link between solidarity and justice. But this link is not essentially about (teleologically) *bringing about* justice, it is (deontologically) about *treating people justly*, that is equitably, whatever the surrounding society looks like. Solidarity is equity for everyday political life.

7

The Ethics of Solidarity

7.1 DEMANDINGNESS

7.1.1 Four Friends

Rosie is determined to meet her duties of solidarity. She recognizes that these are perfect duties of equity, so she struggles mightily to act in solidarity every time she is called upon to do so. She never crosses a picket line. She rarely misses a demonstration. She has her elected officials on speed-dial. She is a "moral saint" in the solidarity department.[1] Unfortunately, Rosie has no life. Her parents feel guilty for imbuing her with this overwrought superego. Her friends feel inadequate around her, but scoff a bit when they discuss her with one another. The legislative staffers roll their eyes when she calls. She looks a bit harried out there holding the line, day in and day out. But she is out there.

Rosie's friend Emma is also dedicated to the struggle. She supports all the right causes. She can also be found on a picket line. Yet she does not let the incessant calls for solidarity prevent her having a life of her own, full of joy. In fact she chooses her objects of solidarity in part on the basis of whether they seem to enjoy themselves and make room for self-expression. "If I can't dance," she says, "it's not my revolution."[2]

Tom is a single-issue man. He occasionally sees Rosie and Emma out in the street, but only when they come out for "his" cause. He sacrifices a great deal in its pursuit. He is an expert on this issue, a point man and frequent public face for the main organization associated with it. He believes in bipartisanship, and so tries to avoid contaminating his cause with any political wedge issues; he thinks that such associations would make his cause less effective.

Finally, Riley has the right opinions, believes in the right things, but most of the time has an excuse that prevents his coming out in support. Usually his

---

[1] Susan Wolf, "Moral Saints," *Journal of Philosophy* 79 (1982). I assume that one can be a moral saint in one department without violating equally weighty moral demands in other departments. If one cannot, then the case to be made is easier for me.
[2] Emma Goldman, *Living My Life* (New York: Penguin, 2006), 88.

excuse is that he is out for a drink with friends. Riley has a lot of friends. He finds the leaders of causes to be blowhards who not infrequently say ridiculous or even offensive things, and he refuses to support organizations led by intellectual or moral lightweights. So for the most part he tunes out. He votes right, donates to the occasional cause and campaign, but rarely lets politics interrupt conviviality.

As laid out so far, the theory of solidarity seems to require us all to be Rosie. Yet intuitively, it is better to be Emma. So I need to show that the theory permits us to be Emma. It is also hard to be too critical of Tom, although the theory seems to regard him as systematically failing in his moral duty. And who wouldn't like hanging out with Riley? Yet we seem to be required to condemn him. The challenge for the current section then is to give good advice to the agent who would want to follow the theory without turning into Rosie.

Let us first briefly review why the theory seems to require us to be Rosie. It is obvious why the theory rejects Riley; opinions notwithstanding, Riley participates in all the inequities of his society, perhaps lifting a finger for the occasional emergency. He thus lays a heavy burden of proof on the activists, since he supposes that he can get on with his life unless they make a particularly powerful appeal that meets his exacting standards; he does not hold friends or bartenders to any similar standard. He presumes to dictate how others should make their arguments so as to avoid offending the sensibilities of people like himself. The theory seems also to reject Tom's single-issue orientation, especially since (we can stipulate that) he did not even choose his issue on grounds of equity, but on personal grounds of relationship or loyalty. And Emma seems to select her objects of solidarity on the basis of whether she enjoys their struggle. This seems trivial and in a way selfish.

Calls for solidarity are ubiquitous, and the theory implies that we have a perfect duty to respond with solidarity when the call comes from those who are treated inequitably. Calls to action can conscript us, giving us an instantaneous choice between treating someone inequitably and participating. Since inequitable treatment is wrongful, we must answer the call. How, then, could we be anyone but Rosie?

7.1.2 Tracking Duties

Christian Barry and Kate MacDonald distinguish between the *stringency* and *demandingness* of a duty.[3] Stringency tracks how serious a duty is—how easy it would be to justify overriding it, whether on the basis of self-interest or

---

[3] Barry and MacDonald, "How Should We Conceive of Individual Consumer Responsibility to Address Labour Injustices?"

competing moral duties. Its demandingness, on the other hand, refers to how much positive action it requires of us—how burdensome it is to comply. Though often conflated, stringency and demandingness pull apart, sometimes quite widely. If I owe you $5, then this debt is very stringent—it is your money, and failing to pay you back would be a kind of theft. But luckily it is not demanding. On the other hand, many people think positive duties of assistance are extremely demanding, but they might not be very stringent if they are easily overridden.

Inasmuch as solidarity is a principle of equity, it is as stringent as they come: other things equal, we never have license to treat others inequitably. And while solidarity need not be especially demanding in any given case, it adds up. This is what we are trying to limit. But it is hard to see how to limit it, because solidarity is an agent-neutral principle, grounded in moral agency itself. It makes no reference to any way we might have contributed to the plight of the victims of inequity, and so the ground of the duty does not rest in our prior culpability. It thus differs from the borrowed-money case since it seems as though I owe you solidarity—here and now, or whenever you ask for it—irrespective of whether I have incurred any kind of debt or obligation to you. So we must be Rosie.[4]

Yet the distinction between stringency and demandingness seems to create an opening for a transition from Rosie to Emma. As a deontological principle, solidarity is more stringent than demanding; it does not require us to seek out opportunities to exercise it. We have a duty to refrain from treating persons inequitably. This is a negative duty: a constraint. Sometimes the only way to refrain from treating someone inequitably is to undertake political action on their terms. This is a positive obligation pursuant to the negative duty. That is, it involves affirmative performances of actions, but the duty is not the affirmative performance, it is the negative refraining. The affirmative performance is agent-relative in the superficial sense that it applies to a particular person in virtue of their being in the relevant situation. Analogously, each of us has an agent-neutral negative duty to refrain from stealing. Sometimes, however, this negative duty involves the affirmative performance of an action. For instance, if I find a lost wallet, the negative duty to refrain from stealing entails the affirmative performance of returning the lost wallet.[5] The affirmative performance is thus simply the way that my negative duty lands on me, given my circumstances. Similarly in the case of solidarity, each of us has a duty to refrain from treating others inequitably, and sometimes this duty entails an

---

[4] I am grateful to Cheshire Calhoun, Sarah Hannan, and RJ Leland for immensely helpful discussion of this challenge, and of attempted solutions to it.

[5] Might I instead just leave it where I found it? I am inclined to think not, or anyway, not *wantonly*. I might do so if I have good reason to think that will maximize the likelihood of the owner's finding it. But otherwise, leaving it to be scattered or stolen seems almost as wrong as stealing it.

affirmative requirement to engage in political action on others' terms—to act in solidarity—when we find ourselves in the right circumstances.

Returning to the wallet case, there is no obligation to maximize instances of wallet-returning, or to seek out wallets to return to people. Nor is there any obligation to maximize the number of people in possession of all and only their own wallets. To refrain from stealing, all I normally have to do is *not steal*, except in the circumstance where I find myself in lost-wallet types of cases; then, there is just an obligation to return those wallets that I do happen to find. Solidarity is again analogous. There is no obligation to maximize instances of solidarity, or to maximize the number of people in solidarity, or even maximize the number of people whose calls for solidarity get uptake. Solidarity is not a maximand.[6] Nor yet is equity a maximand, but rather, a constraint—a requirement that we not treat others inequitably. Sometimes we find ourselves in a situation such that refraining from treating others inequitably entails taking political action on their terms. But not being in such a situation is not something that needs to be remedied. If this is correct, then Rosie is not required to go around searching out cases of solidarity to engage in.

7.1.3 Aggregation

This anti-maximizing solution seems promising. But it might prove too much; it might allow us to be Riley rather than Rosie. As long as no wallet literally lands at Riley's feet—and let's be honest, it's rare that our everyday routine is literally broken up by a face-to-face demand for solidarity—he can go off and live his convivial life. But there are nonetheless massive numbers of calls for solidarity going out over the wires at any one time—and in big cities, typically a not insignificant number of leaflets calling for action against genuine injustice, near and far. Failing to hear *any* of these calls would be tantamount to covering one's eyes and ears. But if I hear one, I hear many more than one. So it seems that we are back to being Rosie, running ourselves ragged.

Marcia Baron suggests that Kantianism avoids the demandingness problem because Kant's theory imposes two coequal and irreducible ends—our own perfection and the happiness of others—and however demanding the latter, it cannot obviate the former.[7] We thus have imperfect duties to pursue our own ends. Nor are we obligated to *maximize* happiness, "but only to take it very seriously, see it as making a normative claim on us, and seek (in some way or other) to promote it."[8] This seems correct, but it cannot inoculate us against

---

[6] I am grateful to Matthew Hammerton for discussion of this issue.
[7] Baron, Pettit, and Slote, *Three Methods of Ethics*, 16.
[8] Ibid., 20.

excessive *perfect* duties. If, as I have argued, deontological solidarity is a perfect duty, then its demands in each instant take priority over the imperfect duties imposed by the compulsory end of self-perfection.

Perhaps we can hold back the tide by appeal to the principle that "ought" implies "can." Since it is impossible to respond to *every* call to action, we are entitled to respond only to some of them. But this does not cut down the burden far enough. For Rosie is answering all the calls she *can*, whereas Emma is not, and Tom and Riley are far from it. A similar reply is that "ought" implies "can will," or in other words, that the agent could, given facts about human nature, actually bring herself to meet this putative obligation.[9] The problem with this option is twofold. First, Tom and Riley, at least, and probably also Emma, *could* will themselves to do more than they do, or at least, we have no reason to grant that they could not. Second, and more seriously, there is no antecedent or immutable fact of the matter about how much a person can will herself to do; this changes over time, partly due to voluntary action, and so even if we cannot *now* will ourselves to be Rosie, we can bring ourselves to be such that we could be her in the future.[10] It still looks, then, as though we should all be or become Rosie. Indeed, once we recognize the malleability of our capacity to will and do what solidarity requires, we might instead wonder whether Rosie isn't a bit self-pitying; she could have a better attitude and maybe do even more.

Let us return to the lost wallet scenario. Suppose that, it is not just one wallet but, for whatever reason, an unending flow of lost wallets. Travelers come through town and then fly out having lost their wallet but unable[11] to come back to search for it. The city consequently receives hundreds of lost-wallet alerts from distressed travelers each day. The new mayor thinks that lightening these wallets would be a no-cost way to avoid raising taxes on city residents, but the city council thinks this would be stealing. The mayor says that he will start taking this money in two weeks unless the city council comes up with a better solution that does not consume scarce budgetary resources. Having no budget for this, the council cannot afford to hire a staff of wallet-returners. So the council sets up a Walle-darity Center where volunteers can pick up lost-wallet alerts from distraught travelers, match owners to wallets, and reunite them by mail. Sometimes matching wallets with owners is easy—the owner clearly describes a highly distinctive and instantly located wallet. Other times, wallets lack adequate identification, the owner's description is vague, or

---

[9] David Estlund, "Human Nature and the Limits (If Any) of Political Philosophy," *Philosophy & Public Affairs* 39, no. 3 (2011). For discussion, see also Nicholas Southwood, "Does 'Ought' Imply 'Feasible'?" Unpublished manuscript.

[10] See ibid.; Avery Kolers, "Dynamics of Solidarity," *Journal of Political Philosophy* 20, no. 4 (2012).

[11] More literally unwilling, but it would be a lot to expect this of them given that they've flown out of town.

whatnot. Sometimes extensive searches come up empty because the wallet was not actually lost here, but the owner does not know that, and neither do we. Dozens of wallets are in each category.

It is extremely rare that a wallet is lost right in front of me such that I can grab it, quickly hand it back to the owner, and be done. Yet I know where the owners send their lost-wallet alerts—they have no other way of asking the people of our city for help, and that's what they are trying to do—and I know that their money is in danger of being stolen by the mayor. Worse, if the mayor's plan succeeds, my tax load will be lightened. So I am no mere bystander; I could benefit from their plight.

This case instantiates both excessive demand and a conflict of inequities. Walle-darity is not correcting just *one* inequity, but hundreds—each case is theft from a different person; they are injustices of the same kind, but they are not the same instance of injustice. The individual wallet-losers would doubt-less be mortified to learn that they were contributing to our being harried and sleepless; but taken separately, no one has made an excessive demand. Each has subjected us to a reasonable demand which it would be inequitable to refuse.

The first step to solving this problem lies in organization and aggregation. Each of us, individually, is overwhelmed by the demand. But suppose we form a walle-darity brigade so as better to coordinate our efforts at solving what we can now fairly treat in the aggregate as the Lost Wallet Problem. Unlike individual initiatives, group efforts are likely to be more effective and make more people whole because the strategy for attacking the wallet problem can be coordinated rather than haphazard, and labor efficiently divided. So our actions as a group are more effective than the actions of the same number of us working individually. Joining together also carries two other important bene-fits. As a group we do not tackle lost wallets severally, one at a time, but the *lost wallet problem*, taken as a phenomenon. Unlike any individual lost wallet, the lost wallet problem confronts us as a single excessive demand. And second, as a group we tackle the problem through our shared agency, with a plan structured around performance of a complex duty. These two benefits work in the following way. First, once there is a single excessive demand we can understand each wallet-owner's inability, or perfectly understandable unwill-ingness, to fly back here to find her wallet as partly constitutive of that demand. It is a reasonable demand for each of them to make, but taken in the aggregate it threatens to exploit our good will in a morally problematic sense. The exploitation is not intentional, to be sure, but it is possible for aggregates of persons to exploit others without intending to, and it is possible for this exploitation to be morally wrongful, even though not culpable.[12] The

---

[12] Barry and Øverland, *The Responsibilities of the Affluent to the Poor: Doing, Allowing, and Enabling Harm*, chap. 7.

aggregate demand turns us into the servants of the wallet-losers, taken as a class. This is not just a heavy burden, but an inequity in its own right since it follows from calls that they have issued. The inequity does not rest in a comparison between the actual degrees of suffering, but rather in the unreasonableness of the demand made on each of us to curtail our lives in service of others. To the extent that the demand is inequitable it cannot give rise to a duty of solidarity. Hence by aggregating and developing a plan for treating all these separate problems as a single phenomenon, we allow ourselves to claw back our lives from the concatenation of demands no one of which is excessive, taken by itself.[13]

Second, once we structure our individual agencies into a shared plan, we give everyone the job that she or he can handle. Our walle-darity group can challenge us to do better, but causing us to burn out would be irrational because the group needs a long-term policy of responding to the lost-wallet problem. This long-term policy might involve asking people to do more than they knew they could—and enabling them to do so over time—but it must stop short of causing burnout. We plan together taking our individual motivations and limitations as realistic inputs into the plan's allocation of jobs. The plan then asks us to perform those jobs, but neither expects us to go above and beyond, nor, in some cases, benefits by our doing so; excessive zeal might just cause confusion. By organizing, then, we turn the demands into a class and meet them more effectively; we return more wallets and achieve more equity. Individual contributions to an organization constitute inputs into the organization's plan, setting limits on what it may demand of each of us. If, even though we address the aggregate demand efficiently, it remains excessive, equity permits us to set boundaries around our own legitimate ends.

In short, our problem was that the cascade of demands for solidarity could force us to be Rosie. But by organizing, we achieve three things. First, we coordinate our efforts more effectively to fight in solidarity. Having a coordinated solidarity movement—an established counterpower to oppressive interests—is a good in its own right, and also makes us more effective at hearing others' calls, coordinating our responses, and efficiently discharging our duty of equity. This coordinated movement may, second, take the cascade of claims for solidarity *as a class.* Taken as a class, the demand is excessive in the sense that fully meeting that demand would exploit each of us, undermining our autonomous moral agency in a way that would itself treat us inequitably. Since no one may treat anyone inequitably, this demand cannot give rise to

---

[13] In a Kantian vein, we might argue that such aggregation is a moral duty, for reasons analogous to those requiring agents in the state of nature to create a state: only through aggregating can we treat cross-cutting claims equally. I am grateful to Sarah Hannan for this observation. See Immanuel Kant, *The Metaphysics of Morals* (New York: Cambridge University Press, 1996).

a duty of excessive solidarity. The duty stops where the inequity starts. And finally, by coordinating, our solidarity group also puts itself in position to take our capacities as inputs in the allocation of jobs. It can, to be sure, treat our capacities as malleable, and thus make a subplan to help build our skills and capacities, as well as to make participation enjoyable, which expands the movement's capacity and reduces the threat of burnout. Coordination thus can solve the problem of excessive demand by both expanding the share of the demand that is met, and protecting us as individuals from bearing excessive burdens ourselves.

I want to draw out a further implication of coordination. Assuming that the wallet-*losers* are not antecedently coordinated, our group's coordination can spur their coming to self-awareness as a class. Our turning from individual s_i into a single S can help the distributed g_i organize themselves as a coherent G. Thereafter, they can also contribute to prioritization, effectiveness, and demand-moderation. Indeed, the g_i may have a *responsibility* to make this shift: each wallet-loser is a version of single-issue Tom, but if they coordinate into G then they can reduce the risk that their own demands might treat others inequitably.[14]

7.1.4 Living for Justice

Solidarity is a perfect duty when and because it partly constitutes equitable treatment of those who have been treated inequitably. The problem is that we are confronted with too many demands for support and solidarity—from victims of unjust war, detention, and violence; to those who suffer and die from the diseases of structural poverty; to workers struggling to organize in fields and sweatshops around the world; to movements for civil and political rights near and far; and so on, and so on. No single demand is excessive. To the contrary, each is eminently reasonable: people's lives and livelihoods are on the line, and we hear their call, and they are entitled to expect our help. You and I would expect the same: if we, in peril of death, cried out to others who were in a position to help us, it would be an added outrage and injustice if we were ignored. Yet taken in the aggregate, these demands could drive each supporter to exhaustion. Moreover, these demands are sometimes not just infeasible because excessive, but incompatible, because what is justice for one would set back the interests of another. Climate justice could harm beleaguered mining towns; economic growth adequate to reduce structural poverty could involve near-enslavement of child laborers; and so on.

---

[14] I am grateful to Cheshire Calhoun for this suggestion.

Aggregation can address these problems—not by magically solving them, unfortunately, but by putting people in conversation with one another and enabling them to light a moral course through. Once we take the demands in the aggregate we can understand them as a single demand that the duty of solidarity makes upon us. Like other deontological requirements, it is grounded in and hence limited by moral agency. A demand that attacks or undermines our moral agency cannot be obligatory. We may, of course, misjudge what counts as such an excessive demand; the mere fact that aggregate demand is excessive does not mean we get to set our own levels of contribution on the basis of our preferences. These duties are owed, not optional. But even if we can miss the mark, and the mark is anyway a variable, the fact is that there exists a point beyond which the demand becomes excessive or unreasonable. I propose to call that point *living for justice*. When others are in peril for life or basic dignity, they may not be able to expect us to sacrifice our own lives or agency for them, but they should be able to expect that we devote ourselves to the struggle in a way that makes it ours.

Living for justice is a kind of "wholeheartedness" about the struggle. Harry Frankfurt understands wholeheartedness as being in a state such that one "has no reservations or conflicts"[15] in one's commitment. One commits oneself to certain ends with such depth and sincerity that one comes to identify with those ends. I think this goes a bit too far. I agree that the person who lives for justice comes to identify with the struggle. She is attuned to the plight of others and has thoroughly internalized procedures for discerning inequity. She might miss some events, but over time she will be among the usual suspects who can be counted on to be out there when it matters, lending her name, her presence, and her intellect to the struggle. Yet it is not the case that she lacks reservations or conflicts. To the contrary, the existence of conflicts underpins the burning sense of injustice: it is precisely because he wants to spend time with his family, rather than walk the picket line, that he understands how important it is to walk the picket line, for the strikers also want to spend time with their families. To live for justice is to identify oneself with the struggle, to engage in it joyfully, not begrudging others our solidarity. Yet in admitting conflict it is a Kantian "purity of heart" rather than a full-on Frankfurtian wholeheartedness.[16]

My claim, then, is that it is fair for others to expect that we live for justice, but not that equity become our sole driving aim. If we genuinely live for justice we take real steps to pursue it, including especially organizing with others to

---

[15] Harry Frankfurt, "Taking Ourselves Seriously. Getting It Right," *The Tanner Lectures on Human Values* (2005), http://tannerlectures.utah.edu/_documents/a-to-z/f/frankfurt_2005.pdf.

[16] My analysis here again follows Baron. See Baron, Pettit, and Slote, *Three Methods of Ethics*, 36; 46–7. To be sure, the closer Kantian wholeheartedness comes to Frankfurtian wholeheartedness, the happier we may be.

do so. If I cannot be bothered to find others and coordinate for justice, I can hardly be said to be committed to it. I do not claim, however, that we have any duty to maximize the amount of justice or benefit we bring about. Causes might seem "small" in terms of the total amount of good that would be accomplished by success, but that is not a reason to deemphasize that cause. By analogy, in baseball, the Second Baseman typically gets the fewest infield balls, but if I am the Second Baseman then I should nonetheless play my position, not interfere with the Shortstop to get more action. I should be the best Second Baseman I can.

If I call upon someone to live for justice, though, I also thereby assume a responsibility to do so myself. I assume a responsibility to ensure that in pursuing justice for myself, I am not unjustly attacking someone else. Hence groups that ask for solidarity also have a duty—indeed the very same duty that they are calling in from others—to think of the movement as a whole. In practice, then, LGBT activists must also support economic and racial justice; civil rights activists, LGBT rights. Workers must support victims of aggressive wars, and the peace movement must support workers. Environmentalists must foreground environmental justice and economic justice, particularly for those who could suffer in a transition to a green economy. This pursuit of coherence in the broader movement requires significant intellectual and emotional work, not least for the purposes of tamping down conflicts of inequities.[17] Calls for solidarity are grounded in justice, but there is no such thing as "me-justice." It is understandable that each of us *starts* from "me-justice," but it is impermissible to remain there. Each of those who call upon others' solidarity may, then, expect that those who hear their call deliver with a wholehearted commitment to justice; but they must also live for justice, or be on the path toward that state.

7.1.5 The Four Friends, Again

It seems clear to me that the life of Riley is morally impermissible. He is wholehearted only in conviviality, which is a fine way to be, taken by itself, but does not meet even a minimal target of justice. He is treating others inequitably. It may be *necessary* to vote right—the state is, after all, in many respects our most effective instrument of justice and equity—but voting right is nonetheless insufficient. *Merely* voting right just makes Riley into Martin

---

[17] I doubt that conflicts of inequities can ever be fully eliminated. One of the benefits of thinking in terms of inequitable treatment rather than justice maximization is that we can side with G even without judging that G's cause is overall just or most just. But it remains possible that G and H will have irreconcilable differences such that each is treated inequitably by any solution to the inequitable treatment of the other.

Luther King's "white moderate." Riley needs to step up. Tom is a different case. As a single-issue man, he may live for that issue, and that issue might in itself be just, but there is a further question of whether this exclusive focus is legitimate. Such behavior is justifiable *only if* it follows from a group plan. The group might in fact delegate Tom exclusively to the job that he is doing, and insist that he be left alone to focus on it, like a Second Baseman. But if this is a case where Tom, like Riley, refuses to join up except on his own terms, then he too is treating others inequitably in the interests of living the life that he has set for himself, unimpeded by attention to the plight of others. Being a "one-issue man" in this way is a kind of selfishness. Again, though, if he is assigned that task then this is no longer true.

Rosie, for her part, would be happier if she thought in terms of the aggregate demand, and the group response to it. She runs herself ragged because she believes—and she is right—that no one is treating her badly but that she would be treating others badly if she stopped answering their calls. But through aggregation she can treat the calls for solidarity as a class, and treat her own participation as part of a group plan for a long-term struggle for justice. She may negotiate her own role in the movement by appeal to equitable treatment of herself, lest she be "slavish," to use Aristotle's term.

May Rosie, then, live Emma's life? *Should* she? If Emma is a "free agent," joining up or not depending on whether she likes the movement or antecedently cares, then she is just a more collaborative version of Riley. Yet suppose instead that Emma joins the movement wholeheartedly, but brings to it an energy and joyfulness that are infectious. She then not only treats others equitably but builds others' capacity to do so as well. Joy in solidarity enhances others' experience and treats them as full human beings rather than as a mass of Justice-Bots. Emma enables others as well as herself, and thus embodies an ethic of solidarity to which we can all aspire.

7.2 INDIVIDUAL INITIATIVE AND CHOICE

Emma negotiates the scope and manner of her participation in the movement. How far may she do this? What principles may she use to choose her causes? And having chosen, how independently may she act in their interests? These are problems of individual initiative. Individual initiative is suspect in solidarity inasmuch as solidarity is action on others' terms. Supporters—especially those drawn from privileged groups—with excessive leeway for pursuing their own interests are likely to follow fads or prejudices, jump from issue to issue, or impose their own ways of seeing or their own loyalties on the group. Yet at the same time, individual initiative seems essential in two kinds of cases: choosing objects of solidarity when too many come calling, and, having chosen, cases where we need to decide upon a course of action before communication with *G* is possible. This section addresses these two general cases of individual initiative.[18]

7.2.1 Selecting Objects of Solidarity

The first thought regarding selection of objects is that if we have been successful—as I recommended above—at blunting the demandingness problem by creating a broad justice movement that uses an actual procedure to allocate resources among calls to action, then space is opened up for participants to divide the labor by interest. If there are enough people with a sufficient diversity of interests, then, much of the work of selection can be left up to individuals.

When such an umbrella organization does not yet exist, or where our interests are not so conveniently complementary, we need strategies for allocating our efforts in a way that does not just collapse back into the prejudiced or unreflective interests of each individual. One such strategy might be to return to those choice methods that, I previously argued, had to be subordinate to structural deference. In Chapter Four, recall, I rejected epistemic and relationship deference as accounts of how to select an object of deference. In Chapter Two I rejected teleological solidarity and loyalty as accounts of the concept and basic justification of solidarity. These principles can, however, serve as subsidiary choice criteria—as means of shaping, out of the raw material of demands that put us under a *pro tanto* obligation, a coherent and feasible all-things-considered obligation. Each criterion has something to be said for it, though they are not all equally compelling.

The most compelling seems to be relationship deference. If we manage to set up a functioning solidarity organization, it will be characterized by intense working relationships. Provided these relationships are regulated by structure—they are part of the justice movement, rather than separate, unaccountably single-issue or mere affinity organizations—such relationships are essential to attaining and sustaining an effective commitment to the struggle. We ought to foster such relationships, and the fact that working on some particular issue will tend to do so can count as a basis for selecting that issue rather than others that are, in other respects, neither more nor less urgent. Epistemic considerations are similar; other things equal, the better we hone our skills at discerning inequity and particularly hearing and trusting the voices of those who are treated inequitably, the better we will do.

---

[18] I am grateful to Seth Lazar, Geoff Brennan, and Nic Southwood for pressing me on the question of counterfactual deference and individual initiative.

Teleological considerations might also make plausible grounds for selection. Individuals or groups might call for solidarity on the basis of dubious factual, moral, or strategic claims. We have no right simply to impose our own judgment on others, and mere disagreement is no basis for failure to support the organization.[19] Still, as others' claims become less plausible or more fantastical, or more morally dubious in particular—and there is a surfeit of meritorious calls for solidarity—it seems more permissible for us to quietly let the more dubious claimants get on with their business, while we throw our energies in a different direction. It is also motivationally easier to focus on cases where conscience, relationships, expectations, and equity all converge.

Yet by readmitting these choice criteria, even in a subsidiary role, we also risk readmitting all the biases and prejudices they carry with them: even well-intentioned white people strangely find the testimony of nonwhite people just a bit harder to believe; they have deeper and more equal relationships within rather than across racial groups; they are more confident that white people's struggles will succeed. And these prejudices can have just enough force to segregate a movement even when people genuinely intend to do justice to others. How then can we guard against judgments that magically track our own prejudices?

In Chapter Five I suggested a "checklist" method for discerning inequities. The idea was that if we use a simple formal procedure that directs our attention at specific sources of moral cognitive error, we force ourselves to confront questions that we would otherwise push under the rug, not through malice (which we are here assuming away), but through inattention and self-deception. I think we can deploy a similar procedure here. First, we can adopt a bias in favor of more fully worked out and coherent plans and analyses, over less developed ones. In general, causal hypotheses and normative conclusions will be more reliable as they become more thoroughly vetted through multiple perspectives and rigorous questioning in meetings. Vetted and coherent claims, be they normative or empirical, should be chosen over one-off or underdeveloped ideas.

A second criterion for assessing the plausibility of factual and strategic claims, and which seems to correlate with the first, is preferring calls for solidarity that come from *groups* over those that come from *individuals*. In addition to the moral work performed by aggregation, discussed above, organization serves numerous essential functions in solidarity. One is *coherence*: groups provide space for conferring with others about analyses and strategies, benefiting from the wisdom of crowds, converging on a single message and maintaining stable plans over time. Another is *commitment*: to the degree that groups are institutionalized and have staying power, they

---

[19] For anyone just reading this chapter, or taken aback by such a brazen claim: arguments to support this conclusion are in Chapters 1, 2, 4, and 6.

maintain their focus and interest and serve as a reliable public voice on an issue. A third virtue of groups is *moderation* or better, *discipline*. However radical they may be, groups tend to tighten up loose cannons and tamp down individuals' high dudgeon. I might be extremely angry about how the IRS treated me, and willing to go to extremes of conspiracy theory, but unless I can convince a group that my experience is emblematic of the IRS's behavior, the group is not likely to make my treatment the basis of a campaign, or still less, lash out wildly as I might have done on my own. A fourth virtue of groups is *efficacy*. Much more than individuals, groups are capable of leveraging multiple skills and viewpoints to plan effective methods for deploying resources. Moreover, in the event of success, groups are much more likely than individuals to be able to capture the benefits thereby gained.

As a general rule, individuals working alone lack all these virtues. They may have half-baked but overheated ideas about the nature of their victimhood and only an incoherent, untested plan for changing it. And they may lose focus or interest as this particular threat passes or is surpassed in salience by something else. Overall, individuals have few resources, and deploy them haphazardly.[20] Thus we should use organization as a criterion for selecting among potential objects of solidarity.

Among organizations, however, third, we can also gravitate toward those that are structured to encourage broad participation in governance and honest input from all levels, rather than a top-down organizational structure; as well as groups that have adopted the formal use of devil's advocates or other methods to guard against group-polarization dynamics.[21] Thus, combining these three criteria, our "checklist" for selecting among potential objects of solidarity ought to aim for those objects that are well-organized groups meeting these rigorous epistemic criteria both in group structure and in the analyses and plans that emerge from this structure. It does not, of course, follow that individuals should be forsaken in favor of groups, but only that if the surfeit of just causes requires us to choose, it is wise and fair to select in favor of organizations meeting these criteria.[22]

---

[20] Cf. Plato, "Crito," in *Five Dialogues*, ed. John Cooper (Indianapolis: Hackett, 2002), 58.

[21] Scholz emphasizes social criticism both as a function of the group in the larger society, and as an internal feature of group discussions. I am suggesting here that the existence of such internal social criticism is a legitimate basis for selecting among objects of solidarity, but not essential to solidarity as such. See Scholz, *Political Solidarity*, 96–7. See also Sunstein, "The Law of Group Polarization."

[22] This is a departure from a view I have defended previously, in "Justice and the Politics of Deference," *Journal of Political Philosophy* 13, no. 2 (2005) and "The Priority of Solidarity to Justice," *Journal of Applied Philosophy* 31, no. 4 (2014). It seems to me the above reasons make it wise to focus on objects that are organized, or to help organize those that are not; however I now see that—contrary to my earlier view—this does not imply that organization should be a necessary condition of eligibility to be an object of solidarity at all. I am grateful to Nic Southwood for extremely helpful discussion.

It might be wondered whether we shouldn't, though, support underdeveloped and "understaffed" causes precisely so as to help organize and thereby bring about the coherence, commitment, discipline, and efficacy just described. Moreover, in a world of organizations, those who are unable to organize might be even worse off than those who, despite their ill treatment, have at least found one another and gotten together. Indeed there might be a further attraction of working with the un- or less-organized, namely, that this way we as individual participants can enhance our own efficacy; we can make a difference. And we can contribute significantly to the culture of the incipient organization, so that it embodies justice rather than a single-issue focus. I think there is no single strategy that is always preferable here. Sometimes leadership and entrepreneurship are called for, not least when unexpected opportunities open up or unrecognized threats material-ize; other times organizations need steady and reliable contributors. Whichever is the case in a given context, however, it should be determined by the group's (or the cause's) needs, rather than the pull of individual efficacy alone. Pursuing a course of action on grounds that it is a means for us as individual contributors to be effective seems to be grounded in improbable judgments about one's own role and about what the future holds. Although the sense of being effective makes it easier to maintain motivation, it is not itself a reliable source of reasons to be in solidarity with one group rather than another.

This last suggestion, however—that we should sometimes be entrepreneurial because that is how we can be effective—raises further questions about features of the individual participant, or her relationship to the victim of injustice, that might be grounds for selecting among objects of solidarity. First, most directly, it might be that we should factor our own personalities into our choices—so for instance, if Emma knows that she needs to be able to dance, then she is exempt from spending her time in dour movements of no-nonsense people who will frown on such carousing. Or if she needs the "buzz" of success, she should join a movement that will bring success. The worry here is, first, that Emma might actually not know herself as well as she thinks; exposure to new types of people might bring joys she did not know about. And second, she might not know *others* as well as she thinks. Their appetite for "nonsense" might just be hidden under a hardened exterior that they show to outsiders, and once she is trusted and known, things might change. It is therefore more reasonable to use joy—or lack thereof—to justify deemphasizing a cause that one has already worked on, rather than failing to respond to a call from people with whom one has not yet worked.

It might, second, be thought that we should particularly support groups to whose plight we have contributed, or from whose plight we have benefited. Many authors have, for instance, defended a responsibility to disgorge unjustly received benefits and, if possible, return them to the victims of the injustice.[23]

---

[23] See Butt, "On Benefiting from Injustice"; Robert E. Goodin, "Disgorging the Fruits of Historical Wrongdoing," *American Political Science Review* 107, no. 3 (2013). See also the papers

Without specifying it precisely, call this idea the Unjust Benefits Principle (UBP), and duties arising therefrom UBP duties. It might then be thought that solidarity could be a means of meeting UBP duties, or that the UBP might replace solidarity.

I do not wish to deny that we can have responsibilities or even duties to pay back unjust benefits. If UBP duties do exist, however, they must not be conflated with duties of solidarity, or used as a means of selecting objects of solidarity. A first reason is that the UBP seems both too strong and too weak to match solidarity. Suppose that S has benefited from injustices against both V and W. S then has *pro tanto* UBP duties to V and W. The existence and stringency of these duties is independent of whether V or W is a victim of inequity or injustice in our society—refugee or Rockefeller. UBP duties depend on the particular unjust benefit, not social injustice. S's UBP duty to V arises when S gains from an injustice against V, and ends no later than when S's quantum of benefit is returned—when S's net benefit from that injustice is zero—and often much earlier. Yet if V is in fact oppressed, she might remain so, and hence continue to be owed solidarity, long after S's individual quantum is paid off. The UBP implies that S must nonetheless stop supporting V, and shift to compensating W. Indeed, if S fails to switch over then V becomes a beneficiary of the injustice against W, since V is receiving benefits that S in fact owes to W. But this seems incorrect. The fact that S's individual quantum of benefit from the injustice against V is paid off says nothing at all about whether S should continue to be in solidarity with V thereafter. It says nothing about whether S should be in solidarity with V at all. Again, despite the one-off injustice, V might be a Rockefeller. Yet S's UBP duties will be unaffected, since they track benefits innocently gained from injustice. Thus UBP duties do not track duties of solidarity.

Second, the return of unjustly received benefits is an agent-relative requirement focused on S, rather than an agent-neutral requirement focused on G. Assuming G suffers inequity, whether and in what form G wants S's support should determine whether and how S contributes, not the fact of S's having benefited and having an obligation to compensate. This is particularly important in the case of movements defined around oppressed identities, when members of the "up" group might try to repay benefits in a way that does not help the "down" group's movement per se. White Americans or men might, for instance, try to pay back unjustly received benefits to nonwhite persons or women. But in doing so they must defer to the recipients' views about how they should contribute.[24] While it would no doubt be very good to

---

collected in Edward A Page and Avia Pasternak, eds., *Special Issue: Benefiting from Injustice*, vol. 31, *Journal of Applied Philosophy* (2014). I have responded to the UBP at greater length in my contribution to that special issue, "The Priority of Solidarity to Justice."

[24] Of course, the recipients will not all agree about how whites/men should contribute. It does not follow that the latter should be free to find the most congenial or least demanding group of

have a sudden glut of antiracist whites or profeminist men, their participation might also skew social movements in unproductive ways, for instance if men started being regularly elected by male majorities to lead feminist organizations, men did most of the talking at meetings, and so on.

Finally, the model of paying back unjustly received benefits trades on a financial metaphor that gives an impression that there is a single currency of benefit received, and that there is a way to pay it back. In fact, though, the currency of benefit and the best means of payback are not plainly evident the way they are when a bank clerk embezzles money. Antiracist whites need to take the time to listen to nonwhite groups to understand precisely what forms these benefits take, and how if at all these benefits can be disgorged. Thus even if UBP duties took moral priority over solidarity, solidarity is *practically* prior to UBP duties, since solidarity helps us determine what UBP duties require. It may nonetheless be true that those who have benefited from injustices perpetrated against others should bear a special responsibility to act in solidarity with the victims of those injustices. If this principle is cashed out in the language of returning unjust benefits, then that language can be motivationally helpful.

An even stronger motivational principle might refer to past contributions to, or complicity in the imposition or continuation of, such injustices, though it might take a certain amount of listening and learning before people who regard themselves as innocent beneficiaries of past injustices graduate to a self-understanding as complicit in ongoing injustices. Nonetheless, analogous considerations apply to the contribution principle. The contribution principle distributes duties to repair injustices among those who have contributed to, or been complicit in, the imposition of such injustices.[25] Contribution is usually understood to be causal, but complicity may be analyzed either causally or noncausally.[26] Noncausal complicity might encompass intentions to contribute or to make a difference even if one is unsuccessful. It might even include identitarian or virtue considerations, such as wrapping oneself in the flags of oppressors, or failing to distance oneself from them.[27] A person who is otherwise reliably in solidarity might still *express* a kind of inequity by, for

---

nonwhites/women, since this just re-enacts the privilege that needs to be overcome. If all the potential recipients are fighting inequity, and none is itself inequitable, then all candidate groups are on a par, and choosing among them should follow the kind of rough-and-ready considerations discussed in the text. We are not limited to supporting only one group in each "category."

[25] See David Miller, "Distributing Responsibilities," *Journal of Political Philosophy* 9, no. 4 (2001); Butt, "On Benefiting from Injustice."

[26] Christian Barry and his coauthors have developed nuanced contribution-based models of complicity in injustice. See Barry and Øverland, *Responsibilities of the Affluent*; Barry and MacDonald, "How Should We Conceive of Individual Consumer Responsibility?" Christopher Kutz has proposed a variously grounded noncausal account of complicity. See Kutz, *Complicity*.

[27] Kutz, *Complicity*, 190.

instance, "dressing the part" of the oppressor, even if they do not thereby *practice* inequity.[28]

Complicity can be a nuanced thing. In deeply and multifariously unjust societies such as we live in, any of these complicity considerations might exert a motivational pull on us. As with the UBP, however, we must not confuse the agent-neutral duty of equity with potentially conflicting agent-relative duties to undo our own past contribution. S's quantum of contribution is independent of the degree of inequity suffered by V; it is the latter that drives duties of solidarity, even if the former drives other duties.

More generally, these personal criteria of benefit from, and complicity in, injustice are a limited ground for choice. We are so deeply entrenched in such a wide variety of injustices that these selection criteria do not much reduce the range of potential objects of solidarity. It might be that the least unhelpful such criterion is found in the identity of the agent, when such an identity is somehow linked to a highly specific injustice. For instance, Canadians might specifically aim to be in solidarity with First Nations in Canada, over and above other groups, not because this is the greatest injustice or the only one in which they are implicated, but because the relation between beneficiary and victim is salient for reasons beyond anything the individual can control, and that relationship is grounded in an ongoing structural inequity.

Selection of objects remains a difficult question that cannot be fully resolved in theory. The "checklist" procedure proposed here can only turn our attention toward and away from certain considerations, and help us to hone our skills over time. It cannot decide the issue from the armchair.

7.2.2 Individual Initiative

We are similarly limited on the problem of individual initiative. The basic question is whether and to what degree it is compatible with deference to take individual initiative in solidarity with G, as opposed to waiting for G to organize or develop a fleshed-out plan that includes straightforward or explicit subplans for S to pursue. The problem of individual initiative can thus be put in the form of two schematic sorts of cases.

Surrogacy: Group G seeks end E, and S is in solidarity with G's struggle for E. In circumstances Z, S believes that doing A can spur amazing progress toward E, but G cannot provide timely guidance and either G's plan is

---

[28] Marilyn Frye, "White Woman Feminist, 1983–1992," in *Race and Racism*, ed. Bernard Boxill (Oxford: Oxford University Press, 2001); Snyder, "'Marking Whiteness'," (2015). It is an open question just how far expression and contribution are separable. For insightful discussion see Lorna Finlayson, "How to Screw Things with Words," *Hypatia* 29, no. 4 (2014).

indeterminate about whether [*S* ought] to do *A* in *Z*, or the plan *rules out* [*S*'s doing] *A* in *Z*.

Entrepreneurship: *S* seeks to relieve the inequity suffered by *G*, but *G* has no plan or cannot provide timely guidance, and circumstances *Z* provide what *S* believes to be an unexpected opportunity to relieve this inequity by doing *A*.

Each case must be answered either with initiative (doing *A*) or deference (refraining from *A*, pending guidance from *G*). Unfortunately, no hard-and-fast rule is available. As a general rule, entrepreneurship should normally be left to those who are most deeply involved: who have put in the time to understand the situation as well as anyone, and have earned *G*'s trust.[29] However, in some entrepreneurship cases, no communication is possible, or the g_i are not organized. Sometimes the g_i are unable to conceive of themselves as a collective, and unable to voice their concerns, as in the case of severely cognitively disabled persons.[30] The g_i may even be intrinsically nonpolitical and nonlinguistic, for instance if they are future generations, most nonhuman animals, or parts of the natural environment.[31] In cases where the g_i are merely contingently unconscious of themselves or lacking in plans, *S* must in the process of acting also try to enable the g_i to organize, and hand off control to the nascent *G* as soon as feasible. Failure to do so will always be *pro tanto* wrong because paternalistic, even if there are decisive moral reasons to go ahead with *A*. *S* must also make some nontrivial effort to discern what is genuinely in the interests of the g_i, rather than simply go on the basis of what seems right to *S*.

Surrogacy, too, is on a continuum: if the plan specifically rules out *S*'s doing *A*, then the presumption against *A* is almost insurmountable, whereas if *S* has built up others' trust, the plan is ambiguous, and the opportunity seems

---

[29] I am addressing here the *legitimacy* of entrepreneurial action, not its *efficacy*. Sarah Hannan pointed out that these can pull apart. However, I think people who lack the legitimacy—as discussed here—to be entrepreneurial cannot claim to be in solidarity when they do so, no matter how efficacious they turn out to be. They may, however, be acting in charitable or beneficent ways, and may be praiseworthy on those grounds.

[30] I have elsewhere suggested the possibility of adopting something like the "prosthetic thinking" proposed by Anita Silvers and Leslie Pickering Francis to enable the articulation of political aims by cognitively disabled persons and hence solidarity with them. I can't develop that idea further here. See Anita Silvers and Leslie Pickering Francis, "Thinking About the Good: Reconfiguring Liberal Metaphysics (or Not) for People with Cognitive Disabilities," *Metaphilosophy* 40, no. 3–4 (2009); Kolers, "The Priority of Solidarity to Justice." Sue Donaldson and Will Kymlicka suggest similar methods for articulating the interests of domesticated animals. I am inclined to agree. See their discussion of animal citizenship in *Zoopolis: A Political Theory of Animal Rights* (New York: Oxford University Press, 2011).

[31] For discussion of these groups/entities/phenomena as political agents, see Christopher D. Stone, *Should Trees Have Standing?*, 3rd ed. (New York: Oxford University Press, 2010); Donaldson and Kymlicka, *Zoopolis*; Sally Scholz, "Political Solidarity and the More-Than-Human World," *Ethics & the Environment* 18, no. 2 (2013).

uncommonly good, then there is a presumption in favor. The gradations between these limit cases are too fine to be decided in theory. What can be said is that S may not, in acting, remain impervious to protestations from G or some g_i. The individual surrogate, like the entrepreneur, must act in a manner that opens up veto points for G, and passes off control to G as soon as is feasible. Moreover, in the event of vagueness there may be a separation between G's *actual* plan and S's *understanding of* the plan. Thus when taking individual initiative, S must take precautions to have correctly understood the plan.

In each case we must aspire to be equitable persons, in the Aristotelian sense of refusing benefits that are not available to all.[32] Then, we tamp down our tendencies to overestimate our own competence or our own sacrifices; we not only decide on behalf of G, but share G's fate. This practice may be the most attractive form of solidarity with the unorganized, as well. Just as it can be politically powerful to try to live on food stamps or minimum wage for a certain length of time, it would also be politically powerful to spend a period of time in a proportionately sized factory-farm cage or symbolically pay the sorts of insurance premiums that would be required given the climate chaos to come. As Sally Scholz suggests, a tree-sit is similarly an instance of symbolically sharing in the unjust treatment of the object of solidarity.[33]

7.3 SOLIDARITY AND MORAL RESPONSIBILITY

We must now consider the inverse of Surrogacy and Entrepreneurship—cases where, so far from s acting independently on her own best judgment, s acts *against* her best judgment, specifically on moral issues, but only in deference to G. Insofar as they are claims about the world, morally dubious claims are on a par with, and sometimes overlap, claims that seem to be factually or strategically misguided. How then should we parse moral responsibility in solidarity?

Among types of action in solidarity, we can schematically distinguish:

(i) s's acting (failing to act) as the group directs;
(ii) s's acting (failing to act) on individual initiative intending solidarity with the group;

And among loci of responsibility we can distinguish:

(a) the choice of object G of solidarity;
(b) the choice to carry out the solidary action (*de dicto*);

[32] Aristotle, *Nicomachean Ethics*, v.10.1137b–38a. For discussion see Chapter Six.
[33] Scholz, "Political Solidarity and the More-Than-Human World."

(c) the choice to carry out act *A* (*de re*) in solidarity; and

(d) the choice to endorse, after the fact, this action (*de re*), or to repudiate it and atone.

The difference between (b) and (c) is that (b) picks out the act under a certain description—for instance, <the course of action that the union decided upon>—whereas (c) refers to the act itself, for instance <enforcing a picket line by physically impeding replacement workers from entering the job site>. And we are restricting our consideration here to actions where there is very strong reason to believe that act (*de re*) to be wrong. I might also emphasize that each of these permutations merits considerably more detailed attention than it can be given here. The challenge is whether the resources of the theory of solidarity can give, or at least gesture towards, plausible answers.

7.3.1 After the Act

Let's start with (d), which might be in play either when the group directs the action (case (i)) or when the action is taken by an individual (case (ii)). If *G* directs an action, then whether it has a duty to take public responsibility for it depends on whether it is morally appropriate for *G* to be clandestine or secretive. Normally, the powerful norms of truthfulness and publicity are undefeated; other things equal, we should take ownership of our acts. Yet openness might sometimes be an unaffordable luxury. Suppose a house that is a station on the Underground Railroad is surrounded by police, and one person is directed to start a diversion by setting fire to a neighbor's barn, enabling the fugitives to flee before the house is raided. If the Underground Railroad has a legitimate reason to remain clandestine, then that reason at least competes with any reason the arsonist might have for publicly atoning. It may be that the arsonist can atone privately to the neighbors, but if we suppose that the neighbors are slave owners or anyway southern sympathizers, even a secretive overture might be impossible.

Similar considerations apply to the question of what happens if the individual agent *s* is caught and prosecuted or publicly vilified for the act. Again, if the group has strong reason to remain clandestine then it may be unreasonable to expect that the group come forward to deflect responsibility. It is a disturbing but, it seems to me, incontrovertible moral fact that there can be conditions under which it is right for me to suffer alone for doing what I was instructed to do by the group, rather than, for instance, name names to the Nazis or expect the Partisans to turn themselves in. But in more democratic conditions, groups are normally required to admit responsibility, back up their members, and atone to victims of the act.

There is a risk here of bifurcating groups into "political wings" and "military wings," such that the former remain publicly pure while the latter do the dirty work; or bifurcating between unblemished public faces of the group and the underlings who plant the bombs. This practice seems to track the above logic: in tyrannical conditions this bifurcation may be justified as self-defense, but as conditions improve it becomes less acceptable.[34]

Finally, we must consider (ii) Surrogacy and Entrepreneurship cases, supposing that *s* acts wrongly. The question is whether G should publicly own *s*'s action, or disavow it. The answer seems to depend on aforementioned considerations such as the depth of *s*'s involvement with the group, as well as whether she was going rogue, whether she acted entrepreneurially without checking in, how ambiguous the plan was, whose interests such ambiguity served, or whether *s* got some semi-official nod before acting. When *s* is deeply involved, G normally bears some accountability, even if *s* has gone rogue. Otherwise, it seems to me—perhaps paradoxically—that groups have both a strong *prima facie* duty to disavow rogue actions, and at the same time an obligation to atone to the victims of such acts. It is important not to imply, through omission, that the group sees the act as acceptable, and important to affirmatively acknowledge that the victims do not merit the treatment they received. This follows from the same logic as the role of solidarity in atonement for inequitable treatment discussed in Chapter Six.[35]

7.3.2 Parsing Responsibility for Wrongful Acts in Solidarity

Returning to the division of cases, type (i) raises the problem of moral responsibility in solidarity par excellence. We begin with locus (a): if G is worst-off, then it is always *pro tanto* right to side with G, and *pro tanto* wrong not to. The agent individually bears responsibility for this choice at (a). G, however, also bears some responsibility insofar as it *represents itself* as worst-off in the situation in question. This claim depends on empirical facts, about which G might be wrong. For instance, G might make claims about how some of its members have been spied on by the police, or subjected to specific forms of oppression, and these are factual claims that G must stand behind. Nativists and White Supremacists often claim to be victimized by immigrants and racial or religious minorities. These claims are factually problematic and those who make these claims are responsible for the messages they thereby convey. Locus (b) is the site of the act *under a description*, namely, the act that G chooses. Normally, locus (b) will inherit its moral character from (a), and S normally bears sole responsibility for (b)—for accepting G's authority.

---

[34] See Chapter 8 for discussion of whether violence is ever acceptable in deontological solidarity. Assume for now that there has been at least one historical occasion on which a violent uprising was permissible.

[35] Radzik, "Moral Bystanders and the Virtue of Forgiveness."

The greatest challenge lies at locus (c): responsibility for the act *de re*. Consider first:

Group Responsibility: G bears full responsibility for A (*de re*) (Table 7.1).

On this account, if *s* does A at G's behest, then *s* bears no responsibility for A (*de re*). It all falls on G. Thus for instance, if the act in question is G's resorting to intimidation or violence in order to enforce a picket line, then *s* bears responsibility at loci (a) and (b) for identifying G and for pursuing G's course of action, whereas G bears responsibility at (a) for representing itself as worst-off, and at (c) for the act itself. That is, G is absolved of (b), and *s* is absolved of (c).

Group Responsibility has important merits. If the act flows from a shared agency structure, then it stands to reason that accountability rests with the group, even if A was carried out by *s*'s hands. Yet *Group Responsibility* seems merely to push the question back a step, to how we should understand such group responsibility. One straightforward option is the following:

Conspiracy: Each participant is jointly and severally liable for A *in toto* (Table 7.2).

Under *Conspiracy*, *s* is not accountable for individually *carrying out* A, but *s* is responsible indirectly for A, by way of participation in G. *Conspiracy* misses something important, though, namely, that *s* acts deferentially against conscience. It thus seems appropriate to treat the g_i as co-conspirators, but not S or the s_i. S and G are not symmetrically situated with respect to the act—most

Table 7.1. *Group Responsibility*

		S	G
(a)	Selection of object	Responsible for selection	Responsible for self-representation as inequitably treated
(b)	Act *de dicto*	Fully responsible	
(c)	Act *de re*		Fully responsible
(d)	*Ex post* aspects	Fully responsible for aftermath of (b)	Fully responsible for aftermath of (c)

Table 7.2. *Conspiracy*

		S	G
(a)	Selection of object	Responsible for selection	Responsible for self-representation as inequitably treated
(b)	Act *de dicto*	Fully responsible	
(c)	Act *de re*	Responsible indirectly as co-conspirator	Responsible as co-conspirator
(d)	*Ex post* aspects	Fully responsible	Fully responsible

saliently, because we have asked S to defer to G's judgment. Moreover, s is already responsible for loci (a) and (b). So it seems unfair to hold s fully responsible for an act that s carries out only in deference to G's moral judgment.

This apparent unfairness is mitigated by the fact that s, unlike G, also gets credit for (b). Since s's solidarity constitutes equity, and failing to be in solidarity in this case would have been inequitable, we can treat s as having been faced with a moral dilemma, neither option of which was morally attractive. Provided G is worst-off, locus (b) constitutes S's following through on the duty of equity, which is obligatory, whereas (c) is the wrongful act itself, which is prohibited. Those who act wrongly only when faced with a dilemma do wrong, but their wrong might nonetheless be the best act for them to do under the circumstances. They can be expected to respond to the victim with remorse, for instance, thereby acknowledging "moral remainders," but they are not blameworthy for acting as they did in this circumstance.[36] Thus under *Conspiracy*, S and G are both fully accountable at (c), yet S's blameworthiness is mitigated by the fact of having faced a dilemma. Making amends and other remainders that are appropriate due to the dilemma situation constitute locus (d).

Conspiracy might still seem unfair since s bears full responsibility at (c) even though s by hypothesis thought act A was wrong. If this seems unfair we could instead adopt

> *Shared Responsibility*: Accountability for A is shared between G (who chooses it) and s (who carries it out) (Table 7.3).

Unlike *Conspiracy*, which posits joint and several liability, *Shared Responsibility* apportions blame based on, for instance, relative contribution. One worry, though, is that if G directs s to perform the act, then even if G is not *solely* responsible, it seems as though G should bear *full* responsibility. That is, if we are going to reject *Group Responsibility*, attention to G's accountability

Table 7.3. *Shared Responsibility*

		S	G
(a)	Selection of object	Responsible for selection	Responsible for self-representation as inequitably treated
(b)	Act *de dicto*	Fully responsible	
(c)	Act *de re*	Responsibility proportionate to contribution	Responsibility proportionate to contribution
(d)	*Ex post* aspects	Proportionately responsible	Proportionately responsible

---

[36] O'Neill, *Bounds of Justice*, 63.

suggests that *Conspiracy* is preferable to *Shared Responsibility*, because these alternatives ascribe full responsibility to G rather than diffuse it.

To determine which of these views is best, we must also check their implications for morally *praiseworthy* acts—those that, in addition to being chosen by the worst-off, also do real good, for instance on teleological grounds. An act that does bring about justice is praiseworthy, so on *Conspiracy*, s gets full joint credit at (c) in addition to credit at (b). On *Shared Responsibility*, praise at (c) is apportioned by contribution. It might be wondered whether *Conspiracy* is not too gushing with respect to s; abiding by deontological constraints is normally not independently praiseworthy, since doing so is morally required. But *Conspiracy* does not need to heap praise on s; it merely insists that s does merit recognition for having met a duty of equity. However, it may be that praise is merited when the constraint is unreasonably costly to the agent.[37] In political struggles, then, *Conspiracy* seems the most attractive solution both on the negative side and the positive side.

I have not given a knock-down argument for *Conspiracy*, but ultimately we do not need to choose. We can instead leave matters with multiple distinct, coherent, defensible models of moral responsibility for actions in solidarity. If even one such model succeeds, then the theory is compatible with an acceptable account of moral responsibility.

---

[37] I am grateful to Seth Lazar for discussion.

8

Equity and the Limits of Solidarity

No theory of solidarity is worth the name if it cannot guide us through divisive and even excruciatingly difficult political challenges. Just as theories of solidarity cannot presuppose that all the "good guys" basically agree where justice lies, or that solidarity, by definition or convenience, always brings about justice, so such theories cannot avoid taking a stand on the hardest cases of agonistic political action.

In Chapter Five I discussed the pro-Palestinian Boycott, Divestment, Sanctions (BDS) movement as a divisive case that any theory of solidarity must be able to answer. More generally, solidarity may dictate certain conclusions for the problem of consumer responsibility. From sweatshops to boycotts to "Buy American" and "Buy Union," participation *via* consumption choices is a staple of contemporary politics and perhaps the most familiar site of (putative) solidarity for most of us. The theory of solidarity must, then, address the mundane role of consumers. On the other extreme, whether it be attacks on private property or political rebellion, we occasionally hear calls for solidarity with violence. The theory of solidarity must also, then, be able to address the terrifying challenge of whether violent tactics may ever be supported, and if so, in what forms. The current chapter takes up these two issues.

8.1 SOLIDARITY AND CONSUMER RESPONSIBILITY

Consumers may communicate directly with companies or urge the government to alter the regulatory landscape in which those companies operate. But *qua* consumers, their essential tool is their money and they may use it in essentially two ways: preference and avoidance. And if they are moved by a recognizably moral—as opposed to straightforwardly consumptive—motive, then they again have essentially two potential sources of motives: conscience and solidarity. By "preference" I mean biasing one's judgment in favor of a particular (brand/unit of) product or service to consume, putting a metaphorical thumb on the scales relative to its inherent attractiveness from a self-interested perspective. "Avoidance" is just the reverse. By "conscience" I mean a moral motive grounded in one's own judgment of right and wrong, whereas "solidarity" is a moral motive grounded in someone else's request that the product be preferred or avoided. For purposes of this discussion I include among "consumers" those who "consume" financial "products" by investing in companies through their pension funds or other layperson investment portfolios. Our question in this section, then, is whether—from the perspective of deontological solidarity—we should be "conscientious consumers," "solidary consumers," or just plain old consumers.

8.1.1 The Very Idea of Consumer Ethics

Although the idea of ethical consumption is widely discussed, it might nonetheless be thought that the whole phenomenon rests on a mistake: that ethics literally has no place in consumption. This might be because all putatively moral motives are best analyzed in terms of consumer utility functions: the so-called "ethical vegetarian" is just someone who disprefers meat. Everyone has idiosyncratic reasons for every purchase, be it the choice of gold over dollars, or of Android over iOS. Beyond idiosyncrasy, then, "ethical" consumption might just amount to trying to change how *others* consume. And if this is not just nosy, then it is a matter for democratic deliberation and legislation, not consumption.

This skeptical view of consumer activism is shared between Milton Friedman, who famously argues that we should maximize utility within the market while using politics to set the market's ground rules, and John Rawls, who thinks that if the basic structure is just, then the day-to-day operations of the system generate "pure procedural justice."[1] As for my idiosyncratic ethical behavior, I can do whatever I want; precisely because markets are a zone of free choice, no one has a right that I buy from them, and so my avoidance behavior does not stand in need of any justification whatsoever.[2]

An obvious reply to this objection is that the sharp line that Friedman assumes we can draw between politics and markets has never existed. It would be one thing to defend profit-maximization within fair ground rules if businesses were effectively barred from using the political arena as an extension of the market; but they are not—quite the opposite—so the major premise of Friedman's argument is false. Similarly, Rawls's account is ensconced within

---

[1] Milton Friedman, "The Social Responsibility of Business Is to Increase Its Profits," *The New York Times Magazine*, September 13, 1970; John Rawls, *Justice as Fairness: A Restatement* (Cambridge, MA: Belknap Press, 2001), 54.

[2] I am grateful to Christian Barry for pressing me to address this objection.

ideal theory, and hence irrelevant for our everyday consumption choices in a grossly unjust world.

I think this obvious reply is true, but not to the point, since it assumes that ethical consumption would have no role in a just society, and many "socially responsible" consumers would balk at that assumption. A better reply is that when we assess ethical consumption we are assessing not consumption per se, but a certain kind of linkage. Just as it is legal to ask a politician for a million dollars, and legal to threaten to publish "innocently acquired" photos of him "on the beach in Acapulco with [his] mistress," but not legal to link these two actions, so it may be perfectly understandable to enjoy Palestinian food, and to desire that the Israeli Occupation end, but puzzling to prefer the former because of the latter.[3] It is this practice of drawing linkages that characterizes consumer ethics. On a deontological view, at least, the moral worth of an act depends on the reason (or the intention) that drives it, not the act itself or still less its outcome. Thus the ethics of consumption is for our purposes the ethics of making consumption decisions on the basis of a particular kind of reason, namely, a reason that links consumption choices to putative moral features of (typically) the good, service, vendor, or production process. The first objection's failure is, then, nonetheless instructive. For we might wonder just what could replace personal utility as a driver of consumption decisions, and could thereby give those consumption decisions moral worth.

8.1.2 Against Conscientious Consumption

I distinguished between preference and avoidance, and between solidarity and conscience. There is, however, no genuine line between preference and avoidance strategies; typically, a consumer who prefers something will manifest this preference by absorbing a certain cost increment in order to buy it, but this is the same thing one will do if one disprefers the alternative. If the cost increment is too great then the preference will have no practical effect; either the consumer will buy the avoided alternative anyway, or will save the money and consume financial products. There is thus no real line between preference and avoidance—preference for one product *is* avoidance of the other. The real division in consumer ethics lies in the other distinction: that between conscience and solidarity.

If we are driven by the motive of conscience, we make consumption choices based on what we believe to be right. We might do so in order to honor or embody a value with no especial concern for any effect that might have. But this orientation is tantamount to moral commitments' being idiosyncratic; any

---

[3] Jeffrie Murphy, "Blackmail: A Preliminary Inquiry," *The Monist* 63 (1980): 156.

linkage between any two phenomena might exercise us. The more relevant cases are those where our consumption choices reflect attempts to either cause a change in behavior or at least express our moral judgment of that behavior. I shall thus briefly assess conscientious and solidarity consumption on these criteria.

Inasmuch as conscientious consumption is undertaken on the grounds of individual moral reasoning, it is done individually. It is hard to see what causal efficacy can be realistically hoped for from individual consumption choices. There might be an actual impact, but the chances of this are extremely low, and even if there is an impact it might be the reverse of what the consumer intends. The initial effect of a decline in demand would presumably be a drop in price, which—if the market is functioning—would stabilize or even increase consumption, rather than reduce it. That is the function of the price mechanism.[4]

It may be more reasonable to hope that conscientious consumption will have expressive properties and hence will communicate something to suppliers. Consumption is not normally a literal speech act, however, and so the supplier must first of all know that something has been expressed, second, know who the target of the expression is, and third, interpret the expression's content. The binary consumption choice—do buy or don't buy—is too coarse-grained to convey the moral judgment or the linkage between moral judgment and consumption choice. Unless the consumer separately informs the company, for instance in writing, why she will or will not buy their product, they have no idea what her reasons were, or indeed, that she had any reasons at all. But ironically, if she does write or call to tell them, then she need not actually follow through, since all the meaningful expression she is capable of is already achieved through the communiqué. So the consumption choice itself collapses into merely embodying or honoring the value, or perhaps a further value of being consistent or true to one's word. But the crucial point is that there is no reason to expect our conscientious consumption choices to express anything to anyone except ourselves and our personal acquaintances. Worse, conscientious consumption may even generate a kind of "moral self-licensing" whereby we feel entitled to act badly after consuming "ethically."[5]

Yet let us imagine that the expression is heard and understood by its intended target. Nonetheless, conscientious consumption suffers from the further problem that it puts the ball in the suppliers' court. The consumer in effect says: "I'm not buying; your move." The seller then has a wide variety of

[4] Paul Wapner and John Willoughby, "The Irony of Environmentalism: The Ecological Futility but Political Necessity of Lifestyle Change," *Ethics & International Affairs* 19, no. 3 (2005), 78.

[5] Anna C. Merritt, Daniel A. Effron, and Benoît Monin, "Moral Self-Licensing: When Being Good Frees Us to Be Bad," *Social and Personality Psychology Compass* 4, no. 5 (2010).

moves at its disposal, only one of which is to bother trying to earn back the boycotter's custom. And even if they try to earn that back, it is at least as likely to be through public relations as through moral progress. Further, among the various actors on the supply side of the equation, those best-positioned to respond will be the most powerful, and they will do so in the way that benefits themselves the most. So even if the consumer's ethical worries are substantively addressed, it might be due to a maldistribution of duties on the supply side. For instance, Wal-Mart might demand organic produce from suppliers, but refuse to pay a premium, thereby imposing even sharper conditions on suppliers and subcontractors.

Conscientious consumption, then, has only haphazard effects if any, and communicates only vaguely if at all. Such effects as it does have are as likely as not to run counter to the intentions of the consumer. And such communicative efficacy as it does have is likely, by and large, to benefit the most powerful actors on the supply side.

These problems beset *conscientious* consumption, that is, consumption choices driven by the individual consumer's moral judgments of what suppliers ought to be doing and what is the best way to make them do this. They do not beset consumption choices driven by *solidarity*. In such cases it is precisely the existence of a victims' movement demanding action on the consumer side that spurs consumers to act. They act this way—for instance, by boycotting lettuce or grapes, or preferring some brands of shirts over others—at the request of the victims of the practices in question. In this case there is a movement, which communicates its aims to the perpetrator, and which explicitly chooses to bear the costs of, say, lost jobs or wages due to the boycott. Moreover, if it is the movement that calls in the consumers' action, then that action puts the ball in the *victims'* court, not that of the supplier. Rather than express "I'm not buying; your move," the consumer expresses, for example, "I'm not buying unless the union is buying." Insofar as the union can determine the fortunes of the company, the consumer action empowers the union.

Equally important, even if solidary consumer action does not have its intended effect, it is not judged by its effects but by which side the agent is on. Solidarity is, as I have argued, agonistic. When there is a workers' or victims' campaign to boycott a certain brand or product or corporation, "to buy or not to buy" is a choice of whether to be on the workers' or victims' side, or whether to be on the side of the company. And if the workers or victims are treated inequitably, then siding with them constitutes equity. Unlike conscience, then, solidarity can require ethical consumption.

There is, however, perhaps one rule-proving exception to this general rule favoring solidarity consumption rather than conscientious consumption. Some supply chains oppress victims who are incapable of effectively rising up against their direct oppressors or communicating with potential supporters. Products made or mined by enslaved persons are a clear case in point here, as may be animal products, where there is an unbroken chain from the purchase of the product back to the death of the animal. A specific quantity of meat is a particular part of an individual animal, and if it is wrong to kill an animal for food then it is wrong to consume an animal that someone else has killed for food; and no amount of causal indeterminacy regarding the number of animals killed and whether a particular purchase makes a difference can change the fact that the piece of meat just is part of a particular animal's body. Similarly, whereas even workers in sweatshops have—under however much duress—accepted these jobs and might not want the work to disappear, enslaved persons have not so consented, and yet typically lack any means of organizing to communicate with consumers.[6] If this is right, it does not revivify conscientious consumption so much as demonstrate that, just as individual initiative has a limited role in solidarity more generally, it has a place in solidarity consumption, when we support those who cannot communicate or rebel. The key is that in whatever way possible, the victims of inequity should be driving the bus, and enhancing their ability to do so can be part of the project of being in solidarity with them.

To conclude this section, then, I have argued that conscientious consumption is of dubious merit, but solidarity consumption may be an essential part of a given movement's tactics.

8.1.3 Back to BDS

These conclusions finally bring us back to the BDS movement. I argued in Chapter 5 that this movement was on its face a legitimate call for solidarity in the interests of those who are treated inequitably, and indeed, a call that did not treat anyone else inequitably in the process. There is, then, an initial argument for the thesis that participation in BDS is a perfect duty.

Yet "BDS is not a one-size fits all movement."[7] Most saliently for our purposes, BDS comes in stronger and weaker forms, and different forms make different moral demands upon us. I'll call "Weak" BDS that range of tactics that targets state officials, government enterprises, corporations, and products that are distinctively or deeply complicit in the Occupation. "Strong" BDS, on the other hand, extends to a cultural and academic boycott of Israel, which entails refusing to perform or attend conferences in Israel, and shunning particular individuals who live and work there. While principal BDS organizations have refrained from calling for specifically Strong BDS—instead using targeted campaigns against specific companies or products, while

---

[6] On this distinction between slavery and sweatshops I agree with Matt Zwolinski, "Sweatshops, Choice, and Exploitation," *Business Ethics Quarterly* 17, no. 4 (2007).

[7] We Divest, "About BDS," https://wedivest.org/p/240/bds.

praising those who participate in a cultural boycott[8]—for the sake of testing the theory it is useful to present these two poles as if they were either demands issued by different wings of a single movement, or by ideologically conflicting organizations each of which claims to speak on behalf of the oppressed. Between Weak and Strong poles, a "Modulated-Strong" BDS would default to Strong but exempt individuals and institutions on the basis of a political litmus test, shunning them unless they publicly oppose the Occupation and support the cause of Palestinian civil society.

There is something to be said for Strong BDS. Israel erects checkpoints throughout the West Bank and has built roads that are open only to Israeli cars. In addition to the arbitrary limitations on movement that fall on everyone irrespective of any culpable acts or intentions, each Israeli army checkpoint causes untold frustration and humiliation for particular Palestinian individuals every day. As of this writing there are 96 "fixed" checkpoints and 361 "flying" checkpoints where Israeli soldiers systematically harass and humiliate Palestinian civilians.[9] Israelis are not likely to take this moral outrage seriously until they have a sense of what it is like to be humiliated or to have their freedom of movement arbitrarily restricted, even if only symbolically. Further, the Israeli government perpetrates collective punishment on whole families, making no distinction between those who commit punishable acts and those who do not. Indeed, the Occupation authority arguably lacks a moral entitlement to mete out *any* punishments, let alone collective ones. Strong BDS thus visits upon Israeli individuals a very soft echo of what the Occupation authority visits on Palestinians every day. An Israeli academic might be disinvited from a conference, for instance, or prevented from getting library privileges at a research institution; and these petty humiliations and limitations on mobility—*precisely because* they are outrageous and spur righteous anger—will perhaps give that Israeli the barest taste of what his country does in his name to others, whether or not he agrees, and whether or not he has ever personally participated in the Occupation. Moreover, since he is a citizen of a democracy, he arguably bears a responsibility for his government's actions such that he is a legitimate target of nonviolent and nonpunitive tactics aimed at defeating the Occupation. This point may be amplified by the fact that most Israeli adults have, indeed, at one time or another participated militarily in the Occupation, though it was within their power to refuse.[10]

Yet this argument faces an important objection from equity. Strong BDS shuns individual Israelis on identitarian grounds. It thus treats them as mere

---

[8] See "What Should I Boycott?" at BDS Movement, "Join the BDS Movement and Make an Impact!," http://www.bdsmovement.net/make-an-impact.

[9] B'tselem, "Restriction of Movement: Checkpoints, Physical Obstructions, and Forbidden Roads," http://www.btselem.org/freedom_of_movement/checkpoints_and_forbidden_roads.

[10] See Courage to Refuse, "Refusing for Israel," http://www.seruv.org.il/English/.

means—as avatars of a collective. There is nothing a shunned individual can do to merit exemption from this treatment. Strong BDS thus engages in the very collective punishment that it abjures. It seems to follow that, if George is practicing Strong BDS against Danny—for instance, George disinvites Danny from a conference or refuses his submission to an art exhibition, simply because Danny is Israeli—then not only should Hannah refuse to join George's boycott, but, insofar as she is an equitable person in the Aristotelian sense, she should side with Danny and refuse the benefits that he is wrongly denied, for instance by herself withdrawing from the conference or art exhibition.

In this scenario, Danny would indeed have a legitimate complaint against George. But in registering his complaint Danny must commit himself, on pain of inconsistency, to the wrongfulness of such treatment *in general*, not just when directed at himself. Suppose that Danny, who complains at this shunning, examines the principle—or in Kantian terms, the maxim—on which he complains.[11] To be worthy of respect, the principle must not just be that *he* should be exempt from inequitable treatment, but that *everyone* should; hence Danny's complaint is believable only if he also works against the Occupation. This suggests that while an exceptionless Strong BDS is unfair, a Modulated-Strong BDS is not unfair. Working against the Occupation oneself is the criterion of legitimacy for a complaint against Strong BDS. Put otherwise: it is through solidarity with Palestinians that Danny merits exemption from being shunned. If he cannot meet his own duties of equity, then he participates in the inequitable treatment that merits the boycott, and he has no legitimate complaint. Modulated-Strong BDS allows him an exemption, but also demands that he earn it.

It might be objected that there are many injustices in the world, and it seems unfair to single out Israel when other countries, such as Saudi Arabia or for that matter the United States have engaged in behavior that was as bad or indeed in many cases much worse. The objector could charge that the reasons for singling out Israelis seem to be, first, that doing so *just might work*, whereas boycotting Saudi citizens is not likely to end that country's oppressive practices; and second, boycotting Israelis is *easier* for the boycotter than is boycotting crude oil, petrochemicals, or Americans. And these are dubious reasons; indeed it is ironically the relative *weakness* of Israelis that makes it possible to carry out this tactic. This shunning then treats Israelis worse than Americans simply because Israel is less powerful than the US, or less hegemonic within the land that it rules.[12] The basic answer to this objection is that

---

[11] I follow Marcia Baron in treating our maxims as objects of discovery, not stipulation. See Baron, Pettit, and Slote, *Three Methods of Ethics*, 37.

[12] For the analysis of (positive, not moral) territorial rights as hegemonic narratives, see Ian Lustick, *Unsettled States, Disputed Lands: Britain and Ireland, France and Algeria, Israel and the West Bank-Gaza* (Ithaca, NY: Cornell University Press, 1993).

perpetrators of injustice do not have the right to choose the time, place, and manner through which their victims demand justice, or to use other injustices, greater or lesser, as distractions. To be sure, Hannah's support for Modulated-Strong BDS does not by any means let her off the hook when there is a call for solidarity against, for instance, the ongoing theft and contamination of American Indian lands. But nor does the existence of other injustices immobilize her in responding to a morally compelling call for solidarity.

It might be worried, finally, that the argument for Modulated-Strong BDS proves too much, since the same argument would also require support for a Palestinian call for, say, a one-state solution that effectively ended the Zionist aspiration of a Jewish homeland altogether—or worse, support for violent organizations like Hamas. I shall address the problem of violence immediately below. But the broader question of the one-state solution has the same answer as the previous objection: perpetrators of injustice do not get to devise their victims' politics. A one-state solution might fall to a charge of inequity just like Strong BDS; but again, only those who are in solidarity with Palestinians have standing to level this objection.

I conclude that in light of the Palestinian call for BDS, Weak BDS is a manifestation of equitable treatment and is an instance par excellence of our perfect duty of solidarity. And although an exceptionless Strong BDS wrongly shuns individuals on grounds of identity, a Modulated-Strong BDS fairly exempts all and only those whose solidarity manifests equity.

8.2 VIOLENCE FOR EQUITY?

Martin Luther King, Jr., rejected violence in favor of nonviolence. Nonviolence served several purposes, but ultimately it was, in his view, morally required because the end, so far from justifying the means, inevitably includes the means. To use violence in the struggle is to will violence in perpetuity:

> The means represent the ideal in the making, and the end in process, and ultimately you can't reach good ends through evil means, because the means represent the seed and the end represents the tree.[13]

Yet, to say the least, not every downtrodden activist is Martin Luther King. What do we do when the oppressed, disagreeing with King, call for violence? Sometimes this call will seem utterly insupportable, but other times the perpetrator of injustice is engaged in systematic killing of a sort that seems to warrant armed struggle and even humanitarian military intervention. The

---

[13] King, *The Trumpet of Conscience*, 71.

theory of humanitarian intervention has its origins in the great Salamanca theologian Francisco de Vitoria; as we saw in Chapter One, he ultimately justified war against the Indians as the defense of victims of human sacrifice and anthropophagy. Thus we come full circle in this final section by engaging the question of whether violence in solidarity is ever justified.

Our dilemma is as follows. If we reject violence we avoid the perilous problem of doing violence at someone else's behest, but then we cannot respond to calls for violent uprising even against the most brutal regimes. For instance, suppose Denmark Vesey's rebellion is being clandestinely organized and we are called to join the fight against the South Carolina slaveocracy. In this event a strict pacifist rule would effectively repudiate the Vesey rebellion and side with the white supremacists. On the other hand, if we accept violence then, even as we might be able to side with Denmark Vesey, we will have difficulty drawing lines without appeal to our own conscientious boundary-setting. We might find ourselves siding with violent terrorists who claim to be freedom-fighters.

Deontological solidarity supports a clear and straightforward prohibition on *aggression*. To aggress against another is to treat her as an object of coercion rather than a fellow rational agent. Thus it is always wrong to commit aggression, and the wrongness follows from the same principle that justifies deontological solidarity in the first place. No call for solidarity can justify aggression. Yet this prohibition does not get us very far. Most perpetrators of political violence frame their actions not as aggression but as response or self-defense. Self-defense is the deployment of the minimal amount of violence necessary to repel an ongoing or imminent violent attack, from the perspective of a reasonable person acting under uncertainty and duress. In contrast, a *response* is an attack by B on A that is putatively justified by A's *earlier, but now ended*, aggression against B. Since A's aggression is no longer underway, B's attack is not strictly speaking an act of self-defense.

Yet this is still too coarse-grained. Some instances of violence, though ended, instantiate patterns of chronic violence rather than one-off attacks. It seems most plausible to treat violent responses to one-off attacks as aggressions, whereas violent responses to chronic attacks constitute self-defense. The result of all these distinctions is then:

Self-defense: the deployment of the minimal amount of violence reasonably thought to be sufficient to (i) repel an attack that is ongoing or (ii) preempt an attack that is reasonably thought to be imminent, or (iii) stop a pattern of chronic aggressions.
Aggression: the deployment of violence otherwise than in Self-defense.

Equity always rules out aggression and solidarity with aggressors, and hence deontological solidarity rejects both. If G requests S's support in such an endeavor, then S must refuse. So suppose S is walking G's picket line when replacement workers arrive. G refuses to let the replacement workers pass. Participation in this refusal is required as long as G is merely standing firm— refusing to move aside or unblock the road. But if G should request S's help in violently attacking the would-be replacement workers, S must refuse. At no point does it become permissible to attack someone who is nonviolent. On the other hand, suppose the situation turns violent because the police try to break the line with physical force. During the struggle, to try to repulse the attack is permissible self-defense. If the police try to separate S from G so as only to attack G, S should refuse to be selected in this way. Now suppose that the police then return the next day, yet make no indication of an intent to attack. Absent any new provocation, retaliation against the police for their previous day's attack would constitute aggression. Yet suppose the police come every day and beat up the strikers. After a few days these attacks cease simply to be one-offs and constitute a pattern, a strategy of defeating the strike through continual violence. At some point, then, G could rightly—if, perhaps, foolishly—ambush the police in self-defense, and call for support. If so, S should heed this call. For the chronic attacks constitute a war of attrition, and it seems bizarre to imagine that the police should get a moral clean slate every day. Thus we now have a preliminary solution to the question of violence in deontological solidarity: self-defense, as defined above and including responses to chronic violence, is permissible, but aggression is not.

Yet this solution is still too simple. G may additionally be the victim of *structural* violence. The concept of structural violence attempts to explain, not one-off interventions that cause particular named casualties, but rather uneven rates of morbidity and mortality, often due to actions all of which fall within the law. No Billy club need ever come into contact with any skull for structural violence to supervene. In such contexts social classifications such as race, gender, and poverty, which are used to distribute opportunities and to marginalize, are essential to the explanation of disparities in outcomes. Paul Farmer describes Haitian women whose poverty leads them to have "consensual" sex with soldiers, through which they contract HIV and, due to a lack of access to anti-retrovirals, die young. The agent of their death is HIV, but the cause of their death is the socioeconomic and gender system that generated their poverty and closed off options.[14] They are victims of structural violence. If these women led a violent Haitian revolution, we could regard that as self-defense.

Ted Honderich considers whether violent means may ever be chosen in response to large-scale structural violence such as South African Apartheid. He refrains from defending an affirmative answer, but insists that neither can

[14] Paul Farmer, "On Suffering and Structural Violence: A View from Below," *Daedalus* 125, no. 1 (1996).

a negative answer be justified.[15] His argument is that political violence may meet five fundamental democratic criteria, and when it does, its moral properties depend on complex empirical facts that cannot be discerned from a lecture hall:

> Violence, then, may [first] serve the ends which are fundamental to the democratic practice. Second, it may, as coercion, share an attribute [namely, the intent to persuade] with procedures that are intrinsic to democratic systems. Third, this violence is by one comparison an attempt to gain equality of influence. Fourth, it is not directed to the ending of democratic systems. It may, finally [fifth], lead to their becoming more democratic.[16]

We could rebut the first and fifth premises on grounds that "civil resistance works" more effectively than violence.[17] But though that might decide something for Honderich, it would not help us. For our question is not that of conscience—whether *we* should ever choose violence—but the question of solidarity, whether we should ever support someone else who chooses violence, even perhaps to the point of joining them in battle. And the final answer seems as if it must be yes: we at least cannot rule out violence for equity. It does not follow that we must ourselves participate in the violent uprising; it may be that in some instance, or perhaps every instance we ever confront, joining in the battle goes beyond what can be demanded of those who live for justice. But nor can we say with confidence that there will never be a time when we, too, must take up arms.

In reaching this conclusion I should emphasize that it goes only to *jus ad bellum*—the "just cause" conditions of the theory of permissible violence. It does not follow that the victims of structural violence are exempt from *jus in bello* criteria such as proportionality and noncombatant immunity. From the perspective of equity, protecting noncombatants must be paramount. Thus solidarity allows support for and participation in violence, but it must distinguish as sharply as possible between legitimate and illegitimate targets and between proportionate and disproportionate means. As soon as civilians are targeted or put at unnecessary risk, equity seems to support the civilians.

This skeptical but ultimately permissive conclusion seems to apply also to humanitarian military intervention. If victims request support, then subject to the equity criteria above it can be permissible or even required to support them in some way. On the other hand, if victims do not request support then we are faced with the further challenge of individual initiative in violent solidarity. It is hard to fathom that individual initiative could go so far as to

---

[15] Ted Honderich, *Violence for Equality*, Enlarged and Revised ed. (New York: Routledge, 1989), 182; 91.

[16] Ibid., 166–7.

[17] Erica Chenoweth and Maria J. Stephan, *Why Civil Resistance Works: The Strategic Logic of Nonviolent Conflict* (New York: Columbia University Press, 2012).

perpetrate violence when it is not requested by an organized group fighting against tyranny. One difficulty in such cases is what the outcome of such violence could be—if there is no "government in exile," then bringing down a sitting government risks even more chaos. On the other hand, there might be no such government in exile precisely because all dissidents are being killed with terrifying efficiency. Like Honderich, I believe that this problem can be solved only case-by-case. States normally have at their disposal an impressive array of means short of military strikes to marginalize and weaken rogue regimes. Philosophers have canvassed many of these, such as refusal to recognize natural resource rights and sovereign debt privileges.[18] In the absence of organized indigenous opposition to tyrannical regimes, it seems most likely that these and other nonmilitary tactics are all that individual initiatives in solidarity can support. Certainly, solidarity must repudiate the *paternalistic* humanitarian intervention defended by Vitoria. If even the victims refuse our help, we must stand down. We may feel conscientious horror at what occurs. We may suggest alternative ways of life and nonviolent means of meeting putative religious obligations. But in the end it is others' struggle, and our actions and omissions must be taken on others' terms.

8.3 CONCLUSION

In his classic article, "Famine, Affluence, and Morality," Peter Singer claims that the massively strengthened duties he derives upset our "moral conceptual scheme" by reclassifying much supposed charity as duty and narrowing the scope of supererogation.[19] It may be that if we followed Singer's recommendations, we would work much harder to alleviate poverty. Yet Singer's recommendations nonetheless fail to challenge one of the fundamental dogmas of our moral conceptual scheme, namely, the authority of individual conscience. Each individual, according to Singer, determines his or her own point of "comparable moral significance," and discerns whether famine relief or population control (or whatever) is the most effective means of helping.[20]

If such talk of conceptual schemes is still useful, I would venture to say that a more profound revision to our moral conceptual scheme is one that topples the unmerited authority of individual conscience and collectivizes or outsources an aspect of our moral judgment. This move enables an embrace of solidarity, while also enabling us to take seriously the genuine danger of solidarity wrongly directed.

---

[18] Pogge, *World Poverty and Human Rights*, 153ff.
[19] Singer, "Famine, Affluence, and Morality," 230.　　[20] Ibid., 240.

I have distinguished between the concept of solidarity and its justification, arguing that the concept is best understood as nonmoral such that even violent Nazis and Novice Nietzscheans can be in solidarity, and that is part of what makes them—and it—so terrifying. Defined simply as *reason-driven, consummated, political action on others' terms*, solidarity is an important political phenomenon. It is not, however, ubiquitous, for solidarity is distinct from alliance, coalition, and association. Solidarity requires deference: the disposition to go along with others' judgment even in the face of disagreement. What could ever justify deference? And could such difficult efforts ever be *morally required*, or are they always mere options? I have argued that solidarity with those who are treated inequitably is a perfect duty because it constitutes equitable treatment. Since equity is an ultimate value, deontological solidarity is intrinsically valuable, win or lose.

I have returned repeatedly to critical moments and movements in modern political struggle, in particular the struggle for indigenous peoples' rights under imperial Spain, the modern labor movement, and the African American-led Civil Rights movement. Movements such as these exert a compelling pressure on us; no matter how well-intentioned, we cannot stand by or get away with mere offers of sympathy or moral support, or even stirring defenses of other people's rights in late-night bull sessions. To do so is to accede to and hence participate in the mistreatment of others. To truly respect others—to treat them equitably—is to defer to their judgment about what is required and why. Without this deference we might be "white moderates," ruining things by our desire to maintain order—an order that serves *us*, at least, just fine; or contrariwise, we might be "loose cannons," making things worse in our zeal to help in ways not requested. What makes solidarity distinctive is deference, and what makes solidarity obligatory is equity. What is demanded of us as political agents is nothing more and nothing less than to live for justice.

LIVERPOOL JOHN MOORES UNIVERSITY
LEARNING SERVICES

Select Bibliography

Alfred, Taiaiake. *Peace, Power, Righteousness: An Indigenous Manifesto.* Toronto: Oxford University Press, 1999.

Alves, André A., and José M. Moreira. *The Salamanca School.* New York: Continuum, 2010.

Anderson, Elizabeth. "Social Movements, Experiments in Living, and Moral Progress: Case Studies from Britain's Abolition of Slavery." *Lindley Lecture.* Lawrence, KS: University of Kansas, 2014.

Anghie, Antony. *Imperialism, Sovereignty and the Making of International Law.* New York: Cambridge University Press, 2005.

Appiah, Kwame Anthony. *In My Father's House: Africa in the Philosophy of Culture.* New York: Oxford University Press, 1992.

Appiah, Kwame Anthony. "What Will Future Generations Condemn Us For?" *Washington Post*, September 26, 2010.

Arendt, Hannah. *Eichmann in Jerusalem: A Report on the Banality of Evil.* New York: Viking Press, 1963.

Aristotle. *Nicomachean Ethics.* Translated by Terence Irwin. 2nd ed. Indianapolis: Hackett, 1999.

Arneil, Barbara. "Citizens, Wives, Latent Citizens, and Non-Citizens in the Two Treatises: A Legacy of Inclusion, Exclusion, and Assimilation." *Eighteenth-Century Thought* 3 (2007): 207–33.

Audi, Robert. *Moral Perception.* Princeton, NJ: Princeton University Press, 2015.

Bales, Kevin. *Disposable People: New Slavery in the Global Economy.* Berkeley and Los Angeles: University of California Press, 1999.

Baron, Marcia W., Philip Pettit, and Michael Slote. *Three Methods of Ethics.* Cambridge, MA: Blackwell Publishing, 1997.

Barry, Christian, and Kate MacDonald. "How Should We Conceive of Individual Consumer Responsibility to Address Labour Injustices?." In *Global Justice and International Labour Rights*, edited by Yossi Dahan, Hanna Lerner, and Faina Milman-Sivan. New York: Cambridge University Press, 2016.

Barry, Christian, and Gerhard Øverland. *The Responsibilities of the Affluent to the Poor: Doing, Allowing, and Enabling Harm.* New York: Cambridge University Press, forthcoming.

Bartky, Sandra. *"Sympathy and Solidarity" and Other Essays.* Lanham, MD: Rowman & Littlefield, 2002.

BDS Movement. "Join the BDS Movement and Make an Impact!" http://www.bdsmovement.net/make-an-impact.

Beever, Allan. "Aristotle on Equity, Law, and Justice." *Legal Theory* 10 (2004): 33–50.

Blee, Kathleen. "How Options Disappear: Causality and Emergence in Grassroots Activist Groups." *American Journal of Sociology* 119, no. 3 (2013): 655–81.

Blum, Lawrence A. "Three Kinds of Race-Related Solidarity." *Journal of Social Philosophy* 38, no. 1 (2007): 53–72.

Branagan, Marty. "Nonviolent Resistance to Nazi Germany: What Occurred and What Could Have Occurred." *Social Alternatives* 33, no. 4 (2014): 31–8.

Bratman, Michael. "Dynamics of Sociality." *Midwest Studies in Philosophy* 30 (2006): 1–15.

Bratman, Michael. "Rational and Social Agency: Reflections and Replies." In *Rational and Social Agency: The Philosophy of Michael Bratman*, edited by Manuel Vargas and Gideon Yaffe, 294–330. New York: Oxford University Press, 2014.

Bratman, Michael. *Shared Agency*. New York: Oxford University Press, 2014.

Brewer, Talbot M. "Two Kinds of Commitments (and Two Kinds of Social Groups)." *Philosophy and Phenomenological Research* LXVI, no. 3 (2003): 554–83.

B'tselem. "Restriction of Movement: Checkpoints, Physical Obstructions, and Forbidden Roads." http://www.btselem.org/freedom_of_movement/checkpoints_and_forbid den_roads.

Buchanan, Allen. "Trust in Managed Care Organizations." *Kennedy Institute of Ethics Journal* 10 (2000): 189–212.

Buchanan, Allen. *Justice, Legitimacy, and Self-Determination: Moral Foundations for International Law*. New York: Oxford University Press, 2004.

Buchanan, Allen. "Institutions, Beliefs and Ethics: Eugenics as a Case Study." *Journal of Political Philosophy* 15, no. 1 (2007): 22–45.

Buchanan, Allen, and Dan Brock. *Deciding for Others*. New York: Cambridge University Press, 1989.

Buchanan, Allen E., Dan W. Brock, Norman Daniels, and Daniel Wikler. *From Chance to Choice*. New York: Cambridge University Press, 2000.

Butt, Daniel. "On Benefiting from Injustice." *Canadian Journal of Philosophy* 37, no. 1 (2007): 129–52.

Card, Claudia. "Against Marriage and Motherhood." *Hypatia* 11, no. 3 (1996): 1–23.

Casas, Bartolomé de las. *In Defense of the Indians*. DeKalb: Northern Illinois University Press, 1974.

Casas, Bartolomé de las. *A Short Account of the Destruction of the Indies*. New York: Penguin, 1992.

Casas, Bartolomé de las. *Witness: Writings of Bartolomé De Las Casas*. Maryknoll, NY: Orbis Books, 1992.

Castro, Daniel. *Another Face of Empire: Bartolomé De Las Casas, Indigenous Rights, and Ecclesiastical Imperialism*. Durham, NC: Duke University Press, 2007.

Chenoweth, Erica, and Maria J. Stephan. *Why Civil Resistance Works: The Strategic Logic of Nonviolent Conflict*. New York: Columbia University Press, 2012.

Christiano, Thomas. *The Constitution of Equality*. New York: Oxford University Press, 2010.

Claes, Jonas. "Libya and the 'Responsibility to Protect'." Published electronically March 1, 2011. http://www.usip.org/publications/libya-and-the-responsibility-protect.

Clayton, Lawrence A. *Bartolomé De Las Casas: A Biography*. New York: Cambridge University Press, 2012.

Cohen, G. A. "The Structure of Proletarian Unfreedom." In *Analytical Marxism*, ed. John Roemer, 237–59. New York: Cambridge University Press, 1986.

Cohen, G. A. *Rescuing Justice and Equality*. Cambridge, MA: Harvard University Press, 2009.

Courage to Refuse. "Refusing for Israel." http://www.seruv.org.il/English/.

Cremer, Peter S. "On Being a Responsible Person." *Southern Journal of Philosophy* 13, no. 1 (1975): 21–9.

Cudd, Ann E., and Nancy Holmstrom. *Capitalism, For and Against: A Feminist Debate.* Cambridge; New York: Cambridge University Press, 2011.

Cumbler, John. *From Abolition to Rights for All.* Philadelphia: University of Pennsylvania Press, 2008.

Daniels, Norman. *Just Health.* New York: Cambridge University Press, 2008.

Davis, David Brion. *Inhuman Bondage: The Rise and Fall of Slavery in the New World.* New York: Oxford University Press, 2006.

Davis, G. Scott. "Conscience and Conquest: Francisco De Vitoria on Justice in the New World." *Modern Theology* 13, no. 4 (1997): 475–500.

Dawson, Michael. *Blacks in and out of the Left.* The W.E.B. Dubois Lectures. Cambridge, MA: Harvard University Press, 2013.

Dean, Jodi. *Solidarity of Strangers.* Berkeley and Los Angeles: University of California Press, 1996.

DeSilver, Drew. "In Late Spurt of Activity, Congress Avoids 'Least Productive' Title." *FactTank: News in the Numbers* (2014). Published electronically December 29, 2014. http://pewrsr.ch/1y13OnQ.

Donaldson, Sue, and Will Kymlicka. *Zoopolis: A Political Theory of Animal Rights.* New York: Oxford University Press, 2011.

Dussel, Enrique. "Orígen De La Filosofía Política Moderna: Las Casas, Vitoria, Y Suárez (1514–1617)." *Caribbean Studies* 33, no. 2 (2005): 235–80.

Epstein, Richard A. "The Ominous Employee Free Choice Act." *Regulation*, 2009: 48–54.

Estlund, David. *Democratic Authority: A Philosophical Framework.* Princeton, NJ: Princeton University Press, 2009.

Estlund, David. "Human Nature and the Limits (If Any) of Political Philosophy." *Philosophy & Public Affairs* 39, no. 3 (2011): 207–37.

Farmer, Paul. "On Suffering and Structural Violence: A View from Below." *Daedalus* 125, no. 1 (1996): 261–83.

Fausto-Sterling, Anne. *Myths of Gender: Biological Theories about Women and Men.* New York: Basic Books, 1985.

Feinberg, Joel. *Offense to Others. The Moral Limits of the Criminal Law.* New York: Oxford University Press, 1987.

Ferguson, Ann. "Gay Marriage: An American and Feminist Dilemma." *Hypatia* 22, no. 1 (2007): 39–57.

Finlayson, Lorna. "How to Screw Things with Words." *Hypatia* 29, no. 4 (2014): 775–89.

Finnis, John. *Natural Law and Natural Rights*, second edition. New York: Oxford University Press, 2011.

Fitzgerald, Chloë. "A Neglected Aspect of Conscience: Awareness of Implicit Attitudes." *Bioethics* 28, no. 1 (2014): 24–32.

Frankfurt, Harry. "Freedom of the Will and the Concept of a Person." *The Journal of Philosophy* 68, no. 1 (1971): 5–20.

Frankfurt, Harry. "On Bullshit." In *The Importance of What We Care About*, 117–33. New York: Cambridge University Press, 1988.

Frankfurt, Harry. "Taking Ourselves Seriously. Getting It Right." *The Tanner Lectures on Human Values* (2005): 169–202. http://tannerlectures.utah.edu/_documents/ a-to-z/f/frankfurt_2005.pdf.

French, Peter A. "The Corporation as a Moral Person." *American Philosophical Quarterly* 16 (1979): 207–15.

Fricker, Miranda. *Epistemic Injustice: Power and the Ethics of Knowing.* New York: Oxford University Press, 2009.

Friedman, Milton. "The Social Responsibility of Business Is to Increase Its Profits." *The New York Times Magazine*, September 13, 1970.

Frye, Marilyn. "White Woman Feminist, 1983–1992." In *Race and Racism*, edited by Bernard Boxill, 83–100. Oxford: Oxford University Press, 2001.

Fuller, Lisa. "International NGO Health Programs in a Non-Ideal World: Imperialism, Respect and Procedural Justice." In *Global Justice and Bioethics*, edited by J. Millum and E. Emanuel, 213–40. New York: Oxford University Press, 2012.

Gaard, Greta, ed. *Ecofeminism*. Philadelphia: Temple University Press, 1993.

Gamson, William A. "Bystanders, Public Opinion, and the Media." In *The Blackwell Companion to Social Movements*, edited by David A. Snow, Sarah A. Soule, and Hanspeter Kriesi, chap. 11. Cambridge, MA: Blackwell Publishing, 2003.

Ganz, Marshall. "Resources and Resourcefulness: Strategic Capacity in the Unioniza- tion of California Agriculture, 1959–1966." *American Journal of Sociology* 105, no. 4 (2000): 1003–62.

Gardiner, Stephen M. *A Perfect Moral Storm: The Ethical Tragedy of Climate Change.* New York: Oxford University Press, 2011.

Gawande, Atul. *The Checklist Manifesto*. New York: Picador, 2011.

Gilbert, Margaret. *Living Together: Rationality, Sociality, and Obligation.* Lanham, MD: Rowman & Littlefield, 1996.

Gilbert, Margaret. "The Structure of the Social Atom." In *Socializing Metaphysics*, edited by Frederick F. Schmitt, 39–64. Lanham, MD: Rowman & Littlefield, 2003.

Goldman, Emma. *Living My Life*. New York: Penguin, 2006.

Goodin, Robert E. "Disgorging the Fruits of Historical Wrongdoing." *American Political Science Review* 107, no. 3 (2013): 478–91.

Goodin, Robert E. "Inconsequential Duties of Consequential Collective Action." Unpublished manuscript, ANU, 2015.

Goodin, Robert E., James Mahmud Rice, Antti Parpo, and Lina Eriksson. *Discretionary Time: A New Measure of Freedom.* New York: Cambridge University Press, 2008.

Goodwin, Doris Kearns. *Team of Rivals*. New York: Simon & Schuster, 2006.

Goti Ordeñana, Juan. *Del Tratado De Tordesillas a La Doctrina De Los Derechos Fundamentales En Francisco De Vitoria.* Valladolid: Secretariado de Publicaciones e Intercambio Científico, Universidad de Valladolid, 1999.

Gould, Carol. *Globalizing Democracy and Human Rights.* New York: Cambridge University Press, 2004.

Gould, Carol. "Transnational Solidarities." *Journal of Social Philosophy* 38 (2007): 148–64.

Gould, Stephen Jay. *The Mismeasure of Man*. New York: Norton, 1981.

Gould, Stephen Jay. "Cordelia's Dilemma." In *Dinosaur in a Haystack: Reflections in Natural History*, 123–32. Cambridge, MA: Harvard University Press, 2011.

Graber, Mark A. *Dred Scott and the Problem of Constitutional Evil.* New York: Cambridge University Press, 2006.

Hampton, Jean. "Feminist Contractarianism." In *A Mind of One's Own*, edited by Louise M. Antony and Charlotte E. Witt, 337–68. Boulder: Westview Press, 2001.

Hanke, Lewis. *Aristotle and the American Indians: A Study in Race Prejudice in the Modern World.* Chicago: H. Regnery Co., 1959.

Harbin, Ami. "The Disorientations of Acting against Injustice." *Journal of Social Philosophy* 45 (2014): 162–81.

Hardimon, Michael. "Role Obligations." *Journal of Philosophy* 91, no. 7 (1994): 333–63.

Harvey, Jean. "Moral Solidarity and Empathetic Understanding: The Moral Value and Scope of the Relationship." *Journal of Social Philosophy* 38, no. 1 (2007): 22–37.

Held, Virginia. "Can a Random Collection of Individuals Be Morally Responsible?." *Journal of Philosophy* 67 (1970): 471–81.

Helliwell, John, Richard Layard, and Jeffrey Sachs. "World Happiness Report 2015." New York: Sustainable Development Solutions Network, 2015.

Hendrix, Burke A. *Ownership, Authority, and Self-Determination.* University Park, PA: Penn State University Press, 2008.

Hendrix, Burke A. "Political Theorists as Dangerous Social Actors." *Critical Review of International Social and Political Philosophy* 15, no. 1 (2012): 41–61.

Herman, Barbara. *The Practice of Moral Judgment.* Cambridge, MA: Harvard University Press, 1993.

Honderich, Ted. *Violence for Equality.* Enlarged and Revised ed. New York: Routledge, 1989.

Hook, Jennifer L. "Gender Inequality in the Welfare State: Sex Segregation in Housework, 1965–2003." *American Journal of Sociology* 115, no. 5 (2010): 1480–523.

Human Rights Watch. "The Employee Free Choice Act: A Human Rights Imperative." New York: Human Rights Watch, 2009.

James, Aaron. *Fairness in Practice.* New York: Oxford University Press, 2012.

Kahane, David, Daniel Weinstock, and Alison M. Jaggar. "Symposium: Diversity and Civic Solidarity." *Journal of Political Philosophy* 7 (1999): 267–329.

Kant, Immanuel. *The Metaphysics of Morals.* New York: Cambridge University Press, 1996.

Kant, Immanuel. *Groundwork for the Metaphysics of Morals.* Peterborough, Ontario: Broadview Press, 2005.

Kant, Immanuel. *Critique of Practical Reason.* Translated by Mary J. Gregor. New York: Cambridge University Press, 2012.

Keller, Simon. *The Limits of Loyalty.* New York: Cambridge University Press, 2007.

King, Martin Luther. "Letter from Birmingham City Jail." In *A Testament of Hope: The Essential Writings and Speeches of Martin Luther King, Jr.*, edited by James M. Washington, 289–302. San Francisco: HarperSanFrancisco, 1986.

King, Martin Luther, Jr. *The Trumpet of Conscience.* Boston: Beacon Press, 2011.

Kolers, Avery. "Justice and the Politics of Deference." *Journal of Political Philosophy* 13, no. 2 (2005): 153–73.

Kolers, Avery. "Dynamics of Solidarity." *Journal of Political Philosophy* 20, no. 4 (2012): 365–83.

Kolers, Avery. "The Priority of Solidarity to Justice." *Journal of Applied Philosophy* 31, no. 4 (2014): 420–33.

Koskenniemi, Martti. "Empire and International Law: The Real Spanish Contribution." *University of Toronto Law Journal* 61, no. 1 (2011): 1–36.

Krugman, Paul. "How Did Economists Get It So Wrong?" *New York Times Magazine*, September 2, 2009.

Kutz, Christopher. *Complicity: Ethics and Law for a Collective Age.* New York: Cambridge University Press, 2000.

Le Grand, Julian. "Equity as an Economic Objective." In *Applied Philosophy: Morals and Metaphysics in Contemporary Debate*, edited by Brenda Almond and Donald Hill, 183–95. New York: Routledge, 1991.

List, Christian, and Philip Pettit. *Group Agency: The Possibility, Design, and Status of Corporate Agents.* New York: Oxford University Press, 2011.

Locke, John. *Two Treatises of Government.* Cambridge: Cambridge University Press, 1988.

Lugones, María. *Peregrinajes/Pilgrimages.* Lanham, MD: Rowman & Littlefield, 2002.

Lustick, Ian. *Unsettled States, Disputed Lands: Britain and Ireland, France and Algeria, Israel and the West Bank-Gaza.* Ithaca: Cornell University Press, 1993.

Lyons, David. *Confronting Injustice.* New York: Oxford University Press, 2012.

McDowell, John. *Mind and World.* Cambridge, MA: Harvard University Press, 1994.

MacIntyre, Alasdair. "Is Patriotism a Virtue?," *Lindley Lecture.* Lawrence, KS: University of Kansas, 1984.

MacIntyre, Alasdair. "Social Structures and Their Threats to Moral Agency." *Philosophy* 74 (1999): 311–29.

Malik, Khalid. "Human Development Report 2014: Sustaining Human Progress." In *Human Development Reports.* New York: United Nations Development Programme.

Marx, Karl, and Friedrich Engels. *The Communist Manifesto.* In *Karl Marx: Selected Writings*, ed. Lawrence H. Simon. Indianapolis: Hackett, 1994: 157–86.

May, Larry. *Crimes against Humanity: A Normative Account.* New York: Cambridge University Press, 2005.

May, Larry. *Global Justice and Due Process.* New York: Cambridge University Press, 2011.

Medina, José. *The Epistemology of Resistance.* New York: Oxford University Press, 2012.

Merritt, Anna C., Daniel A. Effron, and Benoît Monin. "Moral Self-Licensing: When Being Good Frees Us to Be Bad." *Social and Personality Psychology Compass* 4, no. 5 (2010): 344–57.

Meyers, Christopher, and Robert D. Woods. "An Obligation to Provide Abortion Services: What Happens When Physicians Refuse?." *Journal of Medical Ethics* 22, no. 2 (1996): 115–20.

Mill, John Stuart. *On Liberty*, ed. Elizabeth Rapaport. Indianapolis: Hackett, 1978.

Miller, David. *Citizenship and National Identity.* Cambridge, UK: Polity Press, 2000.

Miller, David. "Distributing Responsibilities." *Journal of Political Philosophy* 9, no. 4 (2001): 453–71.

Mills, Charles W. *The Racial Contract.* Ithaca: Cornell University Press, 1997.

Minow, Martha. "Justice Engendered." *Harvard Law Review* 101, no. 1 (1987): 10–95.

Mohanty, Chandra Talpade. *Feminism without Borders: Decolonizing Theory, Practicing Solidarity.* Durham, NC: Duke University Press, 2003.

Moody-Adams, Michele M. "Culture, Responsibility, and Affected Ignorance." *Ethics* 104, no. 2 (1994): 291–309.

Moore, Margaret. *A Political Theory of Territory*. New York: Oxford University Press, 2015.

Mouffe, Chantal. *Agonistics: Thinking the World Politically*. New York: Verso, 2013.

Murphy, Jeffrie. "Blackmail: A Preliminary Inquiry." *The Monist* 63 (1980): 156–71.

Nell, Onora. "Lifeboat Earth." *Philosophy & Public Affairs* 4 (1975): 273–92.

Nussbaum, Martha. "Equity and Mercy." In *Punishment: A Reader*, edited by A. John Simmons, Marshall Cohen, Joshua Cohen, and Charles R. Beitz, 145–87. Princeton: Princeton University Press, 1995.

Nussbaum, Martha. *Women and Human Development: The Capabilities Approach*. New York: Cambridge University Press, 2000.

Nussbaum, Martha. *Frontiers of Justice*. New York: Oxford University Press, 2006.

O'Loughlin, Ellen. "Questioning Sour Grapes: Ecofeminism and the United Farmworkers Grape Boycott." In *Ecofeminism*, edited by Greta Gaard, 146–67, Philadelphia, PA: Temple University Press, 1988.

O'Neill, Onora. *Bounds of Justice*. New York: Cambridge University Press, 2000.

Ochoa Espejo, Paulina. *The Time of Popular Sovereignty: Process and the Democratic State*. University Park, PA: Pennsylvania State University Press, 2011.

Orwell, George. *A Collection of Essays*. New York: Mariner Books, 1970.

Owen, David. "Constituting the Polity, Constituting the Demos: On the Place of the All Affected Interests Principle in Democratic Theory and in Resolving the Democratic Boundary Problem." *Ethics & Global Politics* 5, no. 3 (2012).

Owen, David S. "Othering Obama: How Whiteness Is Used to Undermine Authority." *Altre Modernità/Other Modernities*, no. 3 (2010): 112–19.

Pagden, Anthony. "Human Rights, Natural Rights, and Europe's Imperial Legacy." *Political Theory* 31, no. 2 (2003): 171–99.

Pagden, Anthony. "Conquest and the Just War: The 'School of Salamanca' and the 'Affair of the Indies'." In *Empire and Modern Political Thought*, edited by Sankar Muthu, 30–60. New York: Cambridge University Press, 2012.

Page, Edward A, and Avia Pasternak, eds. *Special Issue: Benefiting from Injustice*. Vol. 31, Journal of Applied Philosophy, 2014.

"Palestinian Civil Society Call for BDS." http://www.bdsmovement.net/call.

Parfit, Derek. "Equality or Priority?" *Lindley Lecture*. Lawrence, Kansas: University of Kansas, 1991.

Pateman, Carole. *The Disorder of Women*. Stanford: Stanford University Press, 1989.

Pateman, Carole, and Charles W. Mills. *Contract and Domination*. Cambridge: Polity, 2007.

Peña, Juan de la. *De Bello Contra Insulanos: Intervención De España En América: Escuela Española De La Paz, Segunda Generación, 1560–1585: Testigos Y Fuentes*. Corpus Hispanorum De Pace, edited by Luciano Pereña. Madrid: Consejo Superior de Investigaciones Científicas, 1982.

Perlstein, Rick. *Nixonland: The Rise of a President and the Fracturing of America*. New York: Scribner, 2008.

Pettit, Philip. "Construing Sen on Commitment." In *Rationality and Commitment*, edited by Fabienne Peter and Hans Bernhard Schmid, 28–48. New York: Oxford University Press, 2007.

Piketty, Thomas. *Capital in the Twenty-First Century*. Translated by Arthur Goldhammer. Cambridge, MA: Harvard University Press, 2014.

Plato. *Crito*. Translated by G. M. A. Grube. In *Five Dialogues*, edited by John Cooper, 56–68. Indianapolis: Hackett, 2002.

Pogge, Thomas W. *World Poverty and Human Rights*. Cambridge: Polity, 2000.

Preuss, Ulrich K. "National, Supranational, and International Solidarity." In *Solidarity*, edited by Kurt Bayertz, 281–92. Dordrecht: Springer, 1999.

Radzik, Linda. *Making Amends: Atonement in Morality, Law, and Politics*. New York: Oxford University Press, 2009.

Radzik, Linda. "Moral Bystanders and the Virtue of Forgiveness." In *Forgiveness in Perspective*, edited by Christopher R. Allers and Marieke Smit, 69–87. New York: Rodopi, 2010.

Rawls, John. *A Theory of Justice, Revised Ed.* Cambridge, MA: Belknap/Harvard University Press, 1999.

Rawls, John. *Collected Papers*, ed. Samuel Freeman. Cambridge, MA: Harvard University Press, 1999.

Rawls, John. *Justice as Fairness: A Restatement*. Cambridge, MA: Belknap Press, 2001.

Raz, Joseph. *The Morality of Freedom*. Oxford: Clarendon Press, 1986.

Redondo Redondo, María Lourdes. *Utopía Vitoriana Y Realidad Indiana*. Madrid: Fundación Universitaria Española, 1992.

Richards, Howard. "Deference." *Ethics* 74, no. 2 (1964): 135–42.

Ricks, Thomas E. *The Generals*. New York: Penguin, 2012.

Rivera-Pagán, Luis N. "A Prophetic Challenge to the Church: The Last Word of Bartolomé De Las Casas." *Inaugural Lecture as Henry Winters Luce Professor in Ecumenics and Mission, delivered at Princeton Theological Seminary* (2003). http://www.lascasas.org/Rivera_Pagan.htm.

Rorty, Richard. "Solidarity or Objectivity?." In *Objectivity, Relativism, and Truth: Philosophical Papers I*, 21–35. New York: Cambridge University Press, 1991.

Rorty, Richard. *Achieving Our Country*. Cambridge, MA: Harvard University Press, 1998.

Rousseau, Jean-Jacques. *On the Social Contract*. Translated by Donald Cress. Indianapolis: Hackett, 1987.

Sangiovanni, Andrea. "Solidarity as Joint Action." *Journal of Applied Philosophy* 32, no. 4 (2015): 340–59.

Scanlon, T. M. *What We Owe to Each Other*. Cambridge, MA: Harvard University Press, 1998.

Schlosberg, David. *Defining Environmental Justice: Theories, Movements, and Nature* (New York: Oxford University Press, 2007).

Scholz, Sally. *Political Solidarity*. University Park, PA: Penn State University Press, 2008.

Scholz, Sally. "Feminist Political Solidarity." In *Feminist Ethics and Social and Political Philosophy: Theorizing the Non-Ideal*, edited by Lisa Tessman, 205–20. New York: Springer, 2009.

Scholz, Sally. "Political Solidarity and the More-Than-Human World." *Ethics & the Environment* 18, no. 2 (2013): 81–99.

Scott, James C. *Two Cheers for Anarchism*. Princeton, NJ: Princeton University Press, 2014.

Sen, Amartya. "More Than 100 Million Women Are Missing." *New York Review of Books*, December 20, 1990.

Sen, Amartya. *Inequality Reexamined*. New York; Cambridge, MA: Russell Sage Foundation; Harvard University Press, 1992.

Serna, Mercedes, ed. *La Conquista Del Nuevo Mundo: Textos Y Documentos De La Aventura Americana*. Madrid: Castalia, 2012.

Shapiro, Scott J. "Massively Shared Agency." In *Rational and Social Agency: The Philosophy of Michael Bratman*, edited by Manuel Vargas and Gideon Yaffe, 257–93. New York: Oxford University Press, 2014.

Shelby, Tommie. *We Who Are Dark: Philosophical Foundations of Black Solidarity*. Cambridge, MA: Harvard University Press, 2005.

Shrader-Frechette, Kristin. *Environmental Justice*. New York: Oxford University Press, 2002.

Silvers, Anita, and Leslie Pickering Francis. "Thinking About the Good: Reconfiguring Liberal Metaphysics (or Not) for People with Cognitive Disabilities." *Metaphilosophy* 40, no. 3–4 (2009): 475–98.

Simmons, A. John. "External Justifications and Institutional Roles." *Journal of Philosophy* 93, no. 1 (1996): 28–36.

Singer, Peter. "Famine, Affluence, and Morality." *Philosophy & Public Affairs* 1 (1972): 229–43.

Snyder, Greta Fowler. "'Marking Whiteness' for Cross-Racial Solidarity." *DuBois Review: Social Science Research on Race* 12, no. 2 (2015): 297–319.

Soper, Philip. *The Ethics of Deference*. New York: Cambridge University Press, 2002.

Southwood, Nicholas. "Does 'Ought' Imply 'Feasible'?" Unpublished manuscript, January, 2016.

Spiekermann, Kai, and Arne Weiss. "Objective and Subjective Compliance: A Norm-Based Explanation of 'Moral Wiggle Room'." *Games and Economic Behavior* (forthcoming; available online 10 December 2015. http://www.sciencedirect.com/science/article/pii/S0899825615001554.

Spivak, Gayatri Chakravorty. *A Critique of Postcolonial Reason: Toward a History of the Vanishing Present*. Cambridge, MA: Harvard University Press, 1999.

Staggenborg, Suzanne. *Social Movements*. New York: Oxford University Press, 2008.

Stilz, Anna. *Liberal Loyalty*. Princeton, NJ: Princeton University Press, 2009.

Stone, Christopher D. *Should Trees Have Standing?* 3rd ed. New York: Oxford University Press, 2010.

Sumner, L. W. *Welfare, Happiness, and Ethics*. Oxford: Clarendon Press, 1996.

Sunstein, Cass R. "The Law of Group Polarization." *Journal of Political Philosophy* 10, no. 2 (2002): 175–95.

Surowiecki, James. *The Wisdom of Crowds*. New York: Anchor Books, 2005.

Thomas, Laurence. "Moral Flourishing in an Unjust World." *Moral Education* 22 (1993): 83–96.

Thomson, Judith Jarvis. *Goodness and Advice*. University Center for Human Values Series, edited by Amy Gutmann. Princeton, NJ: Princeton University Press, 2001.

Tilly, Charles. *Regimes and Repertoires*. Chicago: University of Chicago Press, 2010.

Todorov, Tzvetan. *The Conquest of America: The Question of the Other*. Translated by Richard Howard. New York: Harper & Row, 1984.

Todorov, Tzvetan. *Facing the Extreme: Moral Life in the Concentration Camps*. Translated by Arthur Denner and Abigail Pollak. New York: Metropolitan Books, 1996.

Tully, James. "Political Freedom." *The Journal of Philosophy* 87, no. 10 (1990): 517–23.

United States Congress. *Uniting and Strengthening America by Providing Appropriate Tools Required to Intercept and Obstruct Terrorism (USA Patriot Act)*. 107, H.R.3162.

Van Dyke, Nella. "Crossing Movement Boundaries: Factors That Facilitate Coalition Protest by American College Students, 1930–1990." *Social Problems* 50, no. 2 (2003): 226–50.

Venkatapuram, Sridhar. *Health Justice: An Argument from the Capabilities Approach*. Cambridge: Polity, 2011.

Vitoria, Francisco de. *Political Writings*, ed. Anthony Pagden and Jeremy Lawrance. Cambridge: Cambridge University Press, 1991.

Waligore, Timothy. "Cosmopolitan Right, Indigenous Peoples, and the Risks of Cultural Interaction." *Public Reason* 1, no. 1 (2009): 27–56.

Walzer, Michael. *Interpretation and Social Criticism*. Cambridge, MA: Harvard University Press, 1987.

Walzer, Michael. *Just and Unjust Wars*. 2nd ed. New York: Basic Books, 1992.

Walzer, Michael. *The Company of Critics: Social Criticism and Political Commitment in the Twentieth Century*. New York: Basic Books, 2002.

Wapner, Paul, and John Willoughby. "The Irony of Environmentalism: The Ecological Futility but Political Necessity of Lifestyle Change." *Ethics & International Affairs* 19, no. 3 (2005): 77–89.

Watkins, Kevin. "Human Development Report 2007–2008: Fighting Climate Change: Human Solidarity in a Divided World." New York: United Nations Development Program, 2007.

Watson, Gary. "Free Agency." *The Journal of Philosophy* 72, no. 8 (1975): 205–20.

Weber, Clare. *Visions of Solidarity*. Lanham, MD.: Lexington Books, 2006.

We Divest. "About BDS." https://wedivest.org/p/240/bds.

Weir, Allison. *Identities and Freedom: Feminist Theory between Power and Connection*. New York: Oxford University Press, 2011.

Wicclair, Mark. "Conscientious Objection in Medicine." *Bioethics* 14 no. 3 (2000): 205–27.

Wiggins, David. "Solidarity and the Root of the Ethical." *Lindley Lecture*. Lawrence, KS: University of Kansas, 2008.

Wolf, Susan. "Moral Saints." *Journal of Philosophy* 79, no. 8 (1982): 419–39.

Wolf, Susan. *Freedom within Reason*. New York: Oxford University Press, 1993.

Wolfers, Justin, David Leonhardt, and Kevin Quealy. "1.5 Million Missing Black Men." *The New York Times*, April 20, 2015.

Yi, Joseph E., and Joe Phillips. "The BDS Campaign against Israel: Lessons from South Africa." *PS, Political Science & Politics* 48, no. 2 (2015): 306–10.

Young, Iris Marion. "Responsibility and Global Justice: A Social Connection Model." *Social Philosophy & Policy* 23, no. 1 (2006): 102–30.

Zack, Naomi. *Philosophy of Science and Race*. New York: Routledge, 2002.

Zwolinski, Matt. "Sweatshops, Choice, and Exploitation." *Business Ethics Quarterly* 17, no. 4 (2007): 689–727.

Index

Abolitionists 11, 49, 51–2, 54–5, 56, 61, 68,
    70–1, 112n, 113
Affected Ignorance 112–13, 121
Agency 60, 74, 76, 84
    collective 37, 56
    corporate 54n, 70
    individual 34, 37–8, 40, 42, 44, 82
        socially constituted 44, 47
    moral 143, 147, 149
    shared 57, 64, 67–71, 146
    valuing others' 56, 60–1, 63, 69–70
Agency problem *see* Solidarity
Agency risk 82
Agent-centered options 35–6, 73
Agent-neutrality 47, 50, 73, 119, 140, 143, 158
Agent-relativity 76, 143, 156
Agonism 38–40, 44, 47, 50, 58–9, 63, 73,
    108, 170
    vs. antagonism 39
Alabama 44, 53, 69, 80
Alexander III (Pope) 14
Alexander the Great 20
Alienation 59–60, 63, 64
"Amazing Grace" 52n
Anderson, Elizabeth 49, 70, 112, 124
Anghie, Antony 19
Anthropophagy 11, 19, 22, 175
Apartheid 92, 176
Appiah, Kwame Anthony 1n
Arab Spring 31
Aristotelian(ism)
    in 16th-century Spain 16
    in theory of solidarity *see* Equitable Persons
        and Equity, Aristotelian
Atonement 124, 127, 161–2
Audi, Robert 112
Autonomy 7, 16, 72, 73, 80, 85
    and *anomie* 79
    authorization 75
    compatible with deference 90–1
    moral arguments for 76–7
    Principle of (conceptual) 74–5
    Principle of (evaluative) 74, 75–9, 88
Aztecs 20, 138

Baron, Marcia 149n, 173n
Barry, Christian 86n, 142, 157n, 167n
Bartky, Sandra 31
Beever, Allan 129, 133

"Blue Sword" 80, 102
Boycott, Divestment, Sanctions (BDS) 92–4,
    104, 110, 116–17, 166, 171–4
Boycotts 29, 35–6, 39, 53–4, 63, 100, 166, 170
Brandeis, Louis 88
Bratman, Michael 55n, 56–7, 60, 64, 67–8
Braun, Wernher von 50–1, 68
Brennan, Geoff 152n
Brewer, Talbot M. 65–6
Buchanan, Allen 10n, 11, 125–6
Bulls of Donation (Alexandrine
    Donation) 14, 17–18, 25
Bullshit 127
"Buy American" 111, 166

Calhoun, Cheshire 143n, 148n
Cano, Melchor 10, 20
Capabilities 105–6, 109, 129n
Card, Claudia 58
Casas, Bartolomé de las 8, 9, 11, 15–17, 20, 51,
    61, 74–5, 138
    And slave trade 24–5, 46
    Evolution of 11, 17n, 21–5
    Overcoming conscience 25, 27, 46, 91
Charles V (King/Emperor) 10, 14, 16–18, 20,
    23, 46
Christian X (King) 115–16
Checklist *see* Procedures
Civil Disobedience 2, 32, 84
Circumstance zones 104, 109–12, 158–9
Coercive offers 16
Columbus, Christopher 11, 13–14
Complexity cases 72, 83–4
Conceptual problem *see* Solidarity
Congregation 64–6, 70
Connor, Bull 27
Conquista 5, 8, 10, 14, 16–18
Conscience 4, 10, 16, 73, 76, 95, 118,
    166–70
    and deference 106, 115–16
    as "antipolitics machine" 20–1, 25
    definition 12–13
    in liberalism 7, 24, 37, 75
    in loyalty-solidarity 40–4
    in teleological solidarity 31, 34–7, 73
    parochialism of 8, 11, 13n
    subsidiary to solidarity 5, 8, 13, 22–6, 45–6,
        128, 130–2, 137–8, 163
Conscription 51n, 80, 88–9, 142

Consent 88, 171
actual vs. hypothetical 22, 121
Conspiracy 163–5
Contractualism 120–2
Contribution Principle 156–8, 164–5
Cudd, Ann 127, 129
Cumbler, John 33n, 86n, 132n, 138n

Daniels, Norman 129
Davis, David Brion 46
Davis, G. Scott 19
Dean, Jodi 31, 96
Deference
and individual initiative 53, 115–16, 151–2,
158–60, 170–1
and shared fate 7, 66, 133–4
compatible with liberalism 88–91
counterfactual (dispositional) 39–40, 52,
82, 115–16
epistemic 93–5
essential to solidarity 6–7, 34–8, 45–7, 52
limits of 86–8, 101–2, 135–39
"Moral" (Laurence Thomas) 52
necessary condition of solidarity
on moral questions 4, 7, 84–6, 125–6
relational 95–103
structural 95–6, 103–12
Deference Principle
preliminary (D_0) 76–7
revised (D) 82–3, 89, 93
Deferential Solidary Action (DSA) 63–4,
69, 71
Democratic theory 110–12
Deontology 8, 63, 76, 119–24, 139–40, 143,
165, 168, 179
Difference Principle 2, 129–30
Direction of fit 37–8
Don Corleone 108
Dussel, Enrique 17n, 19
Duties
demandingness of 2, 142–51
nonconsensual 35
of justice 30, 34–5, 107–8, 132, 134
of Rescue 36
perfect vs. imperfect 8, 35, 119, 126–7,
144–5
stringency of 142–3

Encomienda 14–15, 17
Entrepreneurship 155, 159, 162
Equitable Persons 119, 133–5, 136, 160, 173
and sharing fate 108, 133–4
Equity 118–19, 140, 143–4, 147, 164, 172–3,
175–7
and visibility 113
Aristotelian 127–33, 138

as account of well-being 106–9
as Razian ultimate value 8, 119, 126,
140, 179
as structural 106
Kantian 107, 120–27, 137
not principally distributive notion 107, 120
Essentialism 6, 31, 41
Ethical Autopsy 10–11, 18, 25, 28
Eugenics 11, 94, 125–6

Farmer, Paul 176
Farmworkers 35–6, 39, 100–1
Feinberg, Joel 135–6
Francis, Leslie Pickering 159n
Frankfurt, Harry 127, 149
Fraternity 2
Friedman, Milton 167

Gaard, Greta 5
Gardiner, Stephen M. 12n
Gilbert, Margaret 56, 64–6
Goodin, Robert E. 33n, 34n, 62n, 105n, 128n
Goti Ordeñana, Juan 14
Gould, Carol 31, 39n
Gould, Stephen Jay 125–6

Hannan, Sarah 143n, 147n, 159n
Hardimon, Michael 136n
Heteronomy 74–6, 88
Holy Roman Empire 18
Honderich, Ted 176–8
Human sacrifice 11, 19, 21–2, 138, 175
Humanitarian Military Intervention 19–20,
174–5, 177–8

Ideal Theory 3, 128, 132–3, 167–8
Indigenous peoples (Indians) 9n
Under Spanish imperial power 10, 13–17, 61
Las Casas's relationship with 8, 21–3,
24–5, 46
Vitoria on 9, 17–19, 23–4, 46, 91, 175
Intrinsic racism 30–1
Isabella (Queen) 14–15
Islamic State in Iraq and Syria (ISIS) 138–9
Israel 92, 116, 171–3
Ivison, Duncan 91n

Jackson, Frank 89n
James, Aaron 120
Jim Crow 5
Jus gentium 19, 23–4
Justice
and equity 107, 120
as goal *see* Solidarity, teleological
Living for *see* Living for Justice
natural duty of *see* Duties

Justificatory problem *see* Solidarity
Just War Theory 29–30, 177

Kant, Immanuel 113
Kantian(ism) *see* Equity
Keller, Simon 40
King, Martin Luther, Jr. 1, 8, 27, 32, 61, 80, 85, 118, 124, 127, 174
Ku Klux Klan 1, 118, 126
Kutz, Christopher 131n, 157n

Labor law 131–2
Lazar, Seth 152n, 165n
Lee-Stronach, Chad 89n
Left-libertarians 59
Leland, RJ 60n, 143n
LGBTQ community 58, 61n, 66n
Liberalism 5, 36, 38, 41, 73
  And deference 7, 35–7, 75–6, 88–91
  And solidarity 1–4, 5, 30–1
Living for Justice 149–50
Locke, John 88
Lost Wallet problem 8, 143–8
Love Canal 111
Loyalty *see also* Solidarity 12, 28, 40–2, 44–7, 50, 63, 73
Lugones, María 5, 96n, 122–4

MacDonald, Kate 142
MacIntyre, Alasdair 41–4
Magna Carta rights 113, 120
Malcolm X 85
May, Larry 107, 113, 120
Minow, Martha 127
Mohanty, Chandra Talpade 31
Montesinos, Antonio de 1, 14–15, 21, 25, 113
Moody-Adams, Michele 112
Mouffe, Chantal 39n
Mountaintop Removal 86–8

Natural duty of justice *see* Duties
Natural slaves thesis 16, 17, 21
Nazis 6, 7, 42–3, 50–1, 68, 115, 161, 179
Newton, John 112–13
Nicaragua 100
Niger 104, 110
Nonidentity cases 83–4, 88
Nonviolence 85, 172, 174
Novice Nietzscheans 50–1, 68, 179
Nussbaum, Martha C. 128, 129

Occupy Wall Street 59
O'Neill, Onora 36
Organizing 77, 108, 111, 130–2, 146–7, 149, 153–4
Orwell, George 77

Ovando, Nicolás de 14
Oxfam 2

PA_c-man 82, 88–9
Pagden, Anthony 17, 47n
Palestine, State of 104n
Palestinians 92, 104, 116–17, 172–4
Parks, Rosa 28–9, 52–3, 63, 69, 80, 105, 134–5, 136
Peña, Juan de la 10, 20
Peña Echeverría, Javier 20n
Playfulness 122–4
Plural Subject Theory 55–6, 64–7, 71
Polonius 2
Primary Social Goods 105, 109, 129
Principle of Autonomy (PA) *see* Autonomy
Prioritarianism 104–5
Priority Principle *see* Deference, Relational
Procedures 152
  actual vs. hypothetical 33, 120–2
  mechanical (checklist) 113–14, 136–7, 149, 153–4, 158
Prosthetic thinking 159n
Purity of Heart 149

Radzik, Linda 39n, 108n, 124
Rawls, John 2–3, 103, 129, 130n, 167
Raz, Joseph 8, 39n, 89–90, 93, 140
Reason *r* 45–7, 50–1, 63, 66
Reciprocity Principle *see* Deference, relational
Requerimiento 15–16, 18
Respect Principle *see* Deference, relational
Responsibilities 105, 150, 155, 157
Responsibility
  consumer 166–71
  group 163–4
  moral 30, 160–5, 172
  shared 27, 164–5
Revolutionary Association of the Women of Afghanistan (RAWA) 66
Revolutionary Communist Party 59
Richards, Howard 85
"Right-to-work" legislation 131–2

Same-sex marriage 58
"Sandwiching" 101, 139
Sangiovanni, Andrea 34n, 51n, 55–63, 70n, 133n
Scanlon, T. M. 104–5
Schlosberg, David 107n
Scholz, Sally 5–6, 31, 34, 100, 102, 154n, 160
Scott, James C. 20–1
Sen, Amartya 106
Separateness of persons 91, 125
Sepúlveda, Juan Ginés de 11, 16–17, 20–1, 46

Service Employees International Union (SEIU) 27n
Shapiro, Scott 59–60, 64, 67–9, 70–1
Shared Agency *see* Agency
Shared Aims Principle *see* Deference, Relational
Shared Fate *see also* equitable persons 7, 31n, 33–4, 57, 63, 66, 69, 71, 108, 110
Shelby, Tommie 30–1, 38, 110n
Sierra Club 83
Silvers, Anita 159n
Singer, Peter 178
Sisterhood 31, 34n, 41
Slave trade 10, 24–5, 46
Slavishness 134, 151
Social Moral Epistemology (Buchanan) 125–6
Social movements 32, 49, 51, 54–5, 67–9, 78, 81–2, 115, 124, 156–7
Social Security 127–8, 130
Solidarity
　agency problem 27–8, 30, 31, 42, 49–50
　among Nazis 6–7, 179
　and others' agency 60, 63
　as action *see also* Solidary Collective Action; Deferential Solidary Action 38, 53
　　on behalf (surrogacy) vs. *in* behalf (trusteeship) 22, 52–3, 66, 69–71, 158–60
　as Atonement 124, 127
　as legislation for a Kingdom of Ends 123
　as perfect duty 8, 119, 126–7, 135, 142, 148
　asymmetric relation 55, 58–9, 61–3, 65, 101
　conceptual problem 7, 27, 49, 71
　consummation condition 61–2
　definition 71
　　evaluative vs. nonevaluative 6–7, 28, 33, 51–2
　in contemporary political philosophy 1–5
　instrumentally valuable 30, 119
　intrinsically valuable 119, 125–6, 140
　justificatory problem 8
　loyalty- 40–4, 96
　preliminary definitions 7, 28, 50
　purposive 31–3, 58
　teleological 30–8, 119
　varieties of 2, 4–5, 58
　vs. coalitions, alliances, and associations 34–8, 50, 81, 119, 179
　vs. loyalty 44–6, 73

Solidary Collective Action (SCA) 54–6, 64
Song, Yujia 39n
Soper, Philip 74, 92n
Southern Christian Leadership Conference (SCLC) 62, 70
Southwood, Nicholas 152n, 154n
Spivak, Gayatri Chakravorty 51n
Stilz, Anna 35n, 107, 120
Student Nonviolent Coordinating Committee (SNCC) 62
Surrogate decisionmaking *see* Solidarity
Sweatshops 111, 148, 166, 171

Tarrow, Sidney 49
Teamsters 65–6
Tilly, Charles 49
Todorov, Tzvetan 10n, 11, 13, 21n, 22
Togo 104
Trump, Donald 77
Trust 5, 79, 82, 95, 97, 108–9
Trusteeship *see* Solidarity

Ultimate value 8, 119, 140
Underground Railroad 161
United Auto Workers (UAW) 69–70
United States Congress 72, 78
Unjust Benefits Principle (UBP) 156–7
USA Patriot Act 72, 75, 77–8

Valladolid 15, 16–17, 21–2, 24, 27
Vesey, Denmark 8, 31, 175
Victim-blaming 106, 121
Violence 174–8
Vitoria, Francisco de 8, 9, 27, 75, 175, 178
　"Just titles" 18–19, 22
　Proto-liberalism of 19–20, 46, 91, 138–9
　On *jus gentium* 23–4
　"Unjust titles" 9–11, 16, 17–18

"Walle-darity" *see* Lost Wallet problem
Warsaw Ghetto 8, 31
Weber, Clare 100
Welfarism 105–6
Weir, Allison 31, 96, 102–3
White Citizen's Councils 1, 118, 126
"White moderate" 1, 5, 20, 118, 124, 126–7, 151, 179
Wholeheartedness 149–50
Wicclair, Mark 85
Wiggins, David 113
"World"-traveling 122–3